MOUNT SHASTA
A Photo-Novella

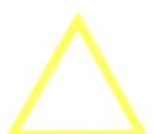

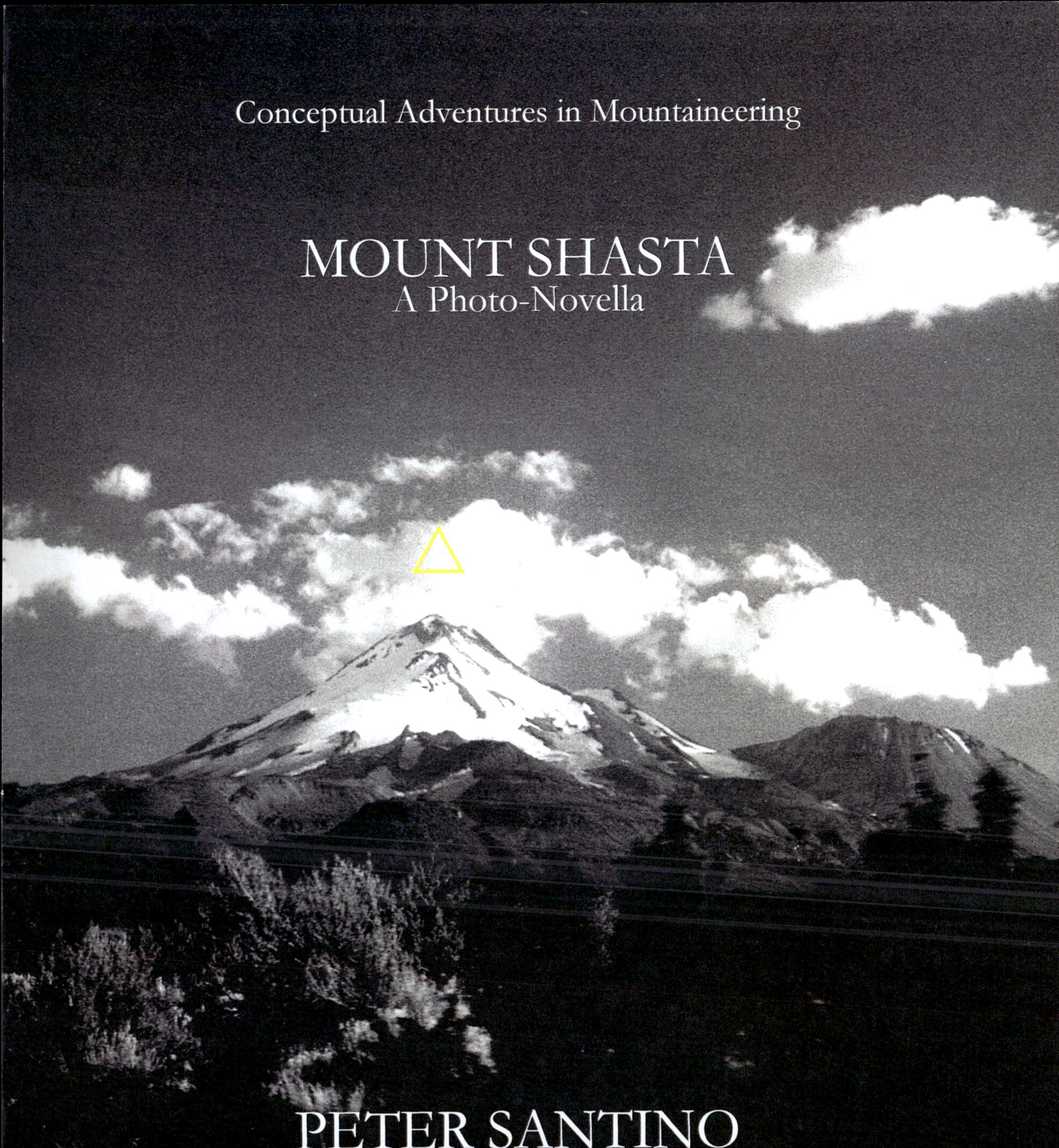

Conceptual Adventures in Mountaineering

MOUNT SHASTA
A Photo-Novella

PETER SANTINO

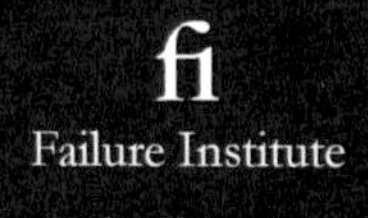

Failure Institute

New York   Firenze   Eureka

2015

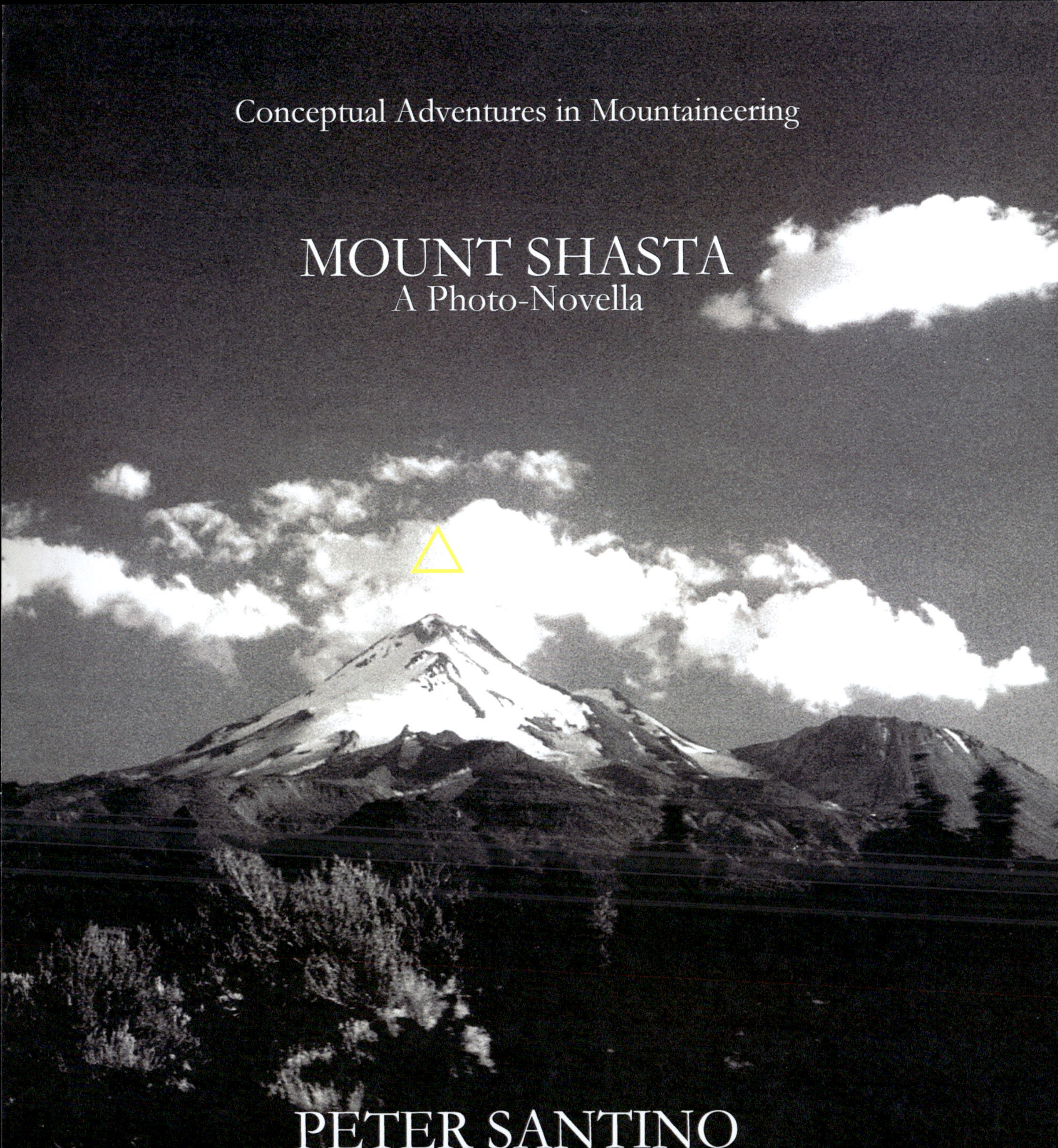

Conceptual Adventures in Mountaineering

MOUNT SHASTA
A Photo-Novella

PETER SANTINO

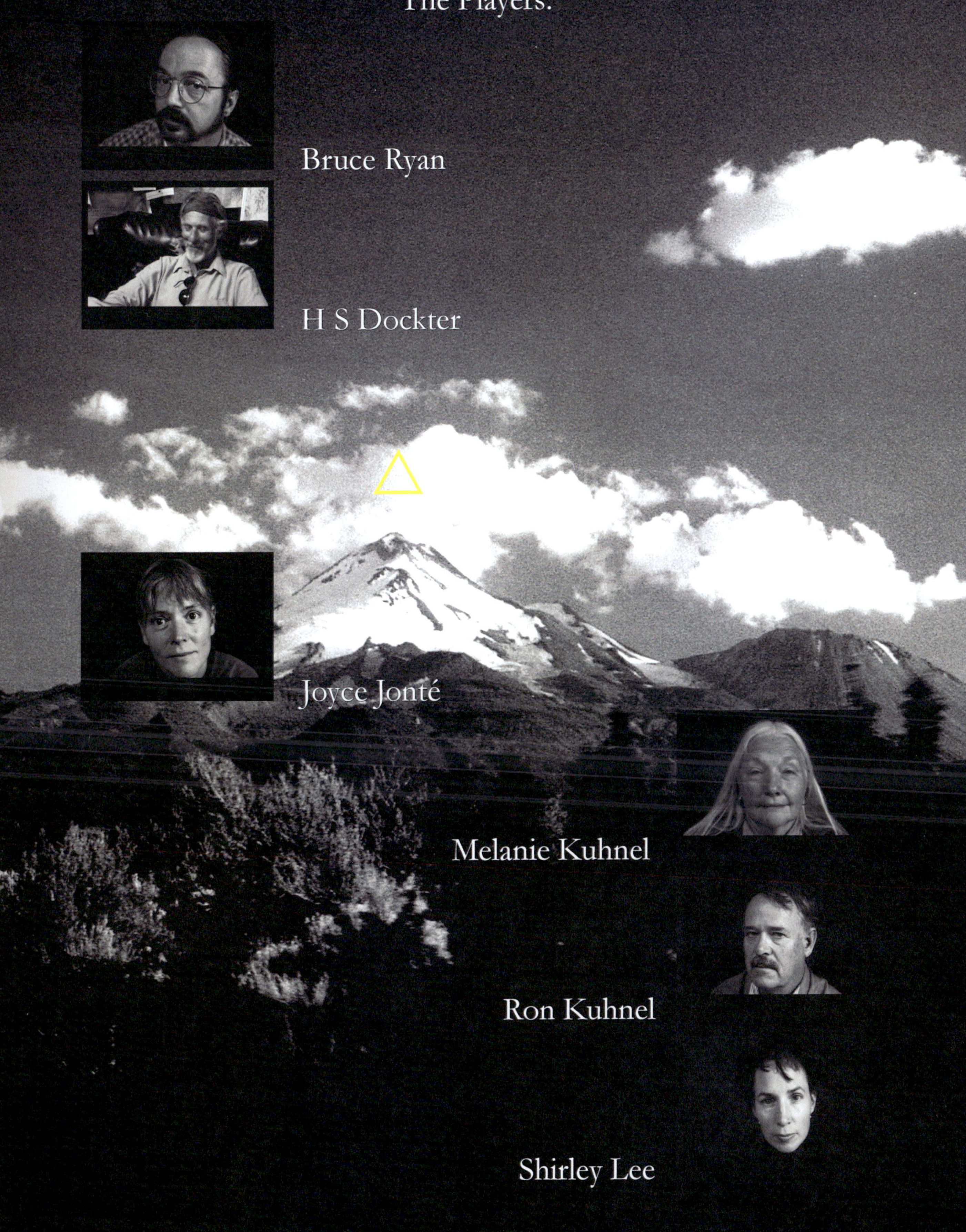

The Players:
Bruce Ryan
H S Dockter
Joyce Jonté
Melanie Kuhnel
Ron Kuhnel
Shirley Lee

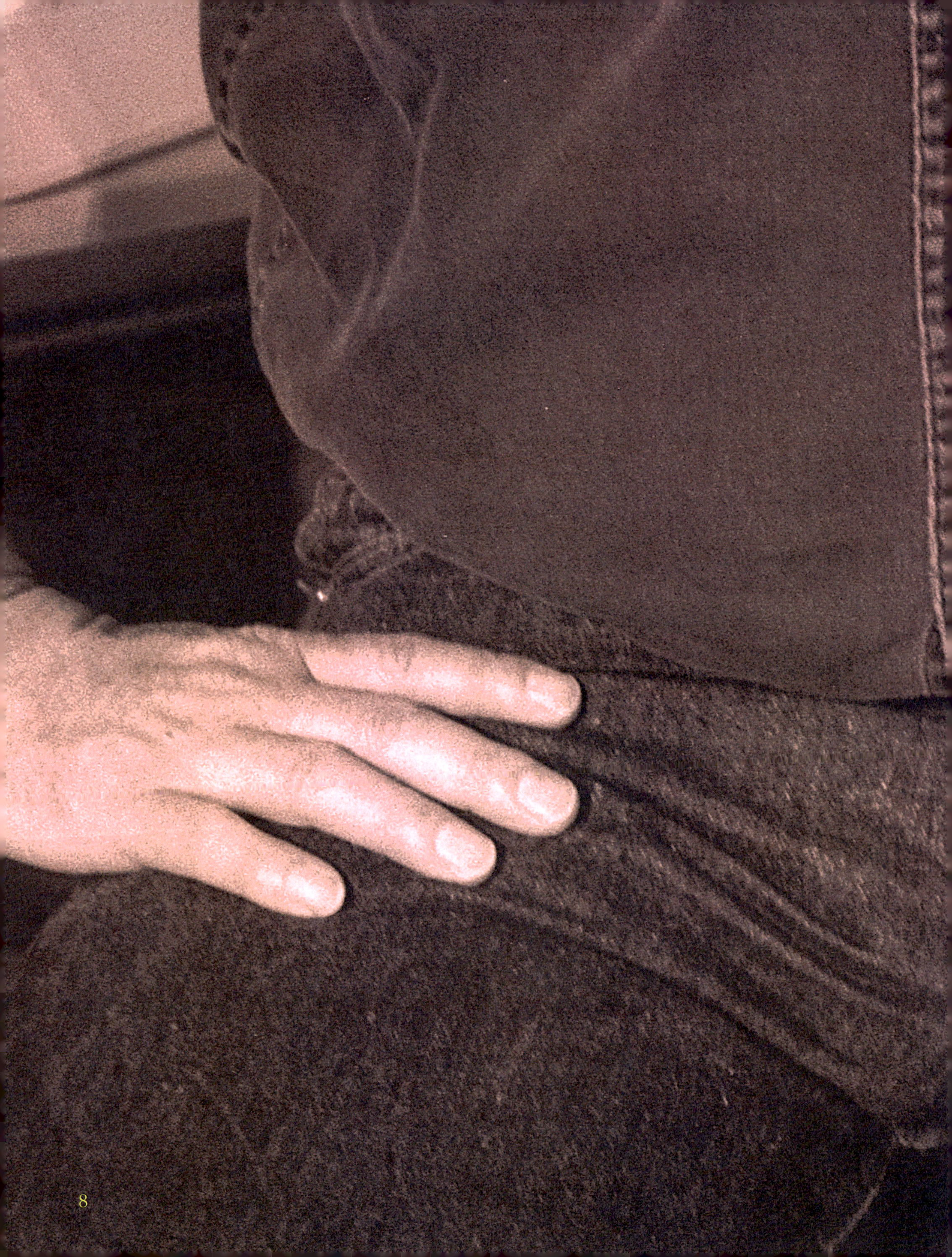

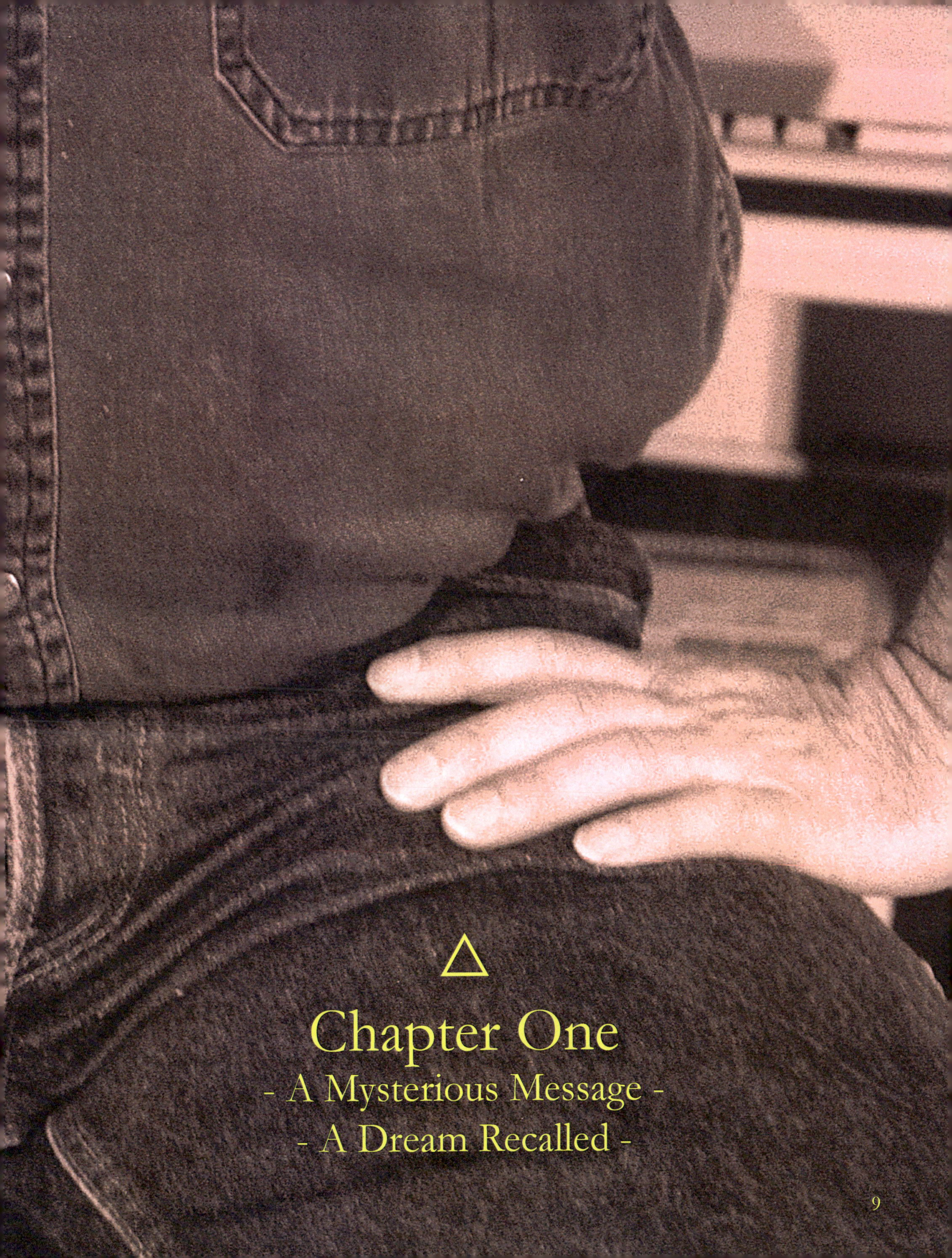
△
Chapter One
- A Mysterious Message -
- A Dream Recalled -

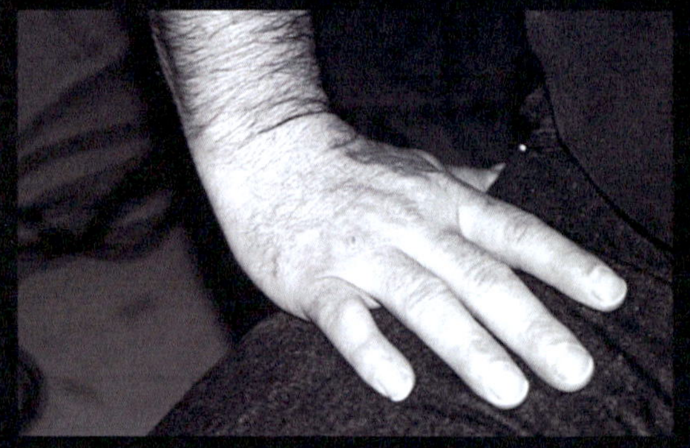

The whole of this strange adventure began

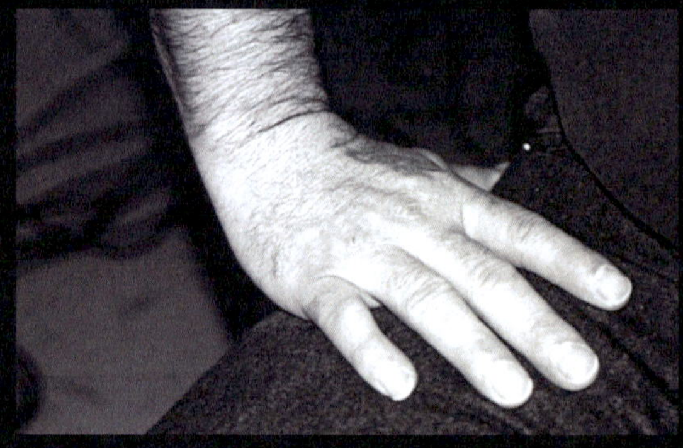

with a peculiar electronic mail message

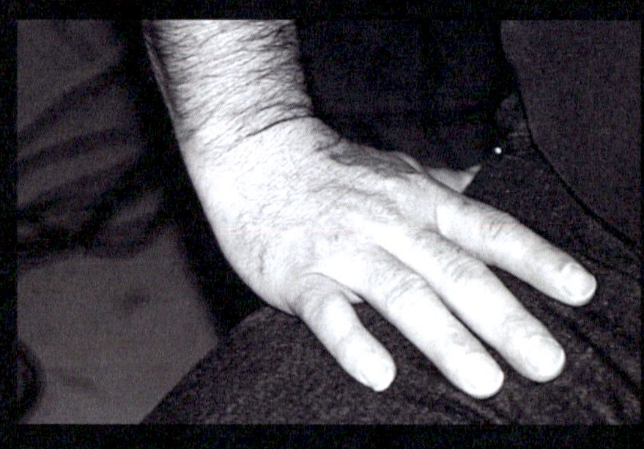

I received several weeks ago,

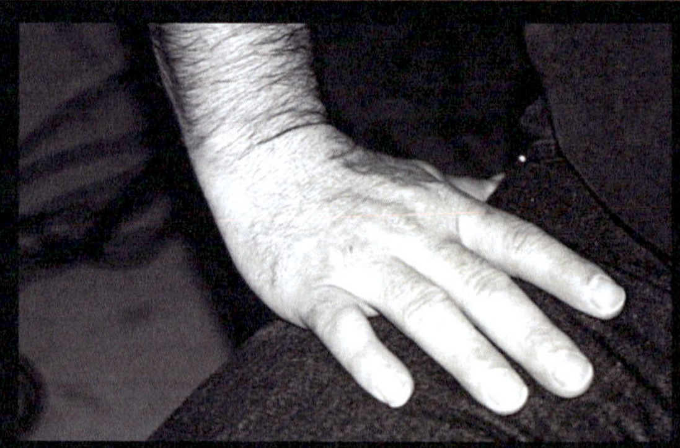

posted to my web site's address.

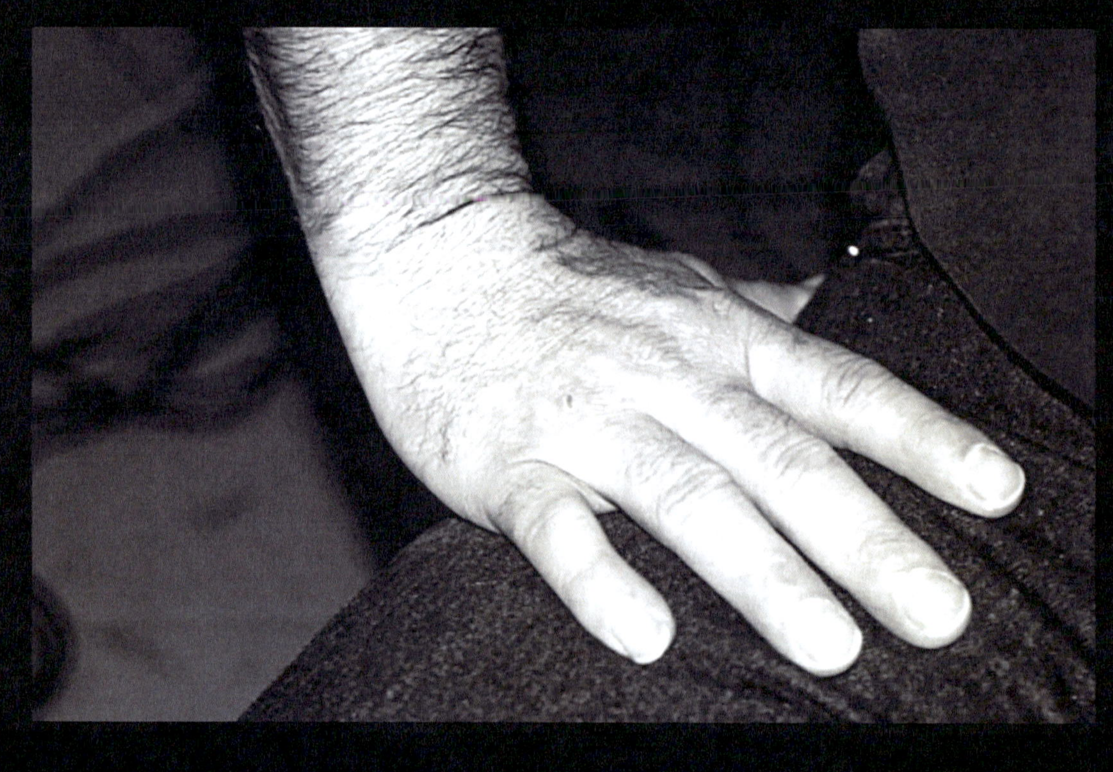

Since the seminal days of the World Wide Web, the project I directed,
FAILURE INSTITUTE,

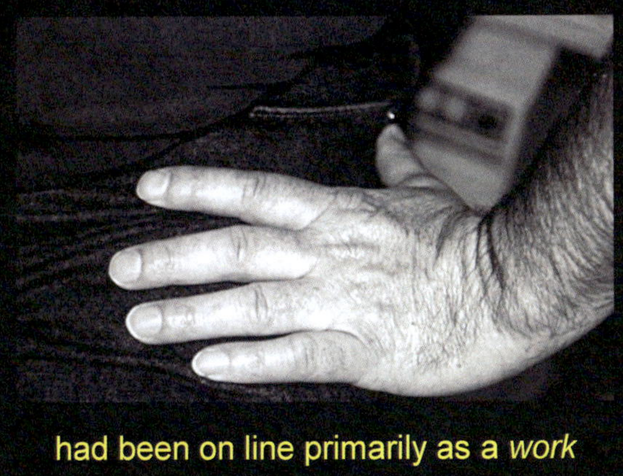

had been on line primarily as a *work*

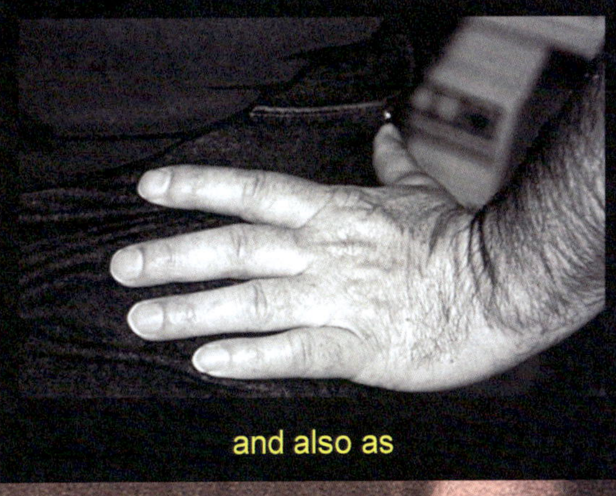

and also as

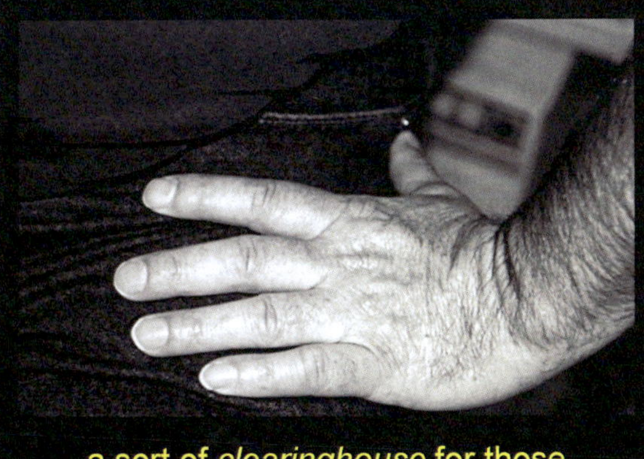

a sort of *clearinghouse* for those

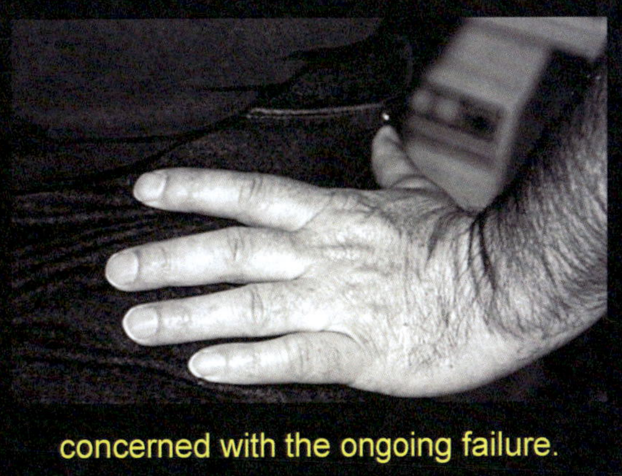

concerned with the ongoing failure.

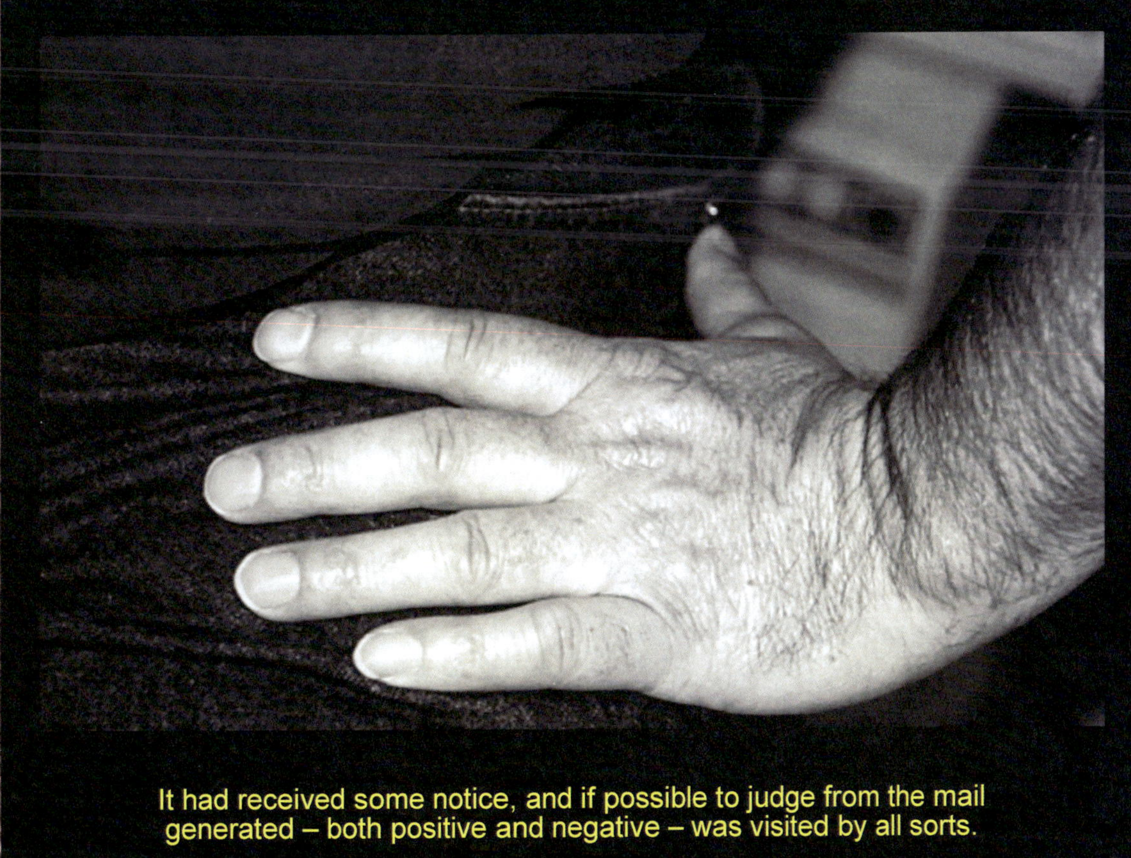

It had received some notice, and if possible to judge from the mail generated – both positive and negative – was visited by all sorts.

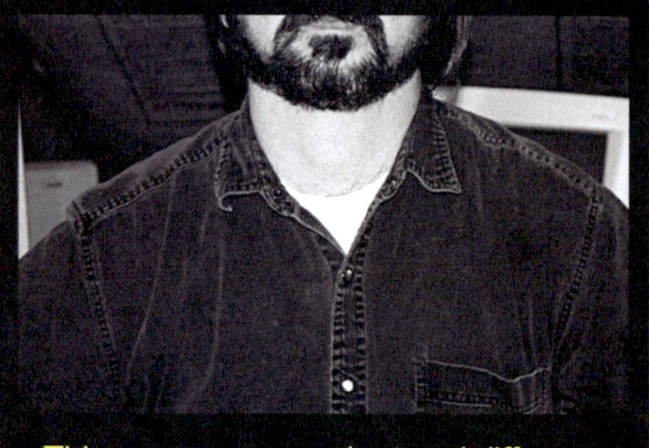

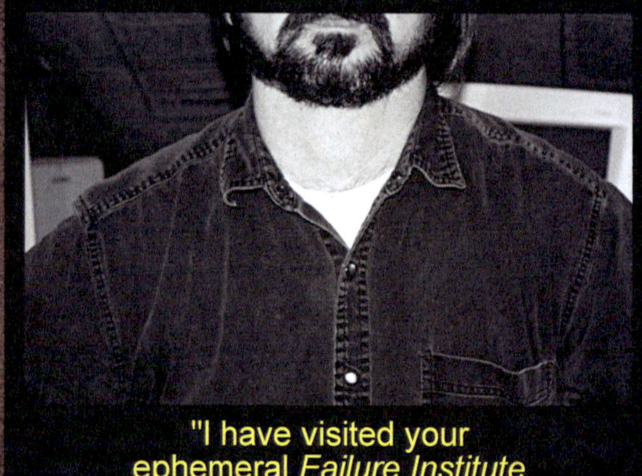

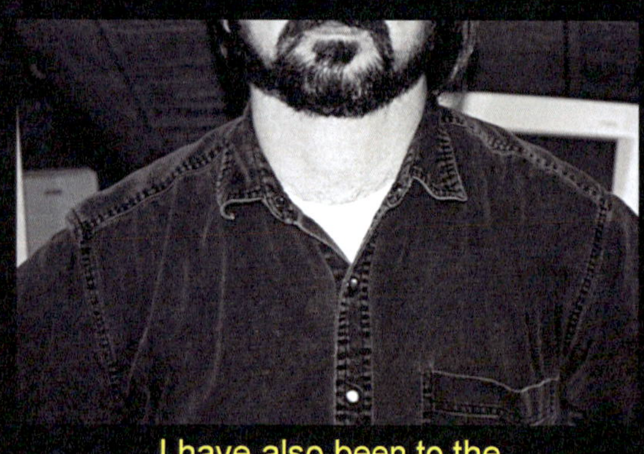

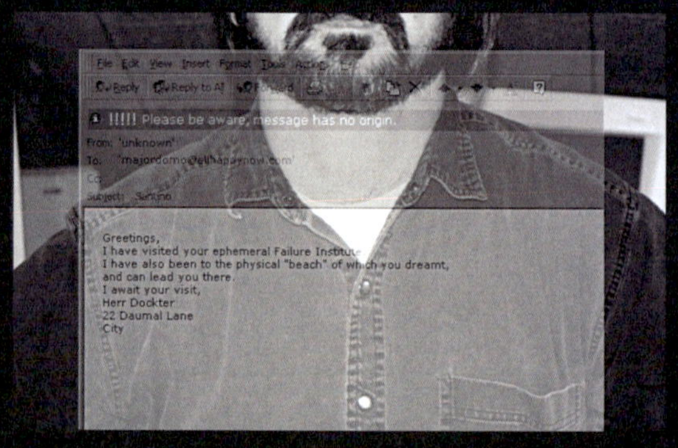

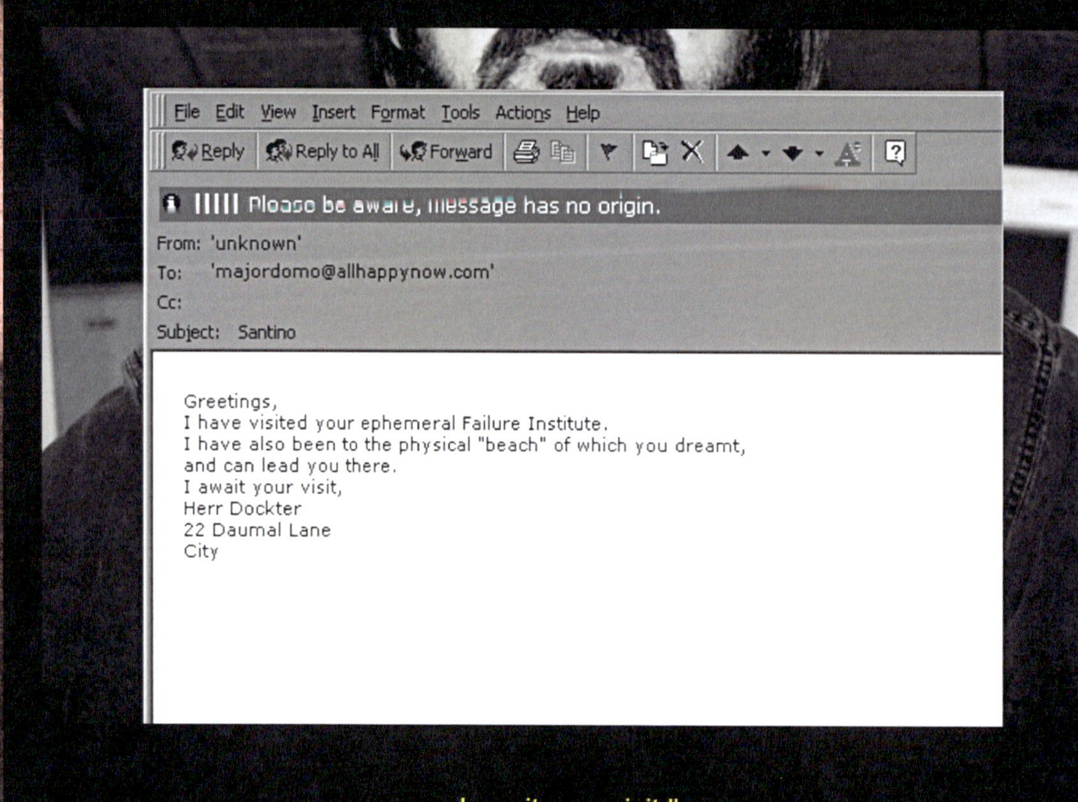

File   Edit   View   Insert   Format   Tools   Actions   Help

Reply   Reply to All   Forward

ℹ️ ||||| Please be aware, message has no origin.

From: 'unknown'
To: 'majordomo@allhappynow.com'
Cc:
Subject: Santino

Greetings,
I have visited your ephemeral Failure Institute.
I have also been to the physical "beach" of which you dreamt,
and can lead you there.
I await your visit,
Herr Dockter
22 Daumal Lane
City

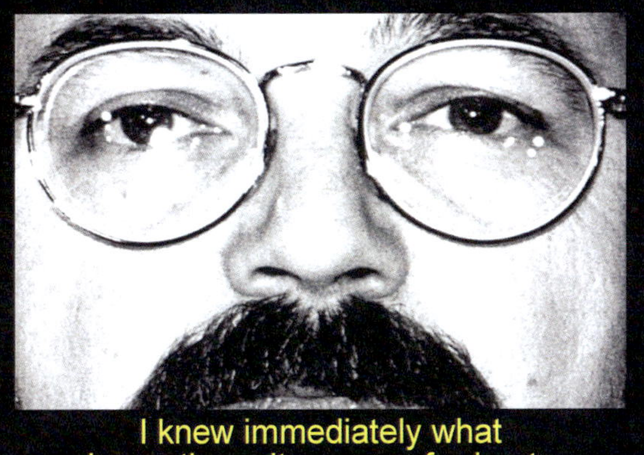
I knew immediately what
dream the writer was referring to.

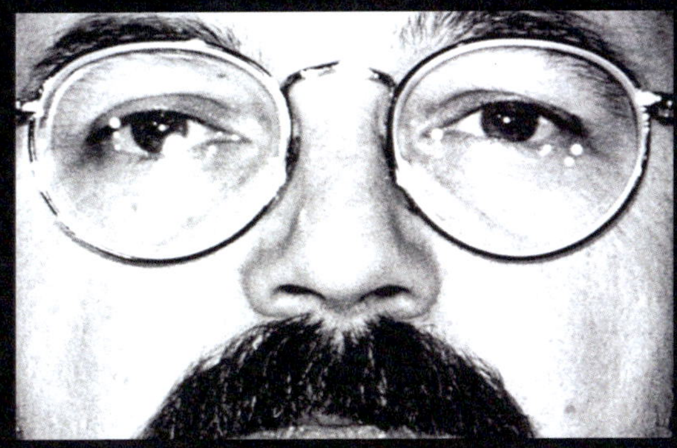
For some time now, there was posted
at *Failure Institute, a text,*

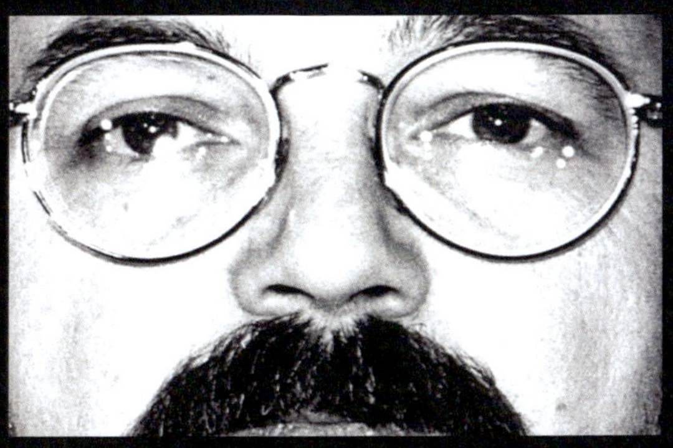
several pages in length, which described

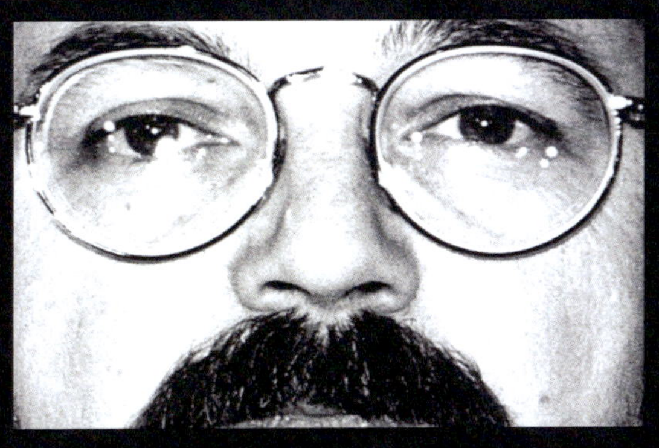
a vivid dream I'd had in Geneva.

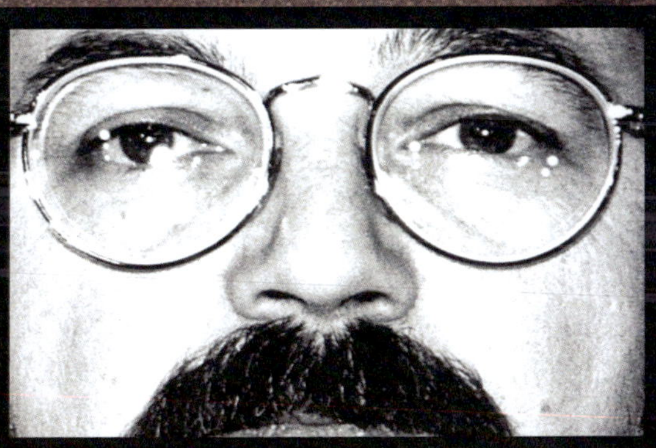
I won't retell the entire dream here,

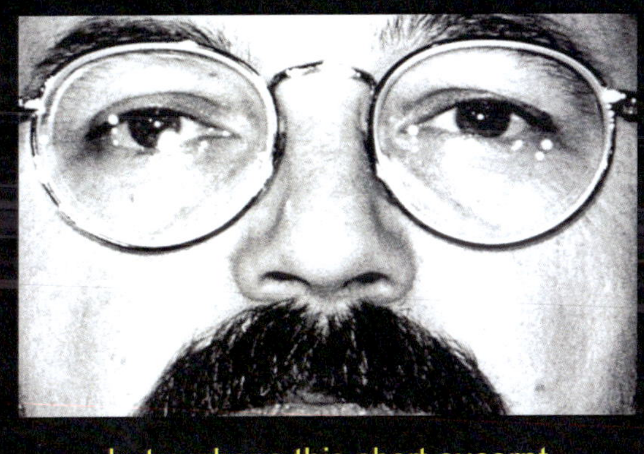
but perhaps this short excerpt

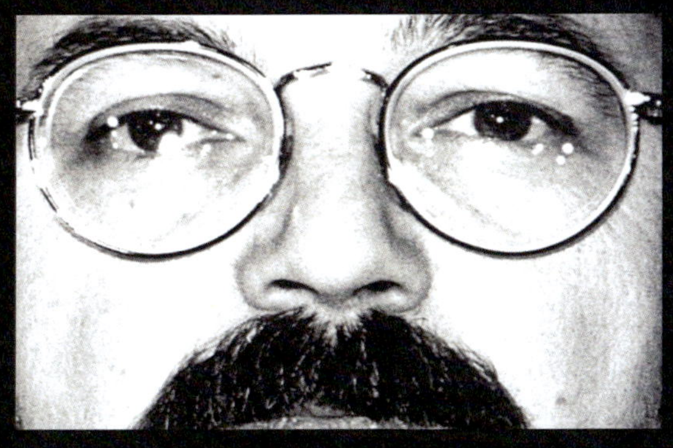
will explain my interest

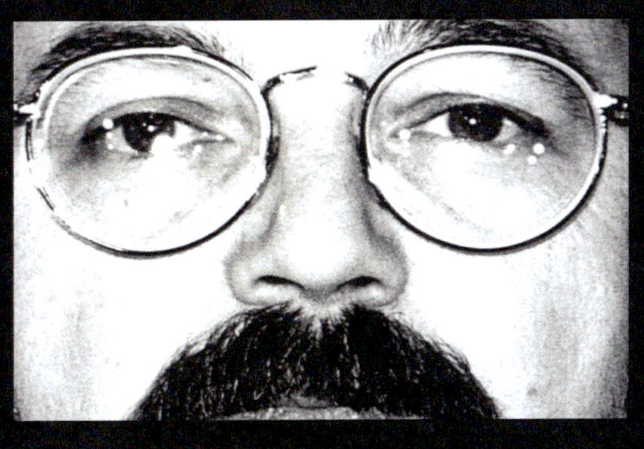
in the mysterious email.

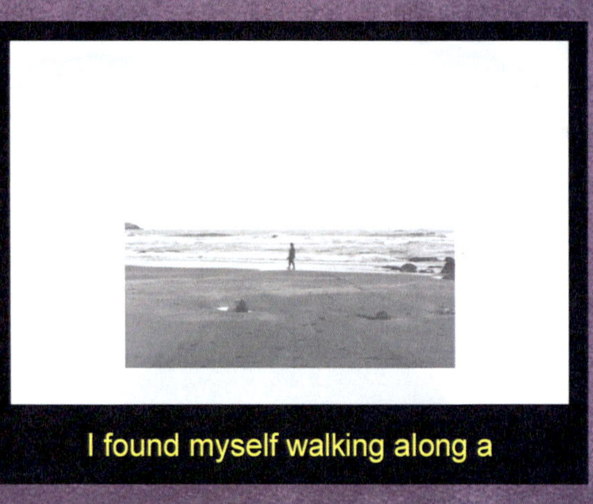

I found myself walking along a

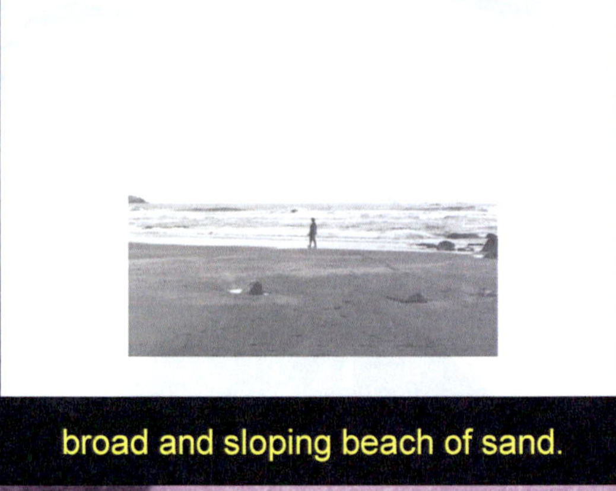

broad and sloping beach of sand.

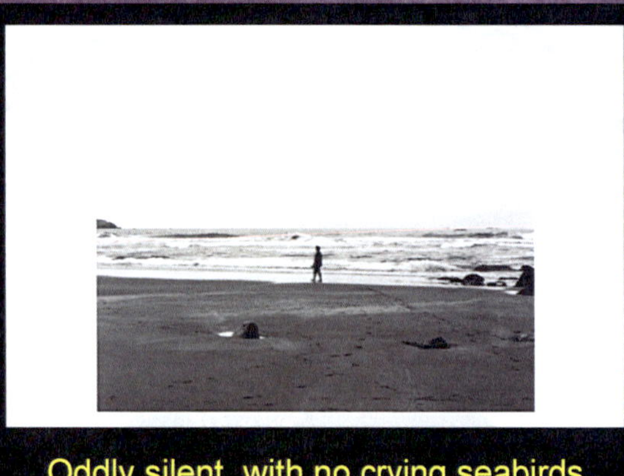
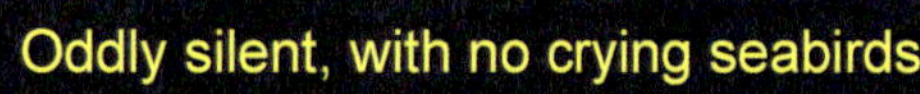

Oddly silent, with no crying seabirds

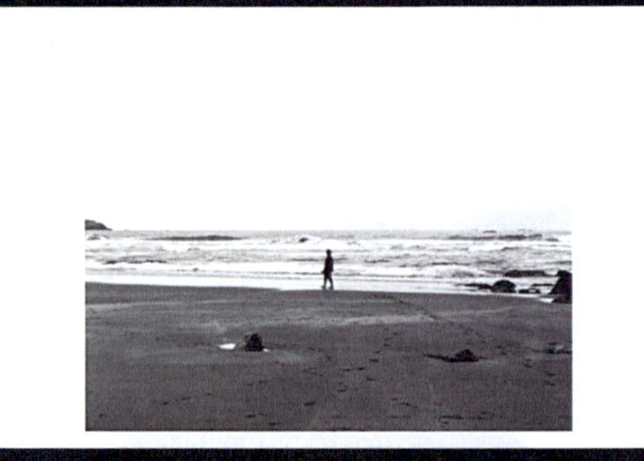
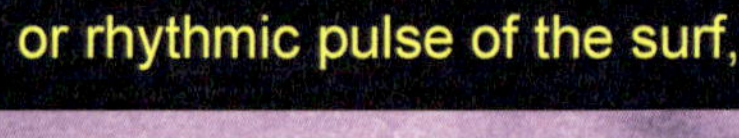

or rhythmic pulse of the surf,

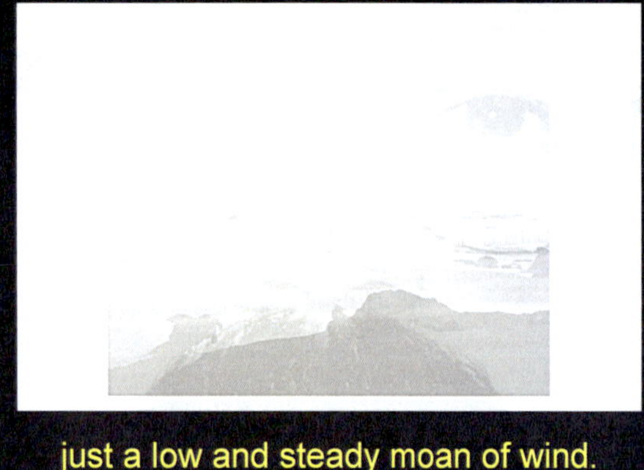

just a low and steady moan of wind.

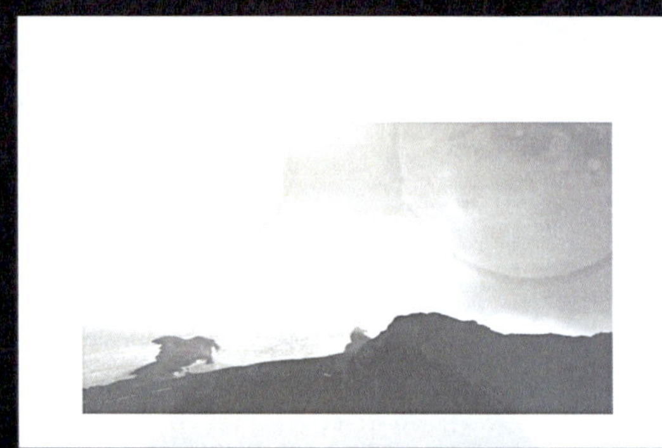

On my left, I sensed a sharply rising cliff.

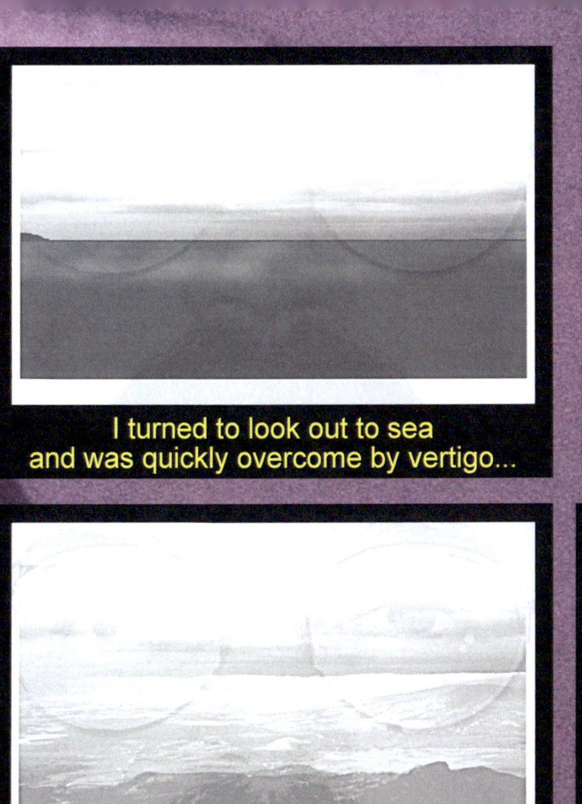
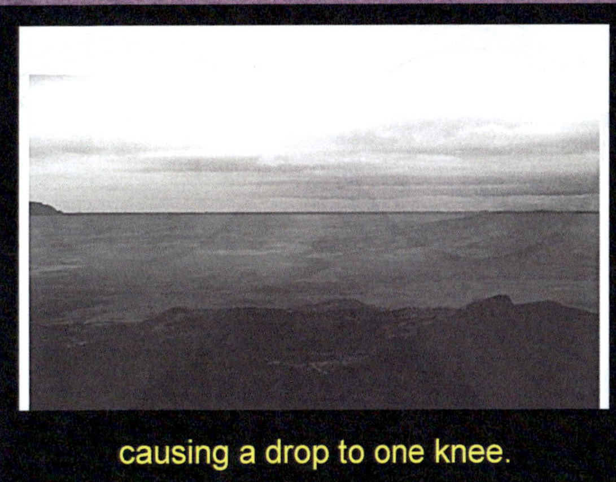

I turned to look out to sea
and was quickly overcome by vertigo...

causing a drop to one knee.

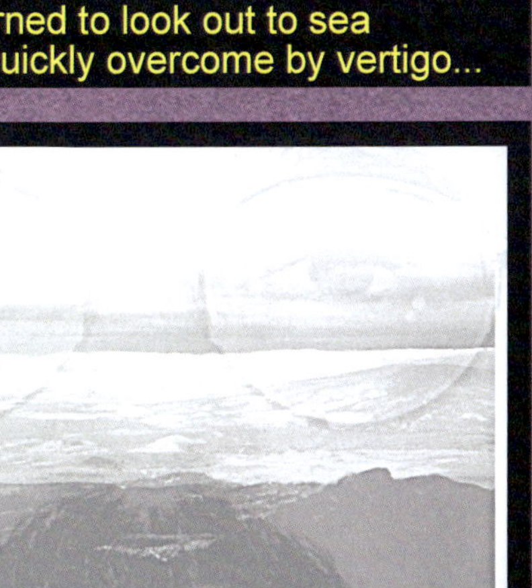
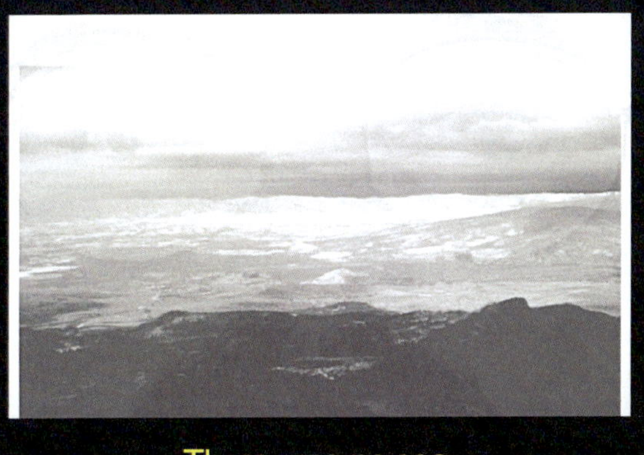

The beach fell sharply away in front of me.

There was no sea.

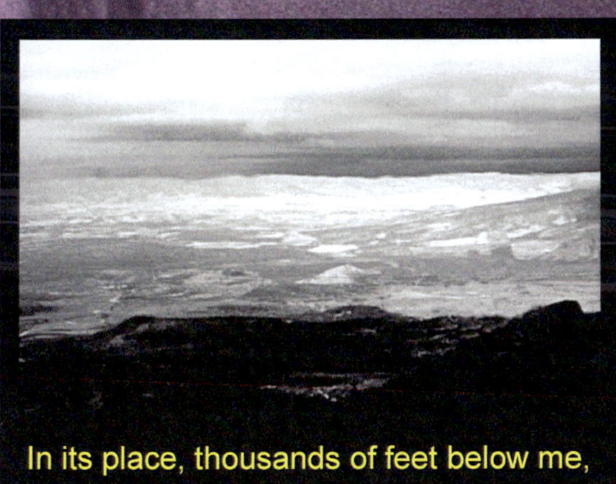
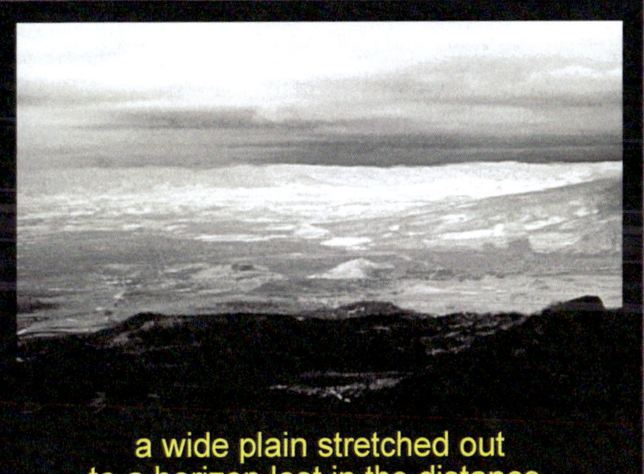

In its place, thousands of feet below me,

a wide plain stretched out
to a horizon lost in the distance.

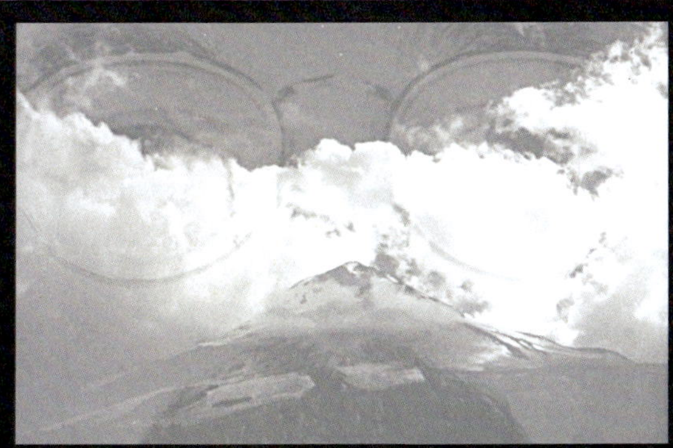
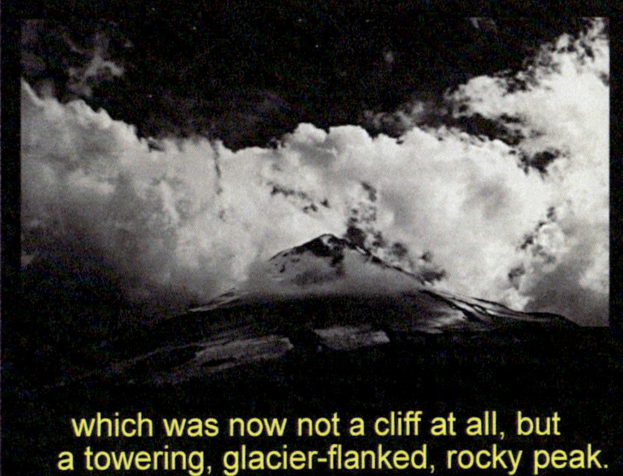

To regain my balance, I shifted and
looked back over my shoulder to the cliff,

which was now not a cliff at all, but
a towering, glacier-flanked, rocky peak.

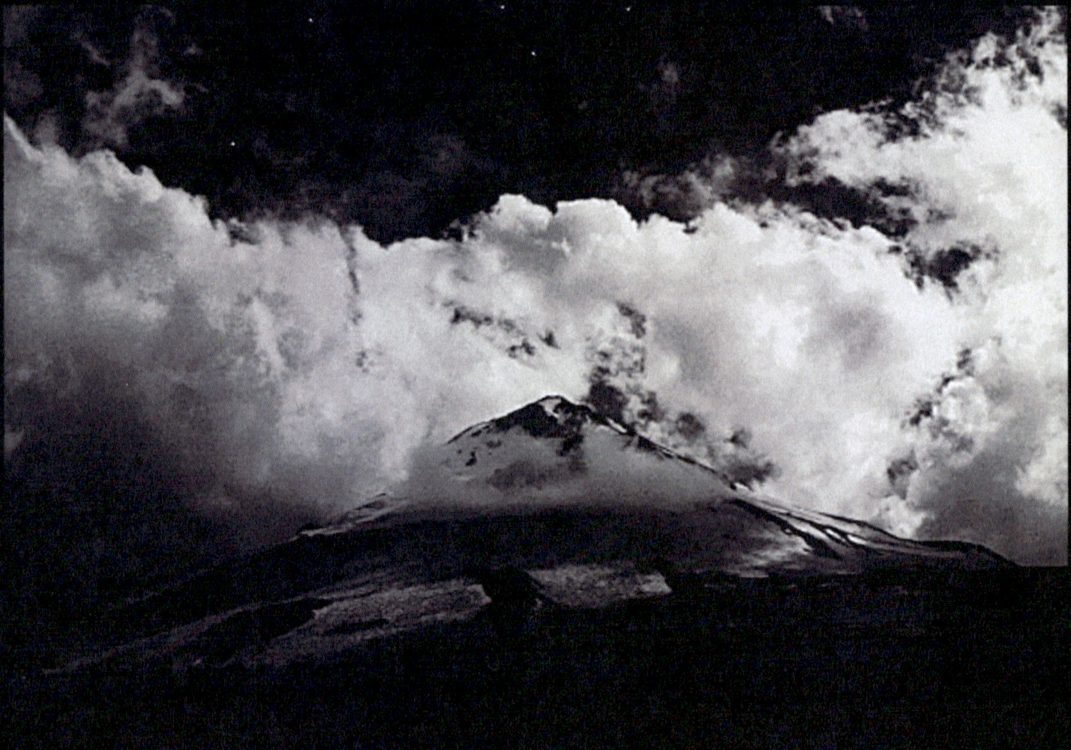

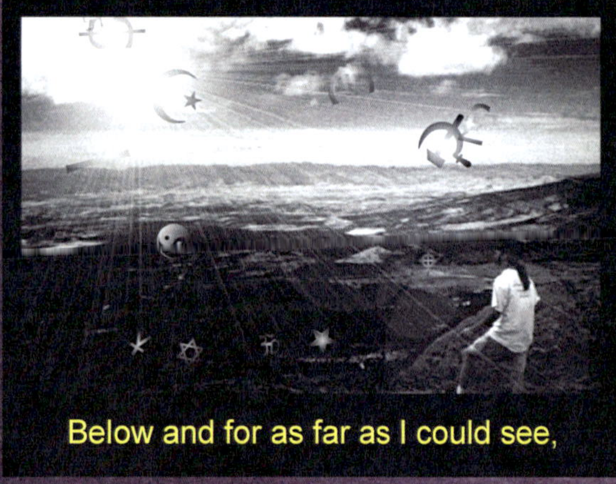

Above me were stars in a sky so deep blue it seemed almost black.
And yet the warm light of a rising, or perhaps setting sun, was still strong.

Below and for as far as I could see,

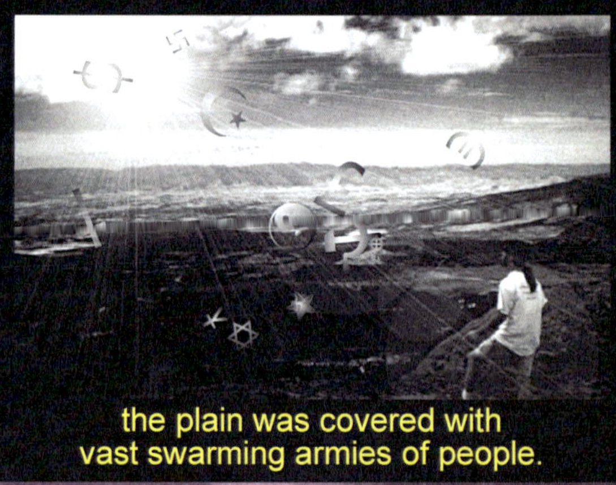

the plain was covered with
vast swarming armies of people.

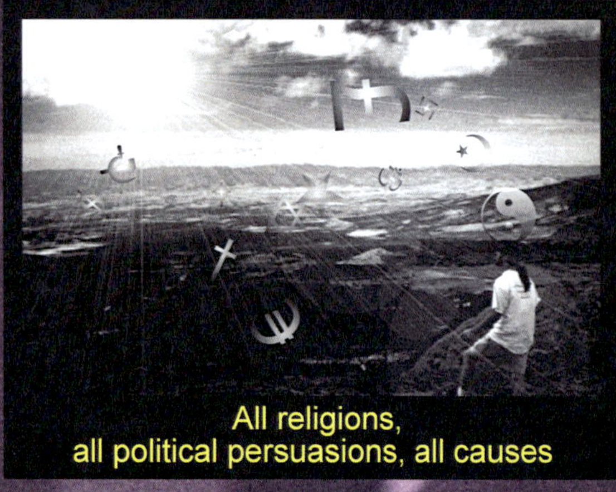

All religions,
all political persuasions, all causes

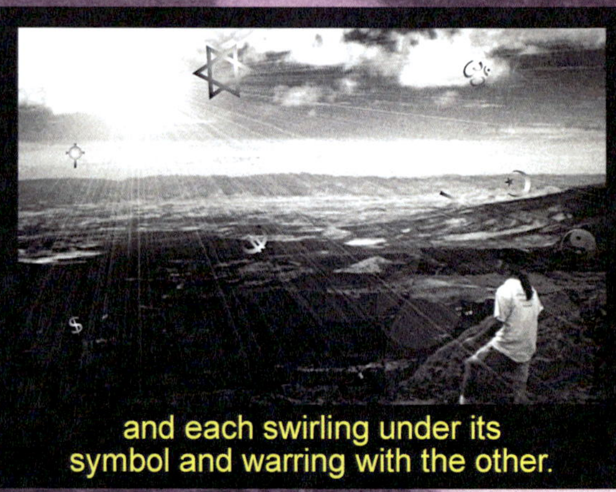

and each swirling under its
symbol and warring with the other.

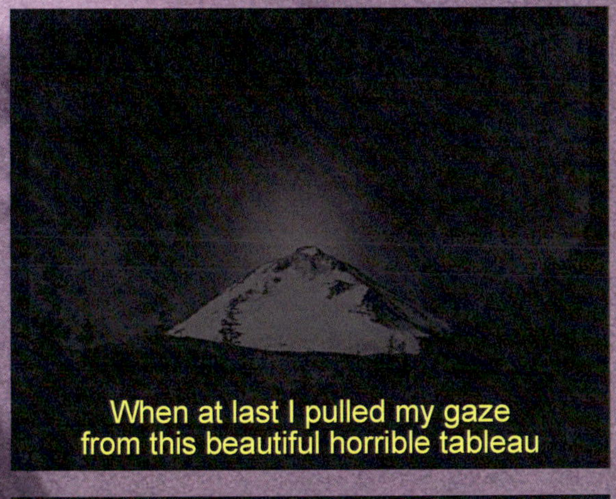

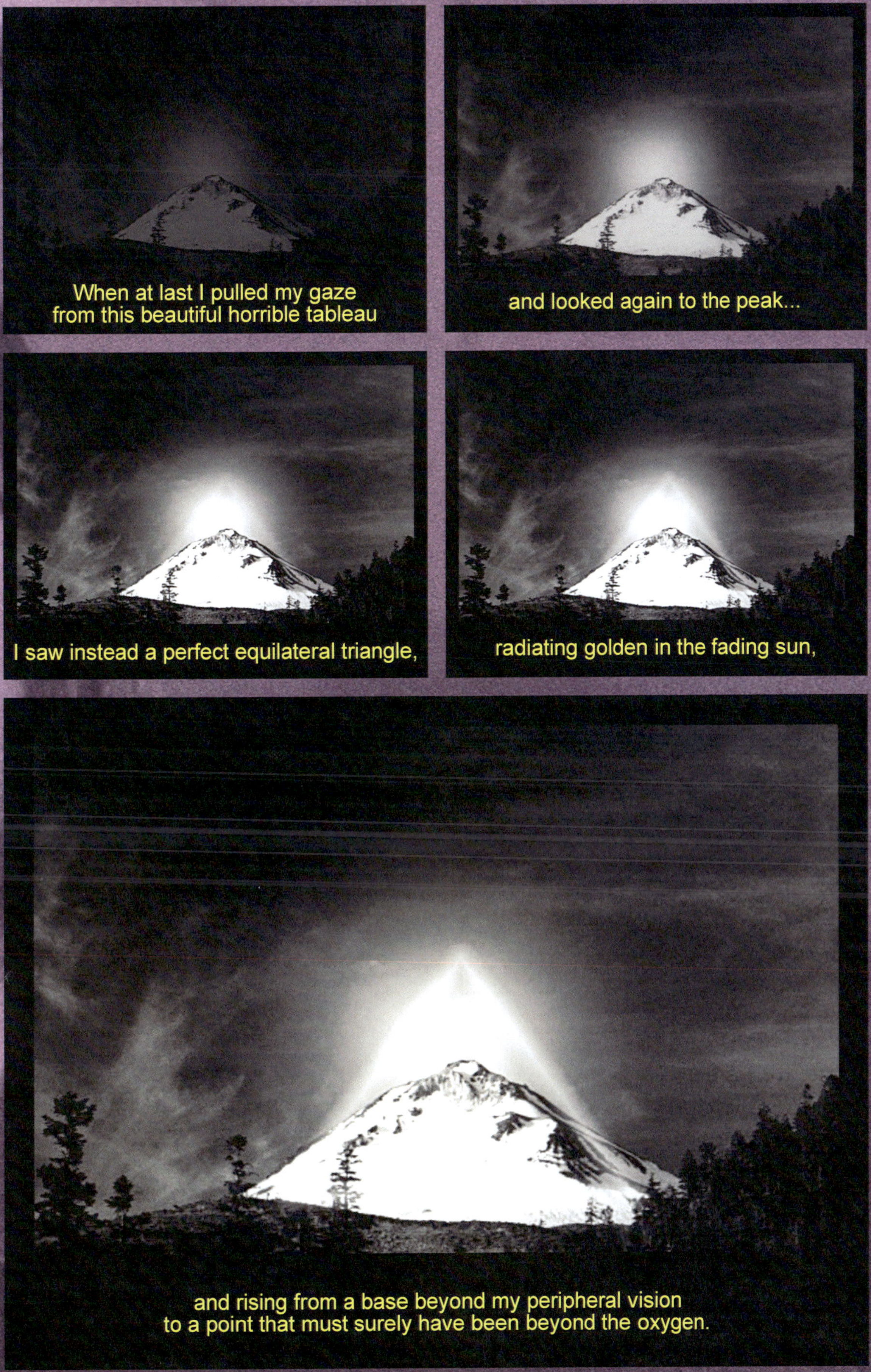

When at last I pulled my gaze
from this beautiful horrible tableau

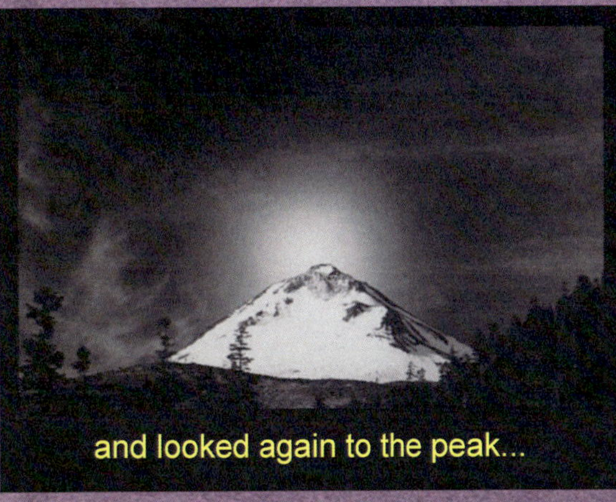

and looked again to the peak...

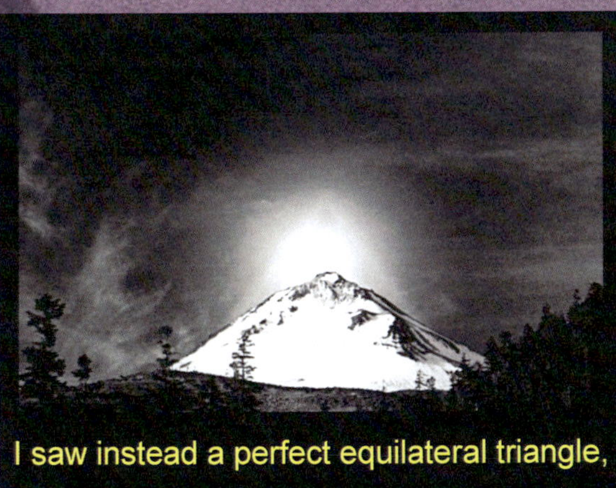

I saw instead a perfect equilateral triangle,

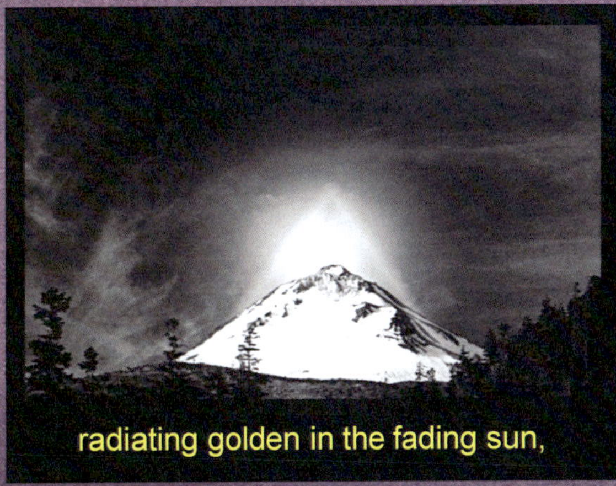

radiating golden in the fading sun,

and rising from a base beyond my peripheral vision
to a point that must surely have been beyond the oxygen.

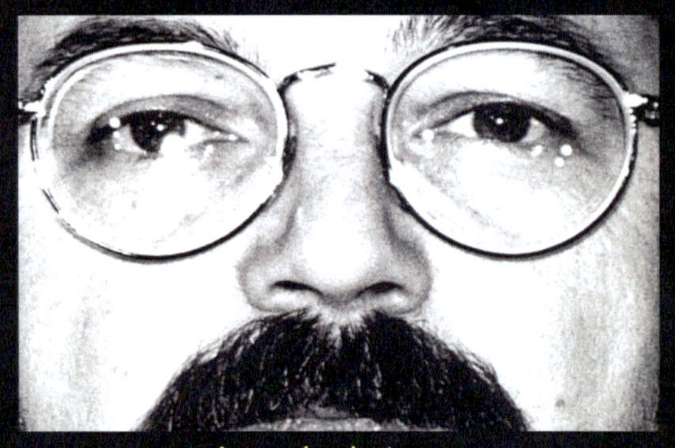

I awoke in tears
with a great sense of longing.

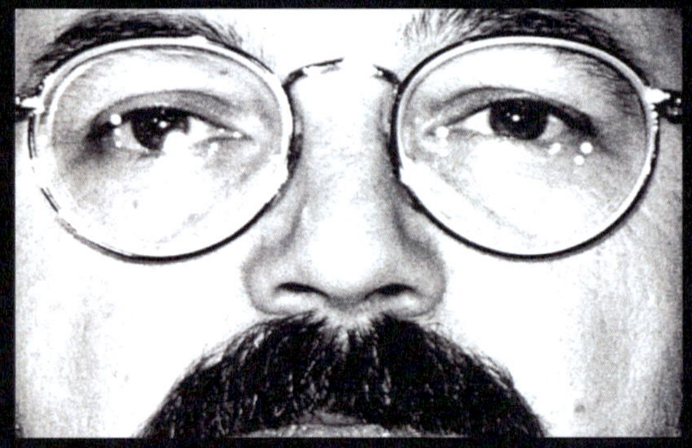

Feeling, at the time,

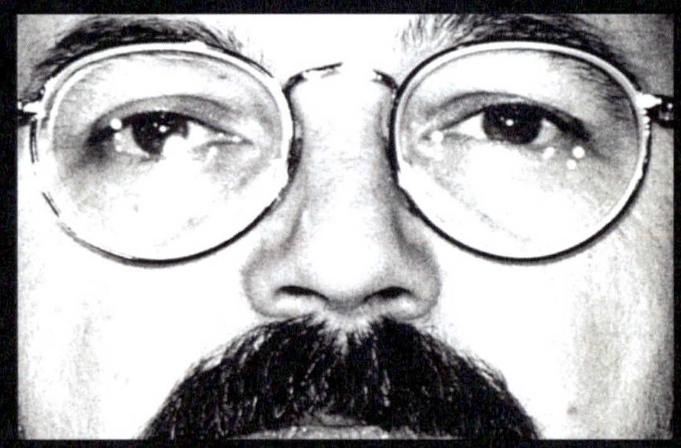

the dream might have
some significance for me,

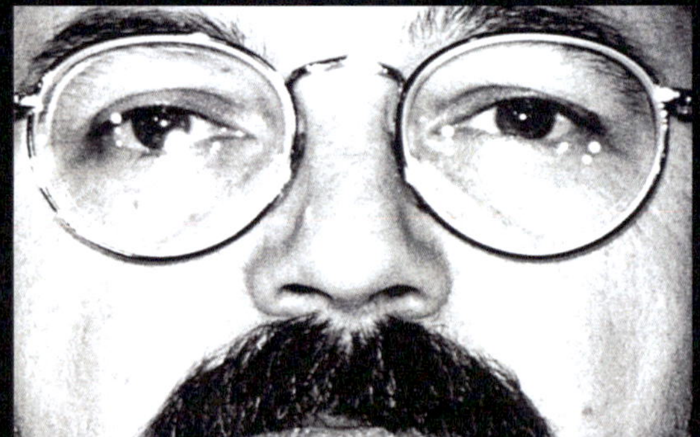

I wrote it down.

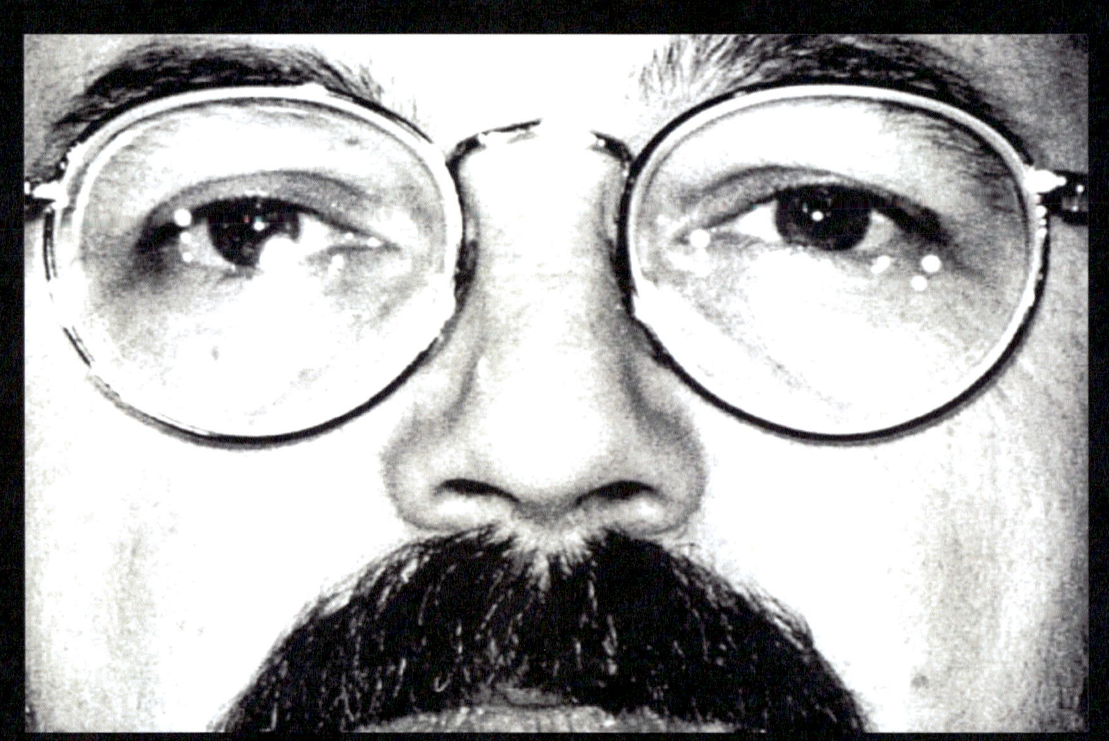

Soon, I was able to dismiss it as having been caused by
nicotine withdrawal during a failed attempt to quit smoking.

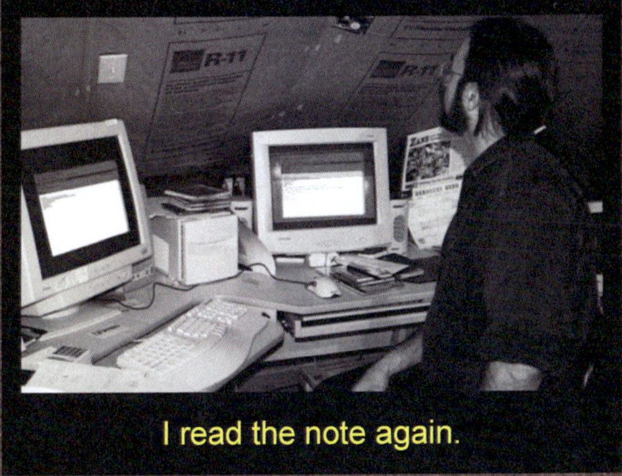

I read the note again.

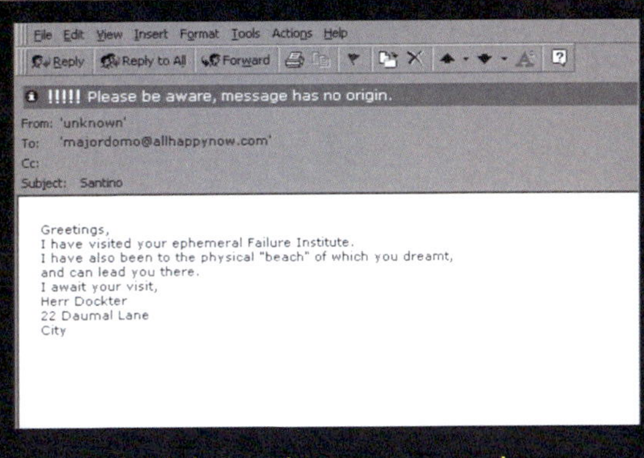

My initial reaction was uneasiness.

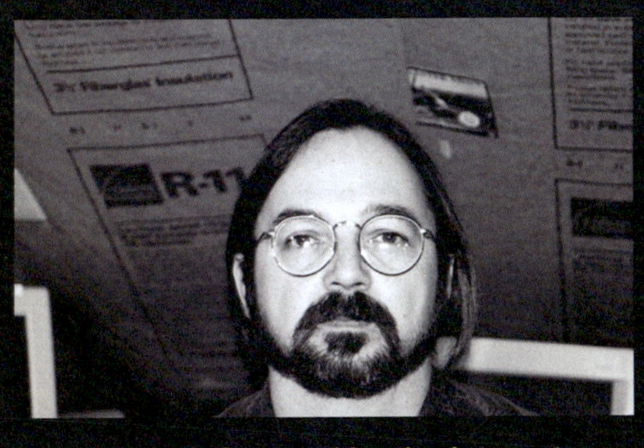

Although flattered by the interest,

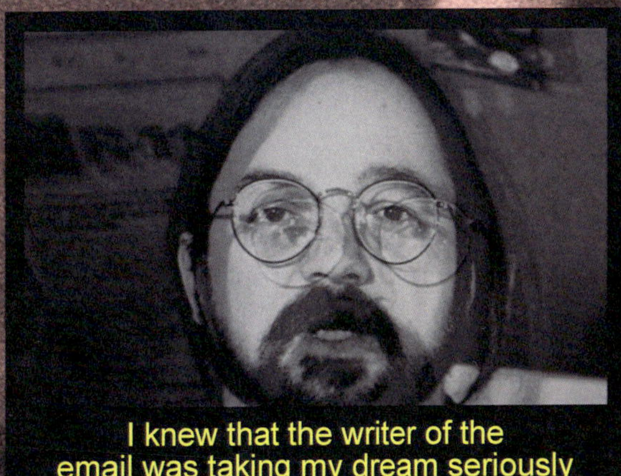

I knew that the writer of the
email was taking my dream seriously

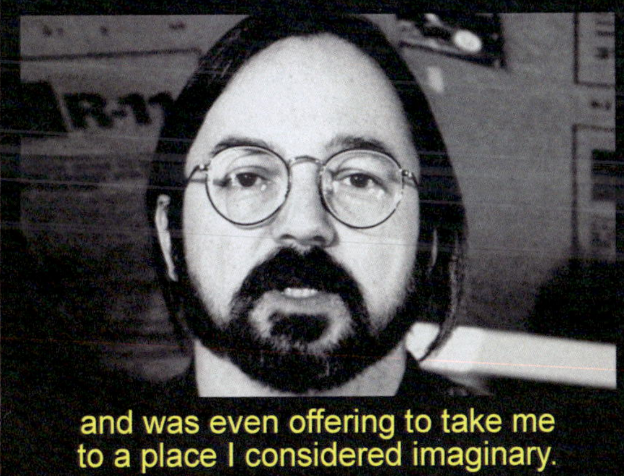

and was even offering to take me
to a place I considered imaginary.

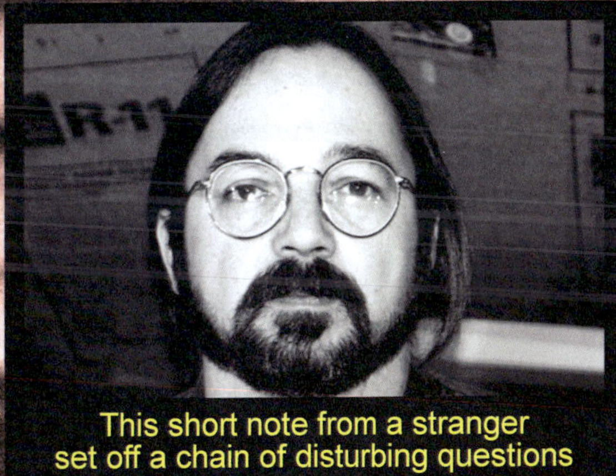

This short note from a stranger
set off a chain of disturbing questions

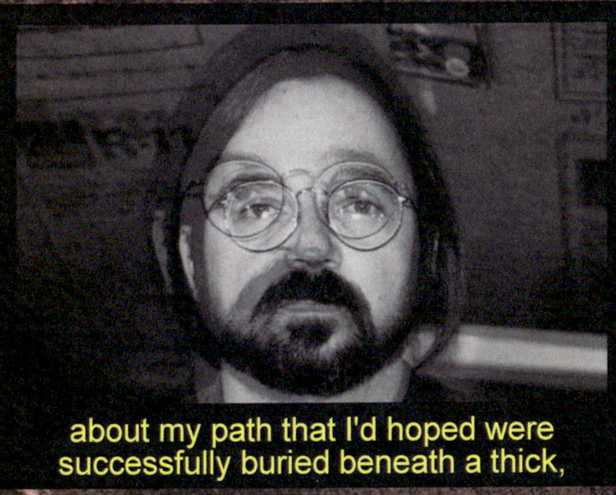

about my path that I'd hoped were
successfully buried beneath a thick,

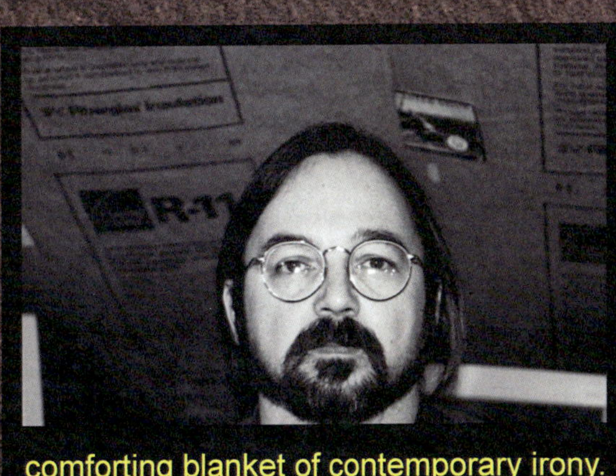

comforting blanket of contemporary irony.

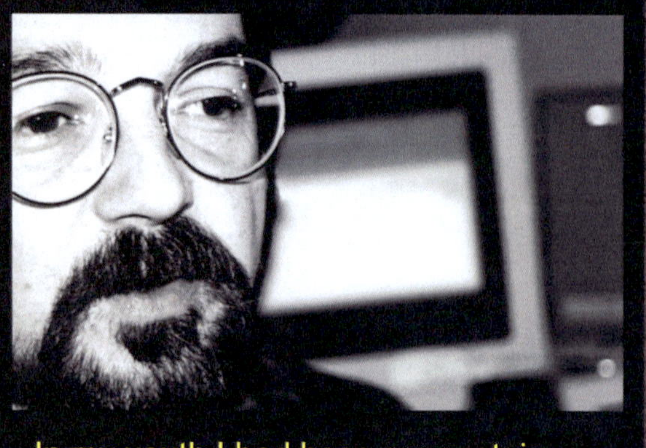

In my youth I had been a mountaineer.

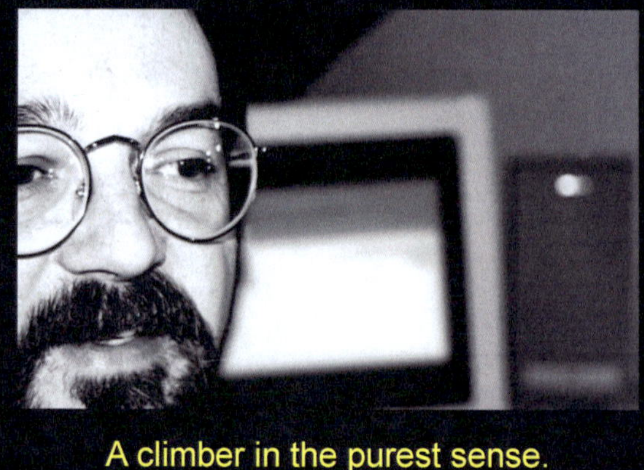

A climber in the purest sense.

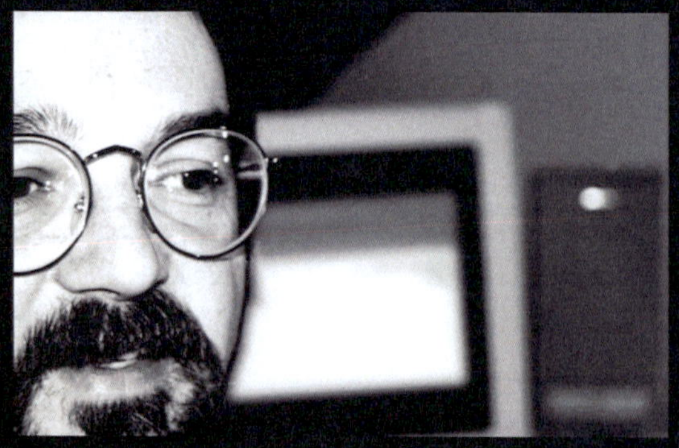

I knew, full well, what
the mountain in my dream signified.

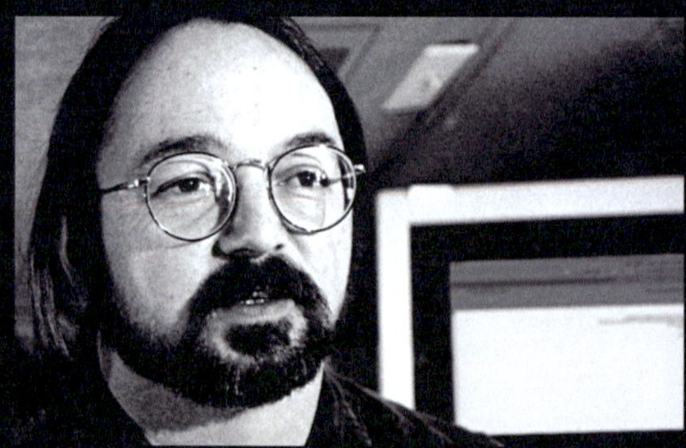

Thirty years of smoking had made me a
solid companion of altitude sickness;

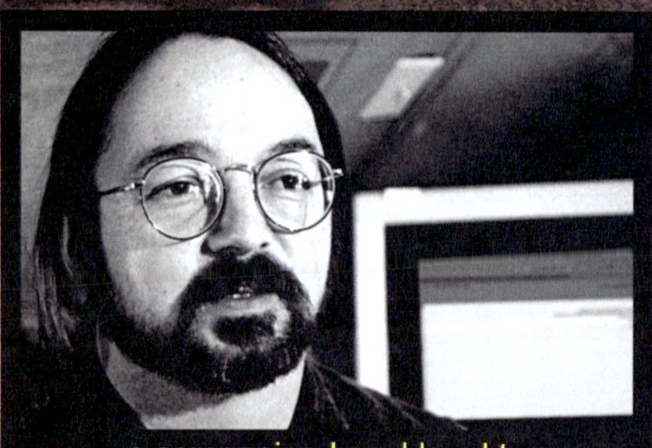

a companion I could nod to
when asked to go climbing.

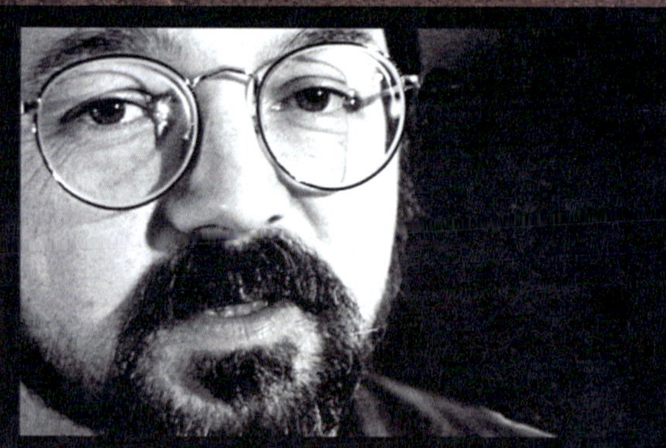

With the coming of the new millennium,
I had been re-exploring some of

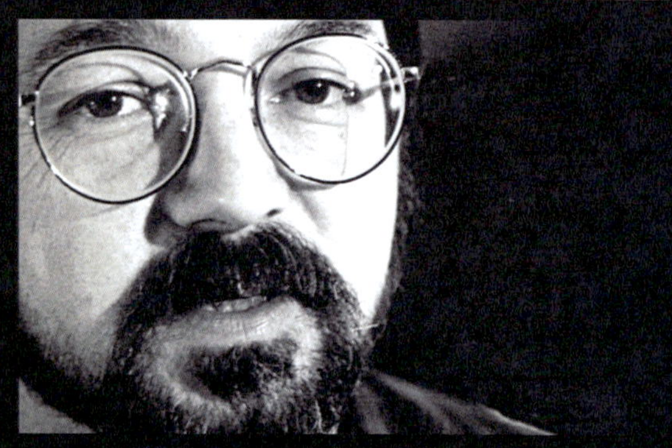

the more spiritual thoughts
of those early days.

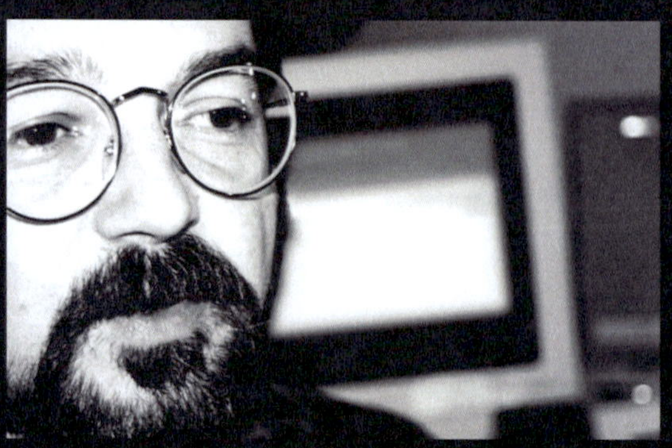

An idea that stayed strong was that of
the *Sacred Mountain,*

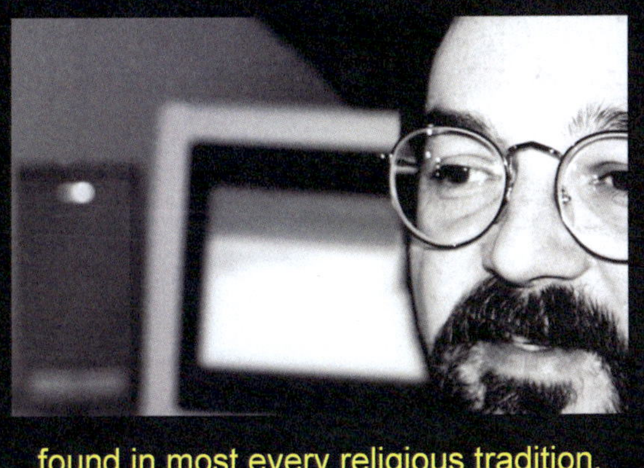

found in most every religious tradition.

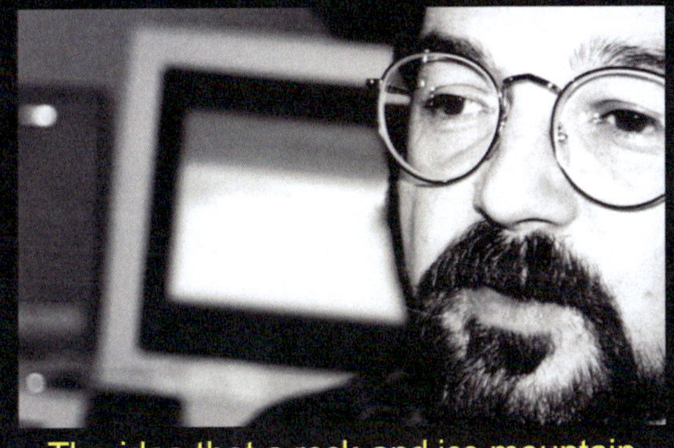

The idea that a rock and ice mountain exists somewhere on the planet,

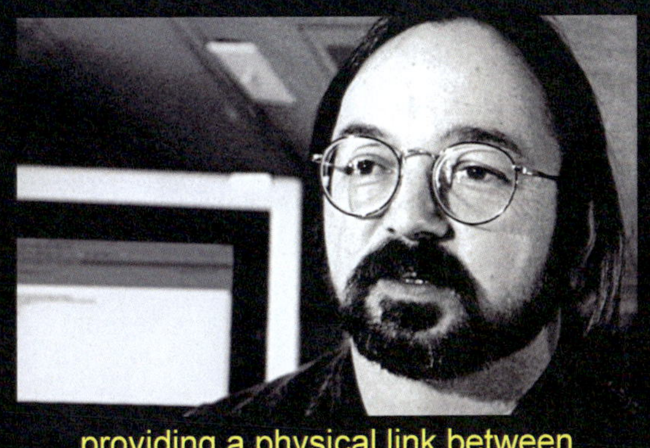

providing a physical link between Earth and Heaven, body and spirit.

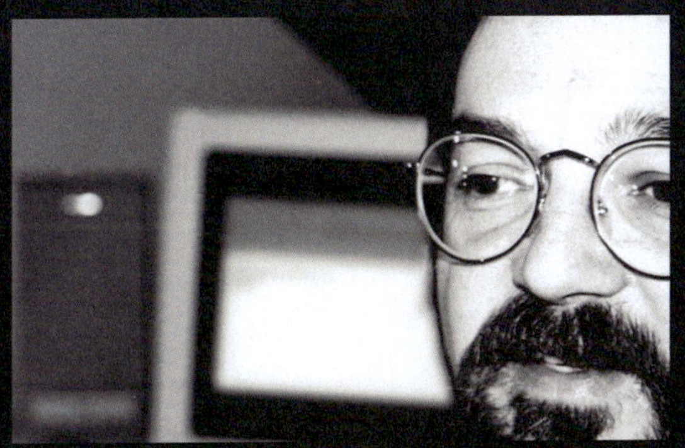

To function as this link, the mountain would have to be visible and accessible

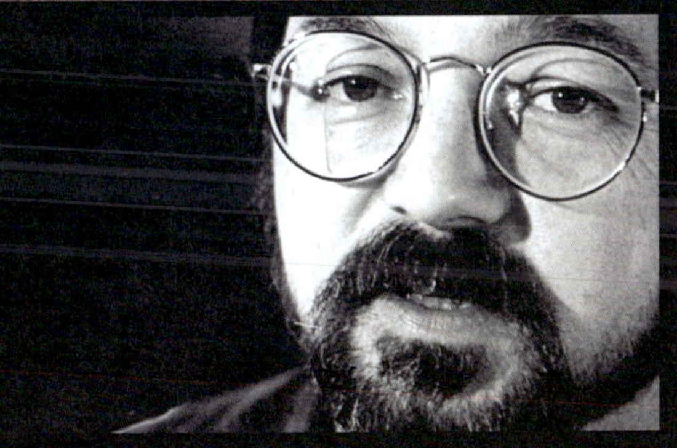

to the average human, not just an "enlightened" guru.

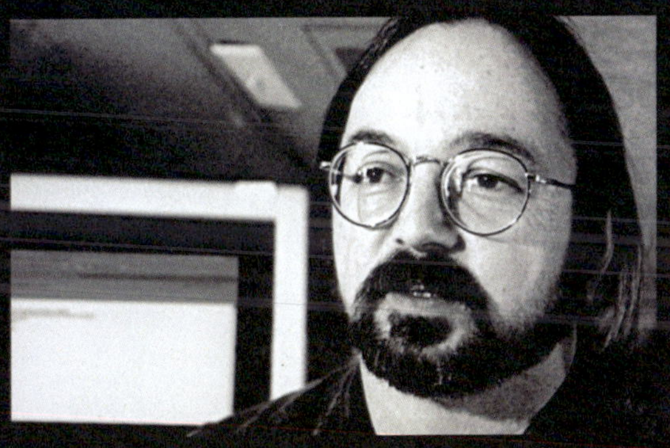

To believe in the existence of a mountain many times higher than Everest,

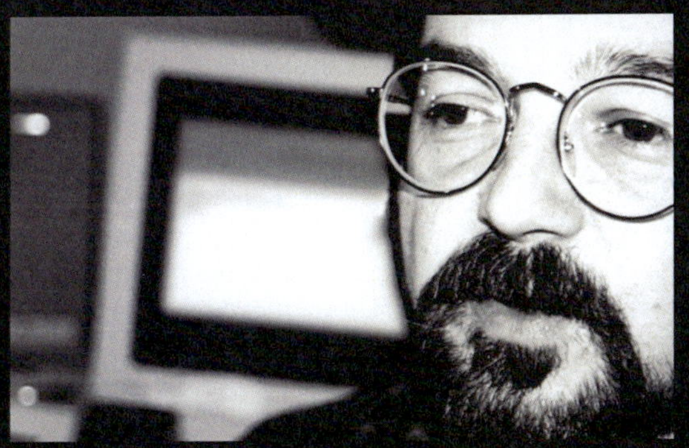

still undocumented in this age of satellites and holographic maps,

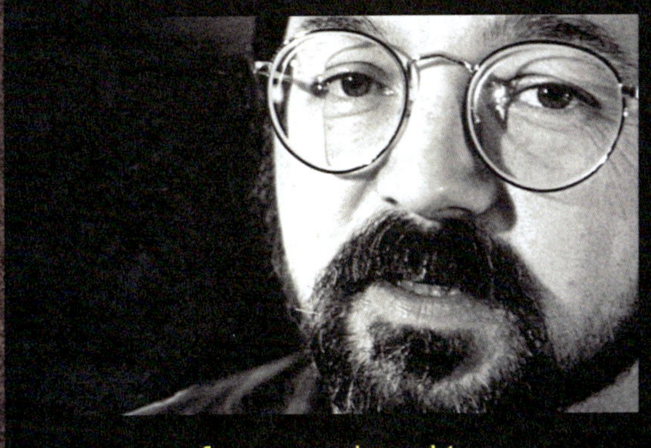

seems, of course, absurd to me now.

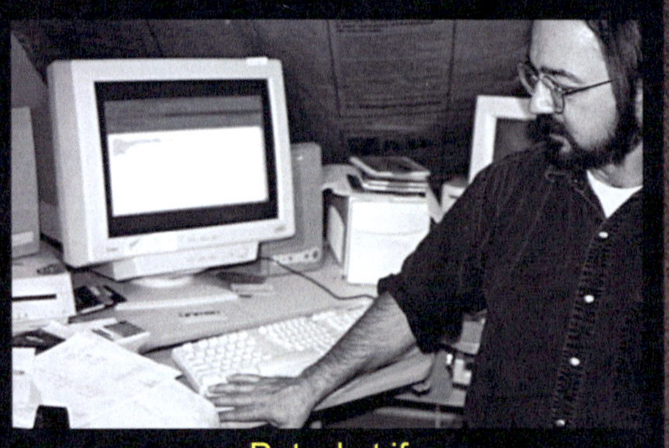
But what if
the mountain weren't always there,

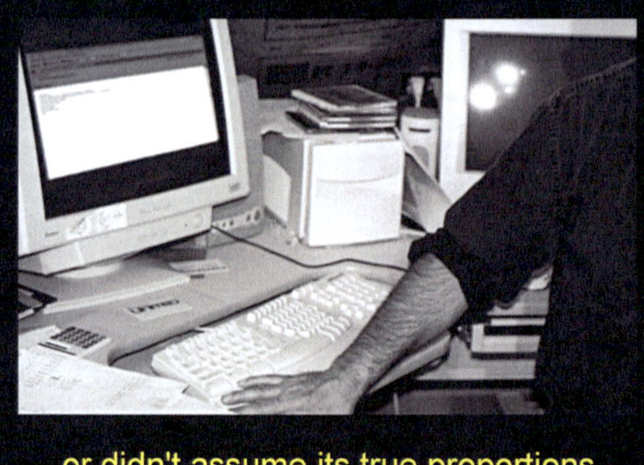
or didn't assume its true proportions

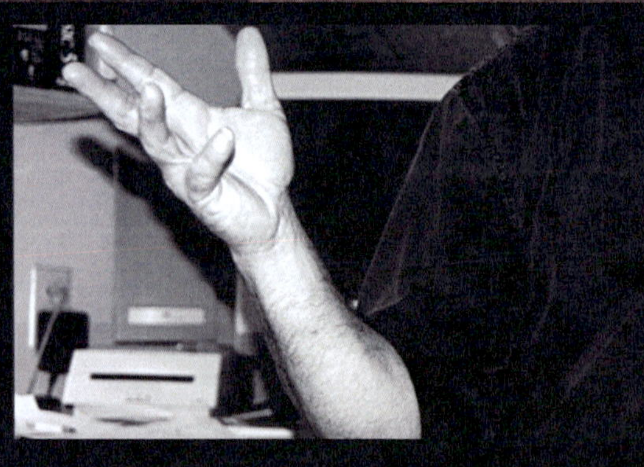
until certain conditions were met?

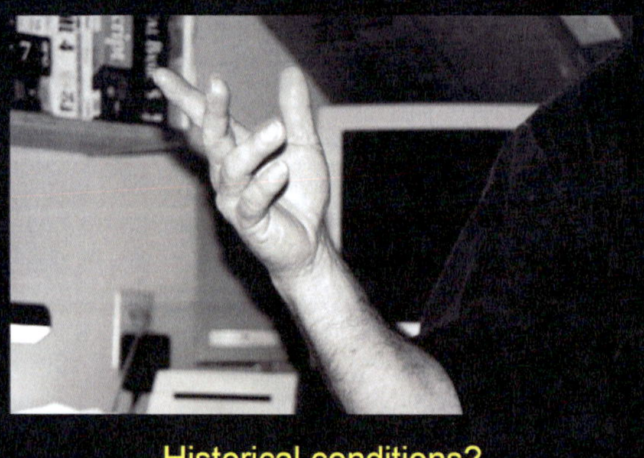
Historical conditions?

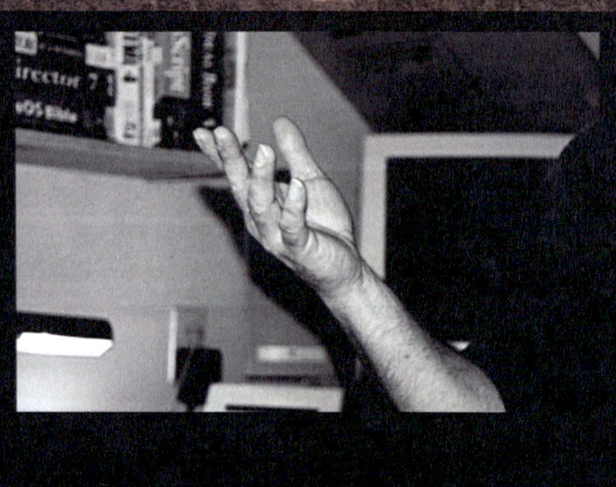

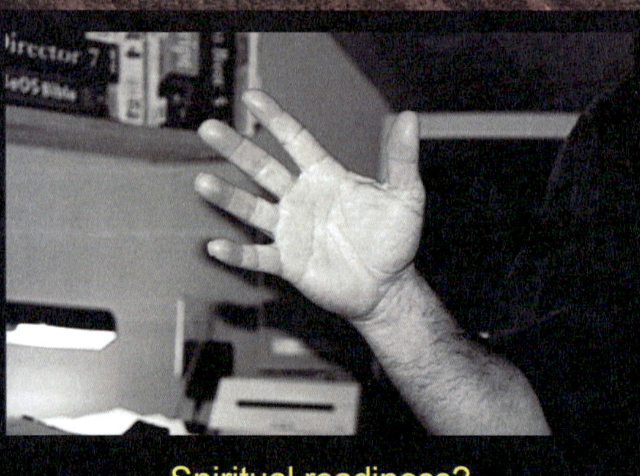
Spiritual readiness?

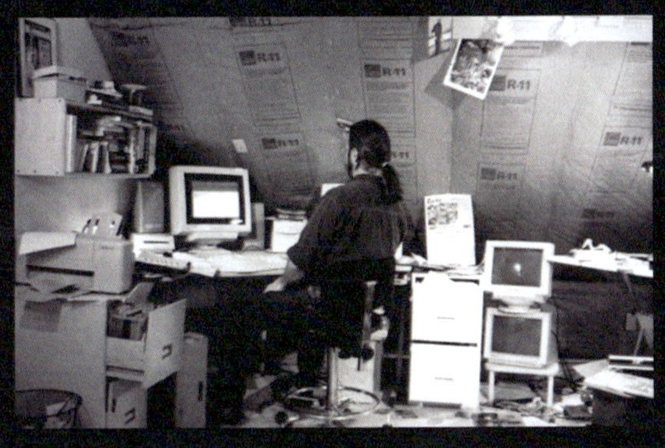

As all of these thoughts came flooding in,

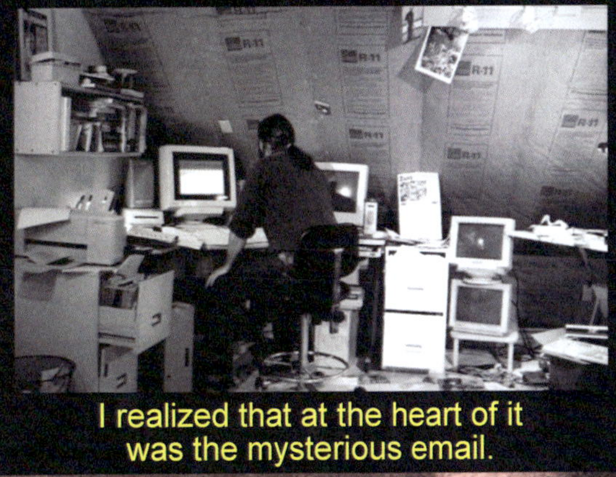

I realized that at the heart of it
was the mysterious email.

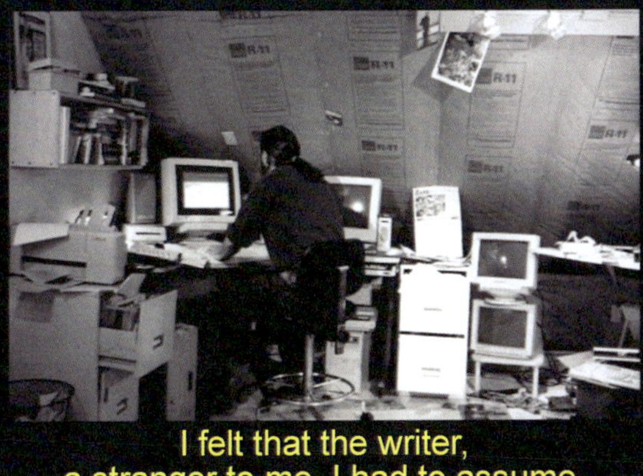

I felt that the writer,
a stranger to me, I had to assume,

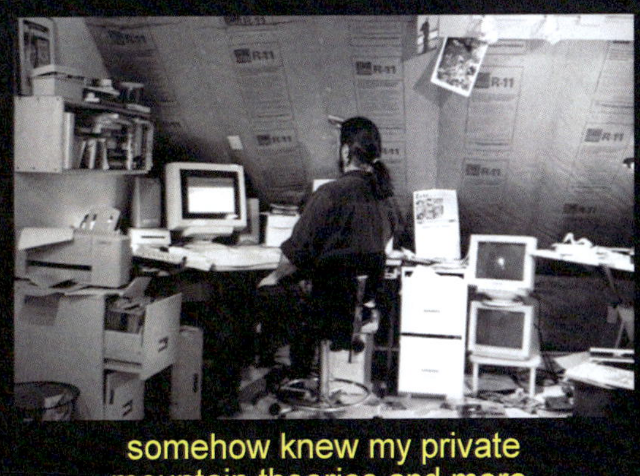

somehow knew my private
mountain theories and more.

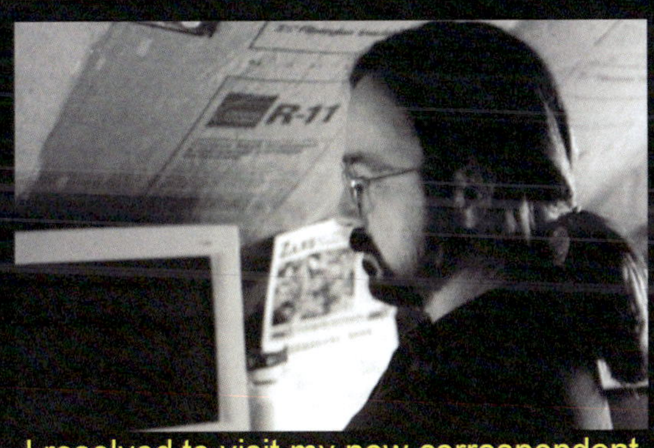

I resolved to visit my new correspondent
and replied to the message that very day.

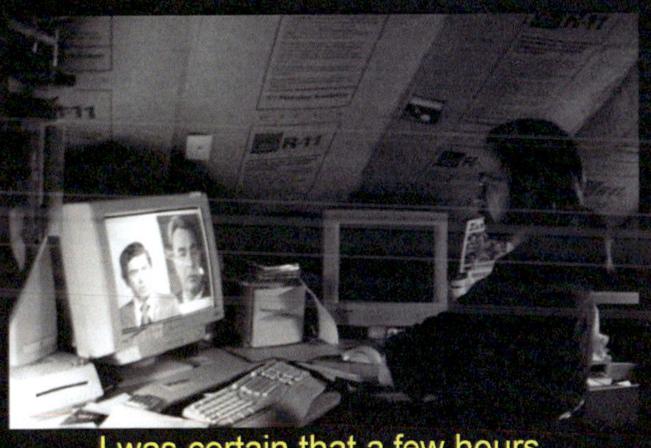

I was certain that a few hours
with this eccentric – a few hours

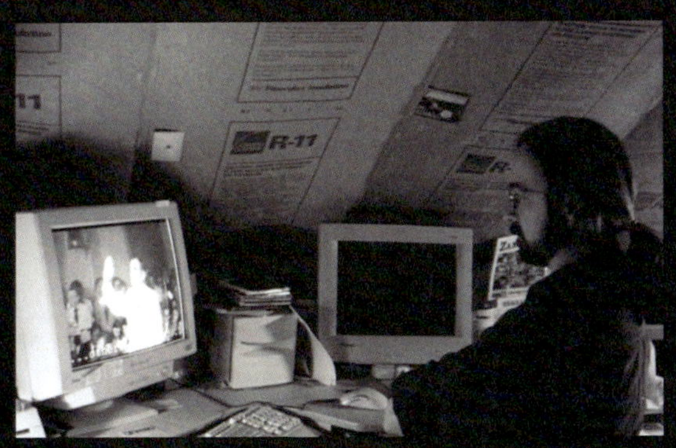

would assuage my guilt about
avoidance of things mystical – and

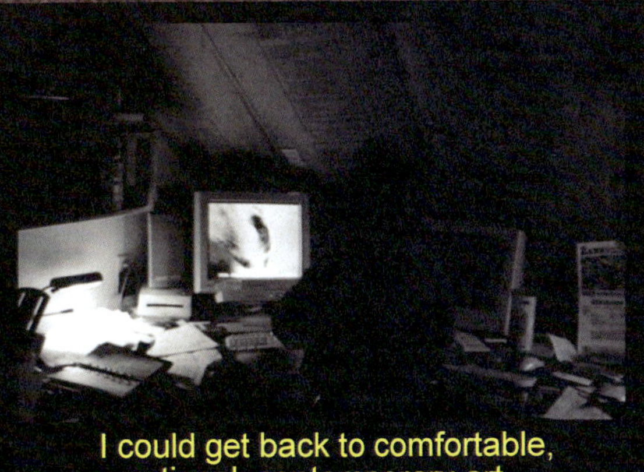

I could get back to comfortable,
rational, contemporary art.

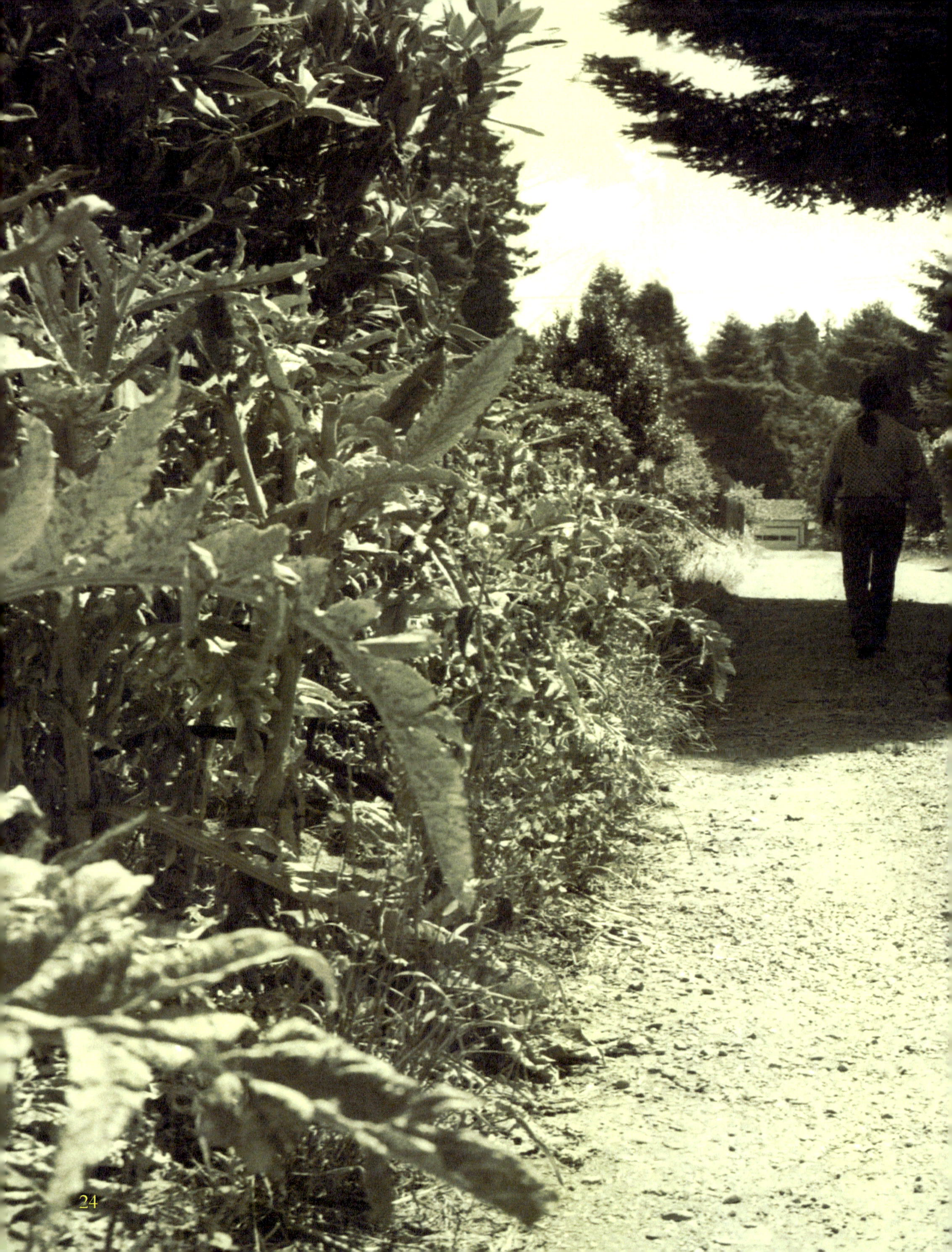

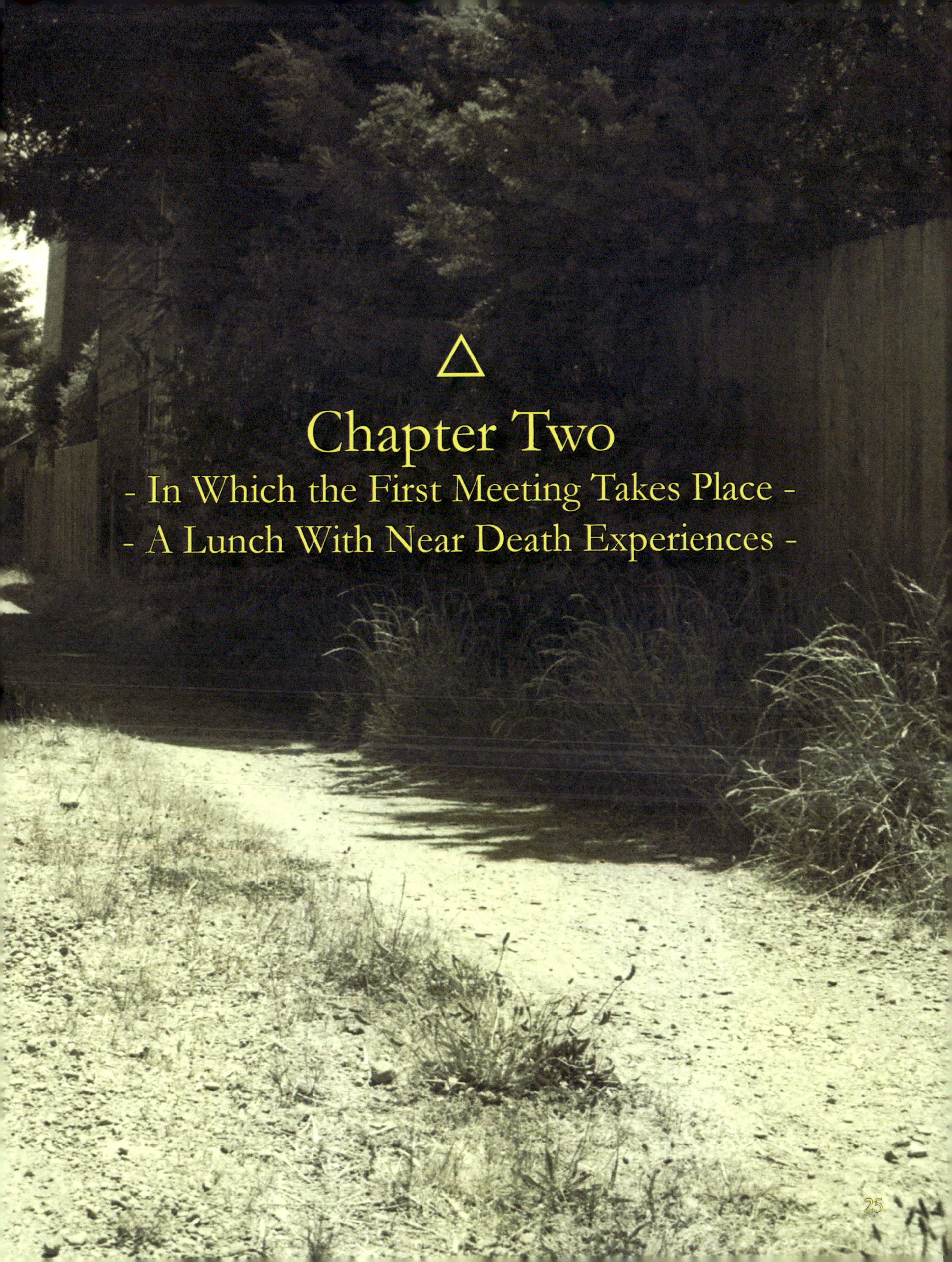
△

Chapter Two

- In Which the First Meeting Takes Place -
- A Lunch With Near Death Experiences -

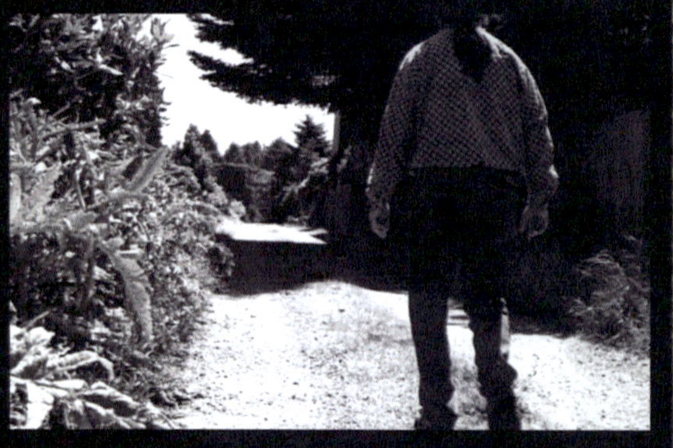

The address Herr Dockter had given me

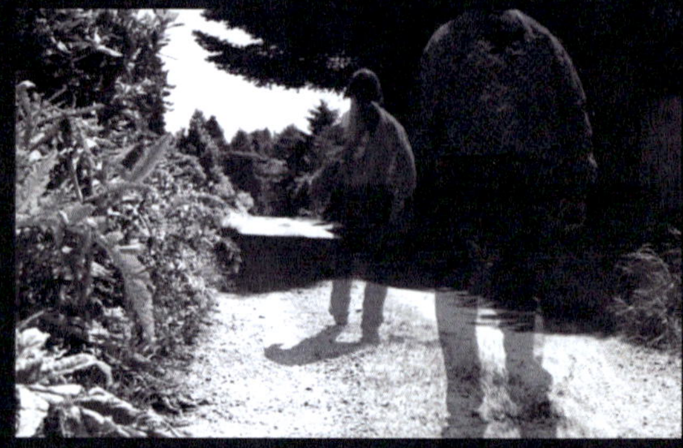

was not too far from my own home,

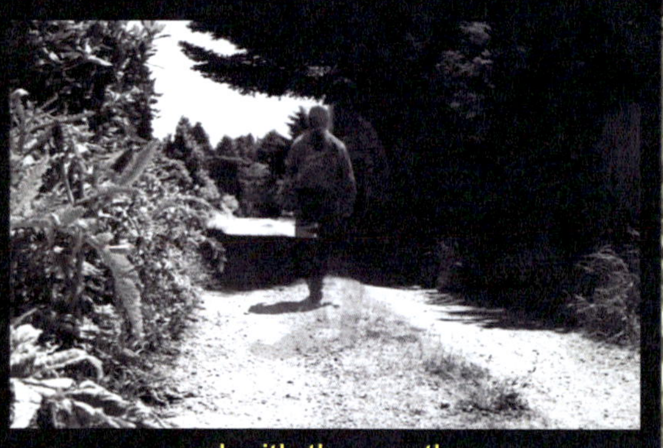

and with the weather
being fine the following day,

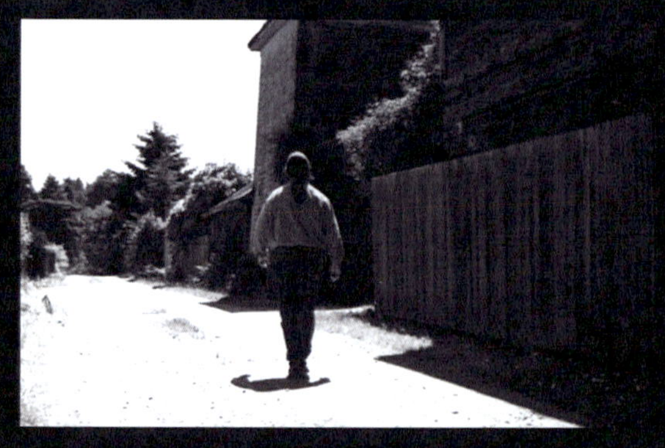

I chose to walk.

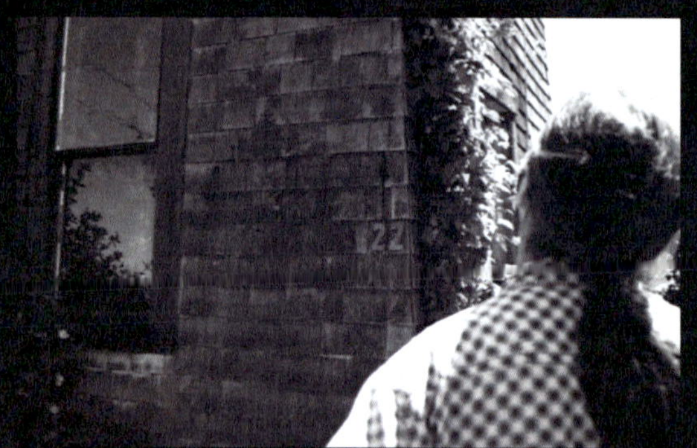

The house at No. 22 Daumal Lane
was an odd wooden structure.

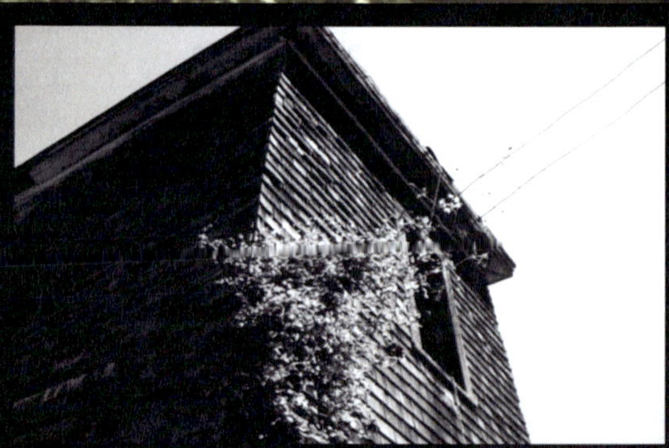

A two story shingled affair.   Taller than it
was broad, it seemed more a sort of tower.

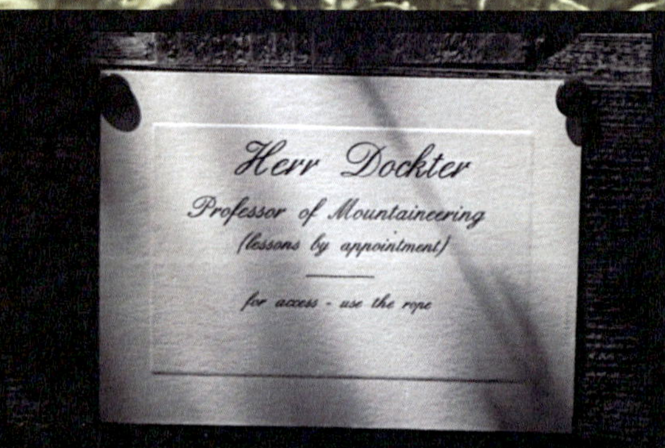

On the entrance was tacked a small card
which read: Herr Dockter (et cetera)

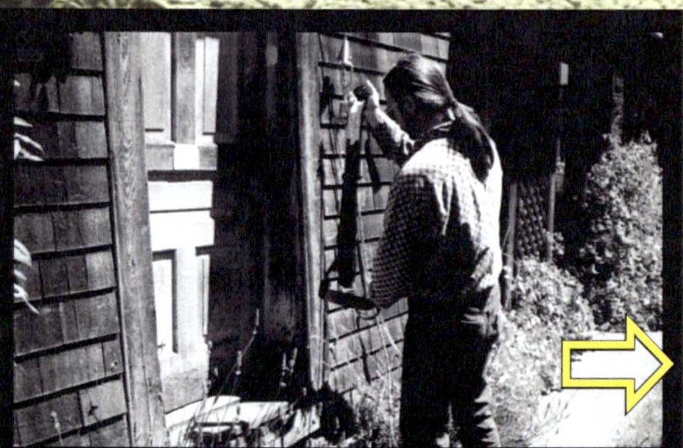

Next to the door, hung a nylon climbing
rope, and affixed to it:

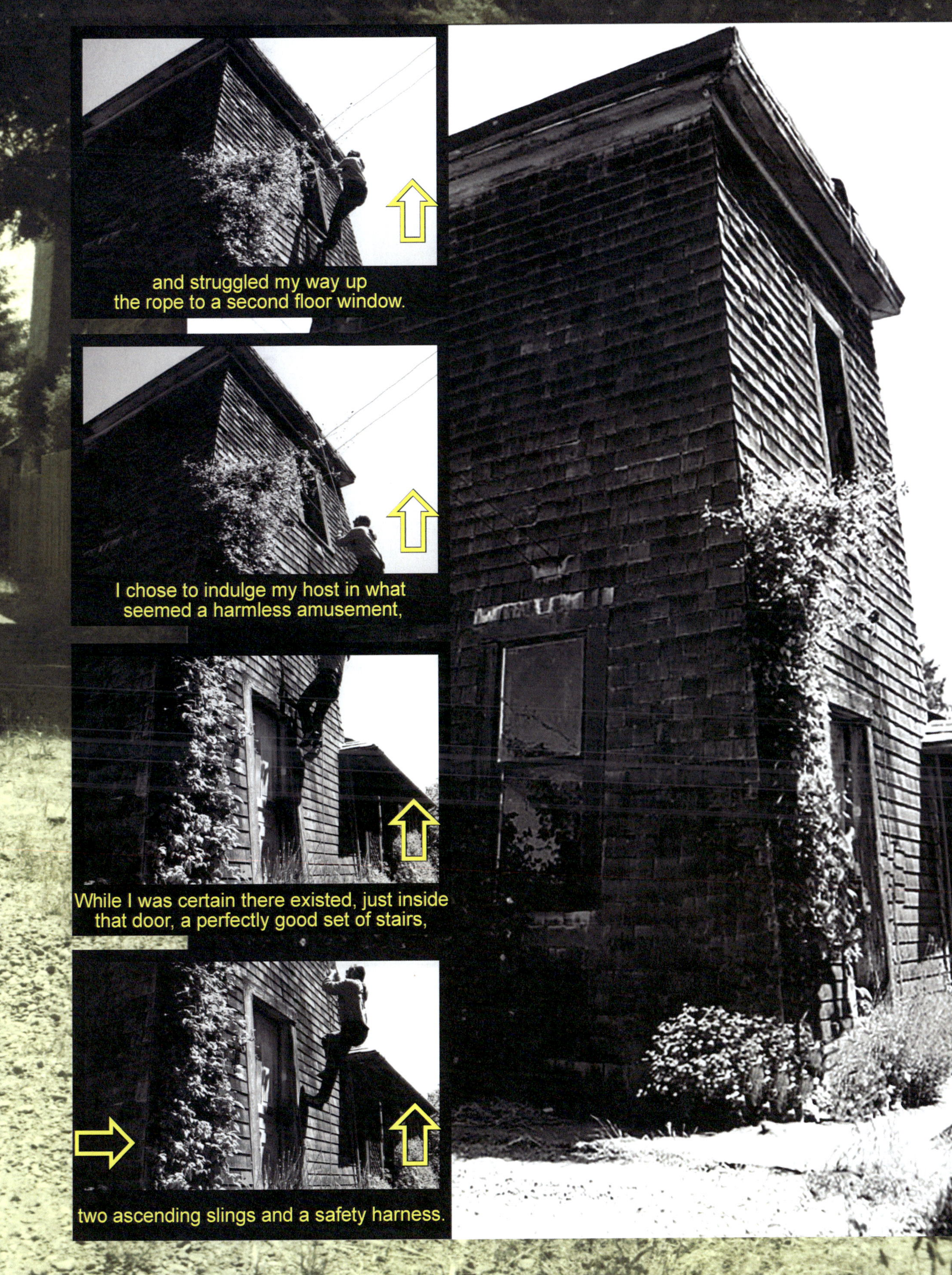

and struggled my way up
the rope to a second floor window.
I chose to indulge my host in what
seemed a harmless amusement,
While I was certain there existed, just inside
that door, a perfectly good set of stairs,
two ascending slings and a safety harness.

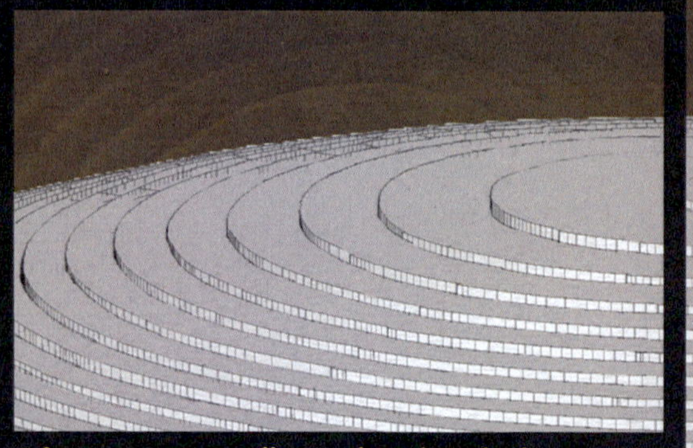

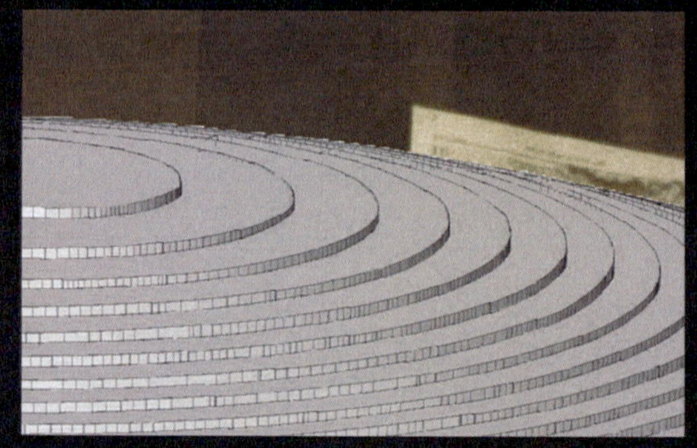

As my eyes adjusted to the darkness, I saw the room was tiny and its walls covered with maps, symbols... and spirals, everywhere spirals.

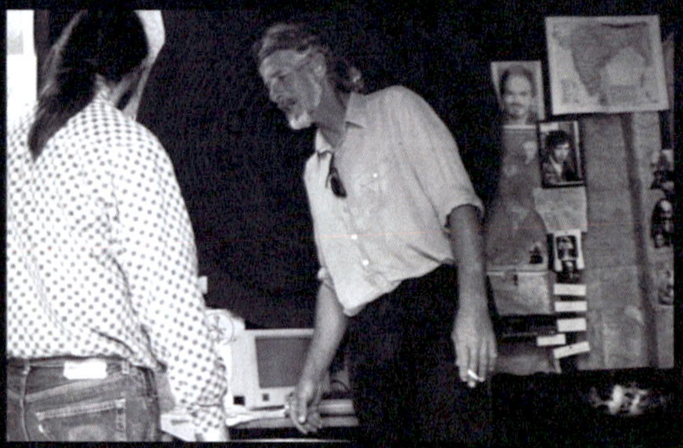

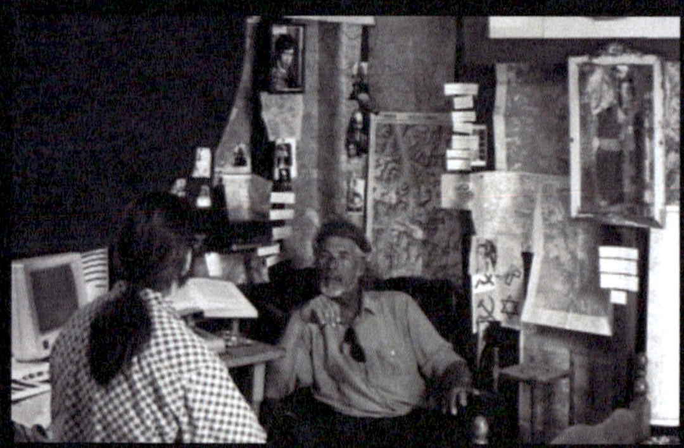

Herr Dockter rose to greet me and once seated, we naturally began talking about mountaineering. I was immediately charmed by his easy manner.

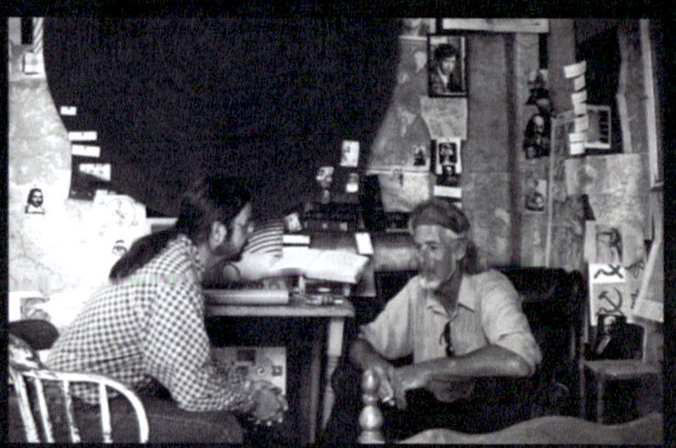

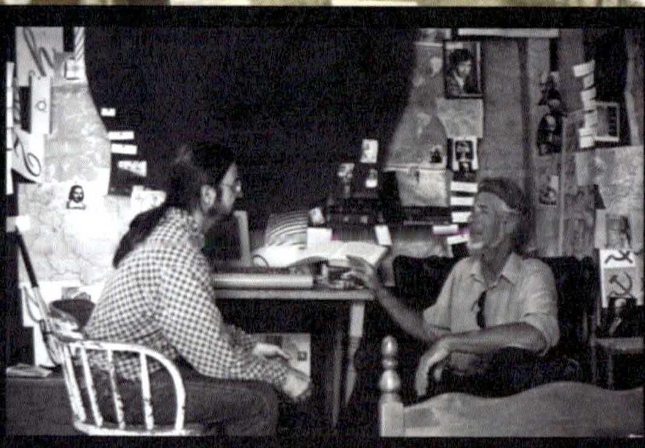

"You and I must get to know each other in the next few hours," Herr Dockter said, in a voice that held traces of an eastern European accent.

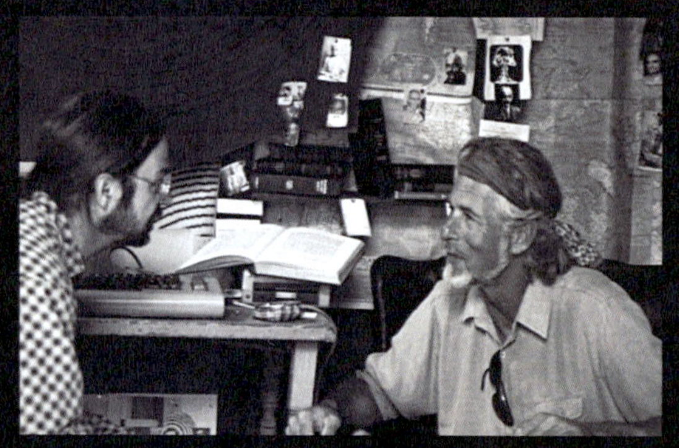

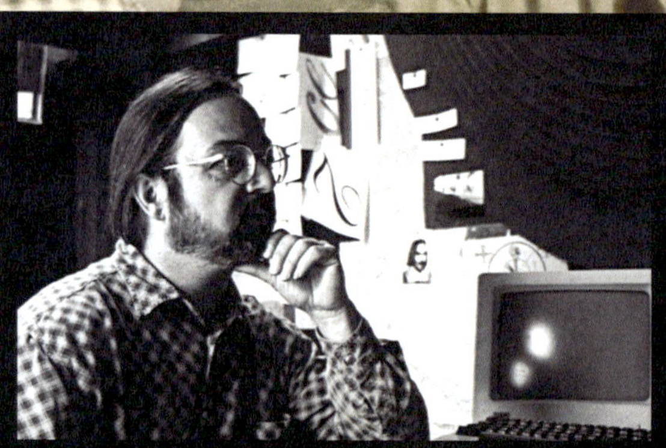

"I'm confident that soon we will embark on a great adventure. We hold a certain belief in common."

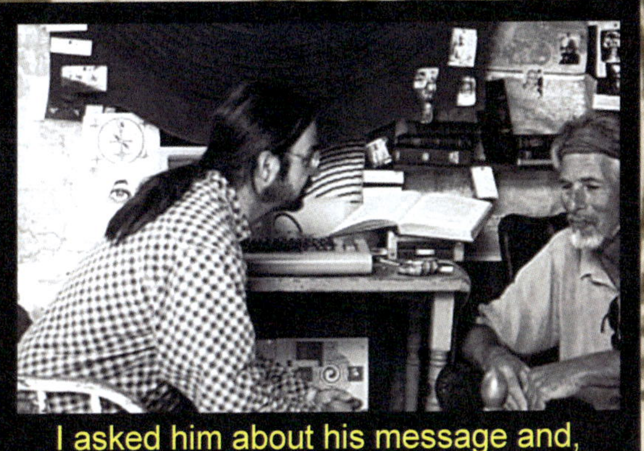

I asked him about his message and, of course, the meaning of "the beach".

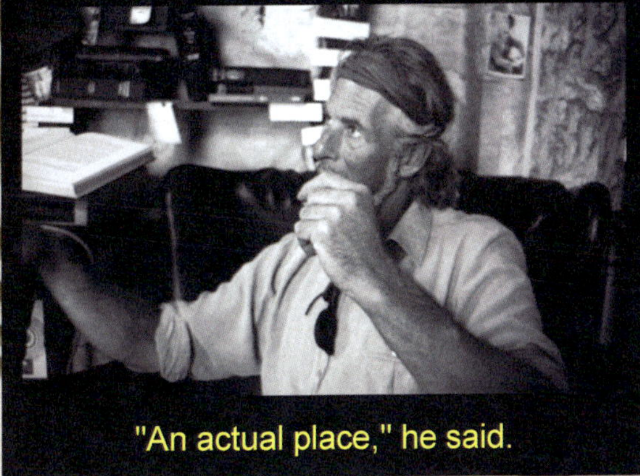

"An actual place," he said.

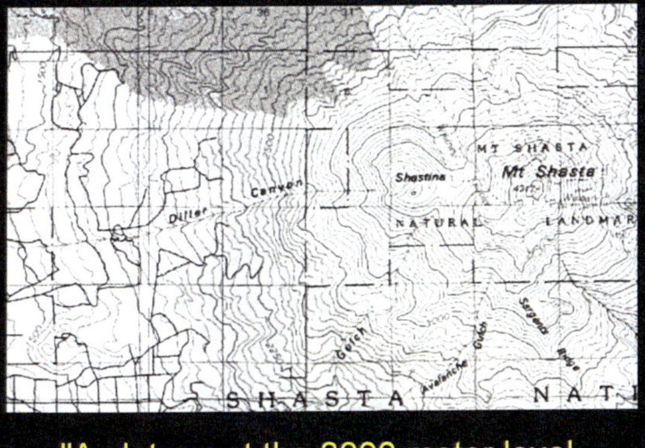

"A plateau at the 3000 meter level,

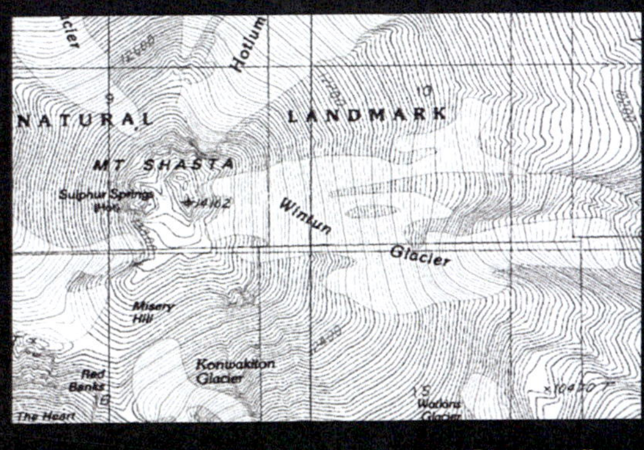

on the north side of Mount Shasta."

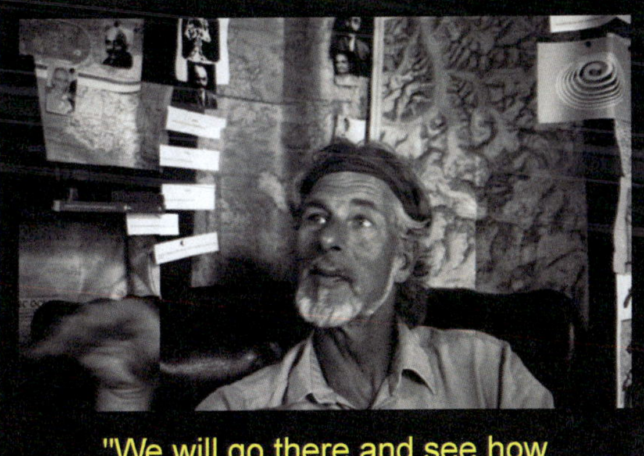

"We will go there and see how

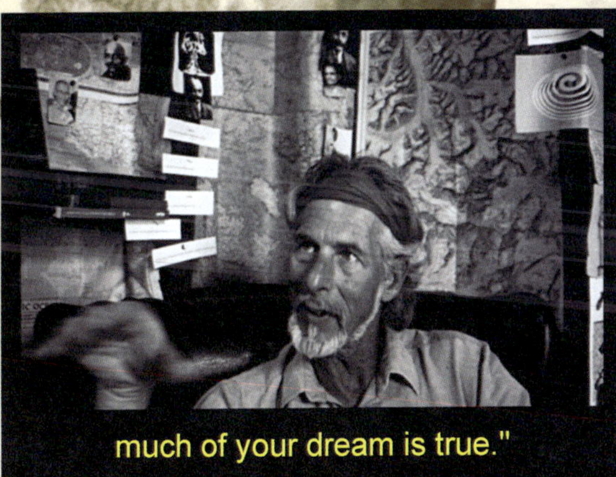

much of your dream is true."

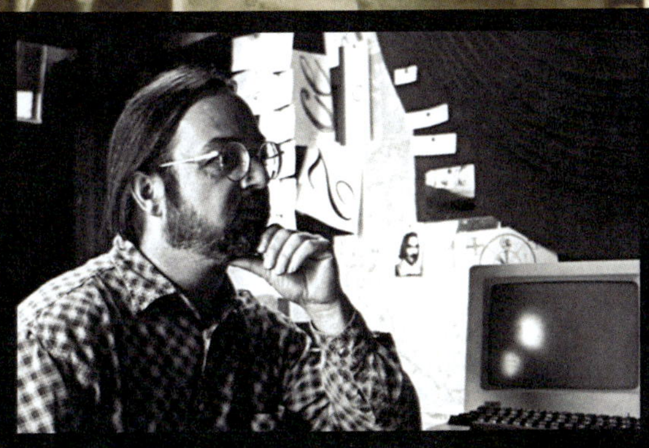

"I am quite sure this dream

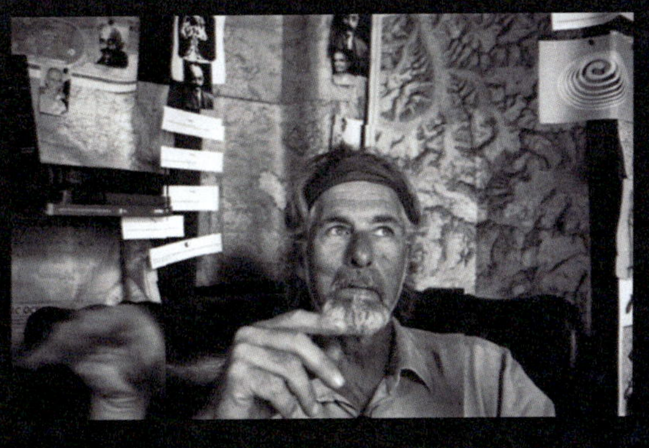

was more a vision," he said with a smile.

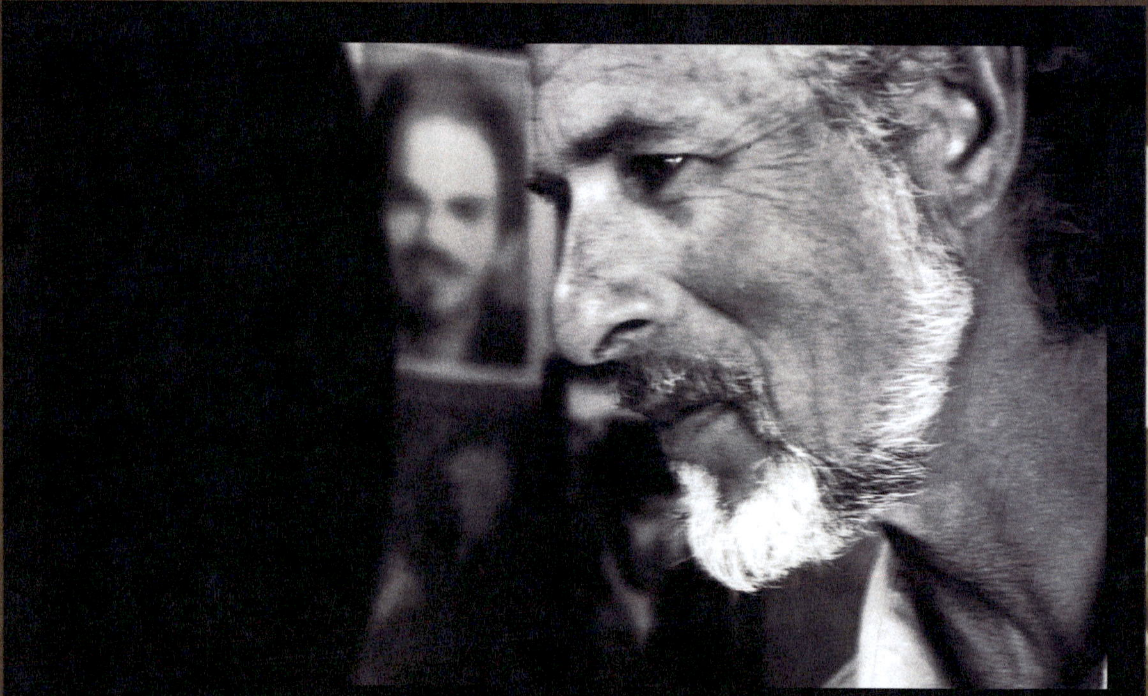

Herr Dockter told me of his many climbs of the mountain; how its proximity was the main reason for his moving here. He told me of stories and legends dating back thousands of years. Fantastic tales that made it clear, to him anyway, that Mount Shasta was a... no, perhaps, *the*... sacred mountain.

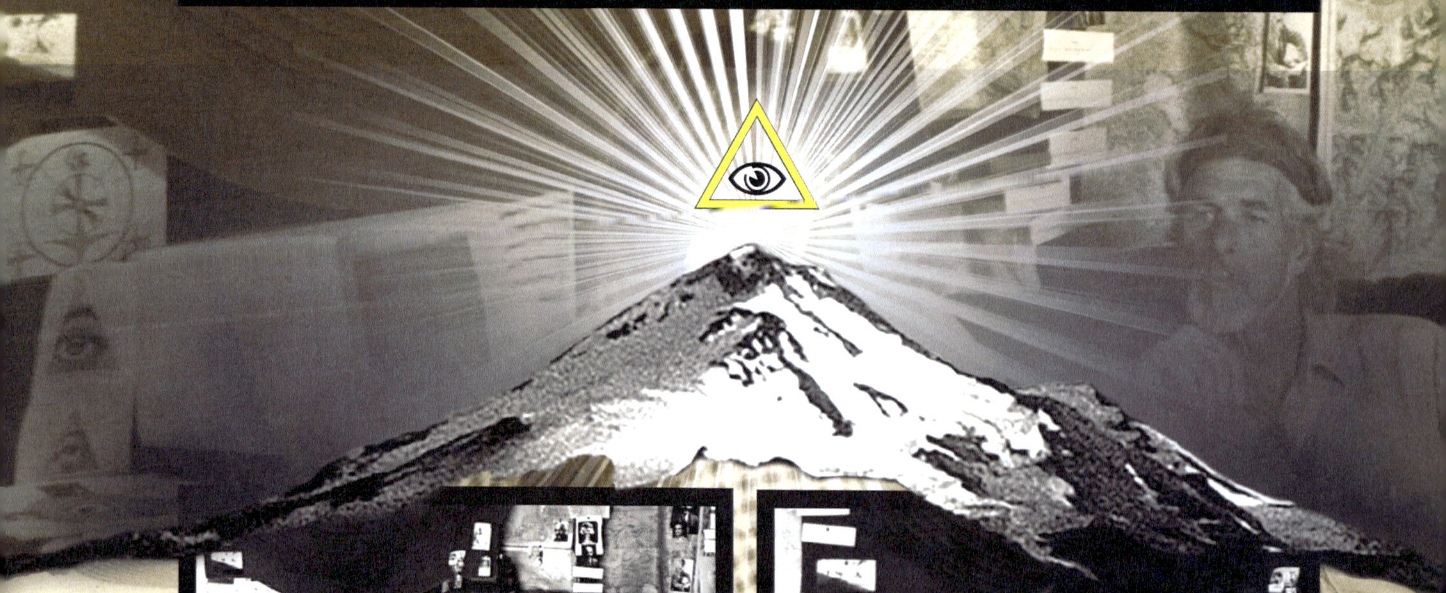

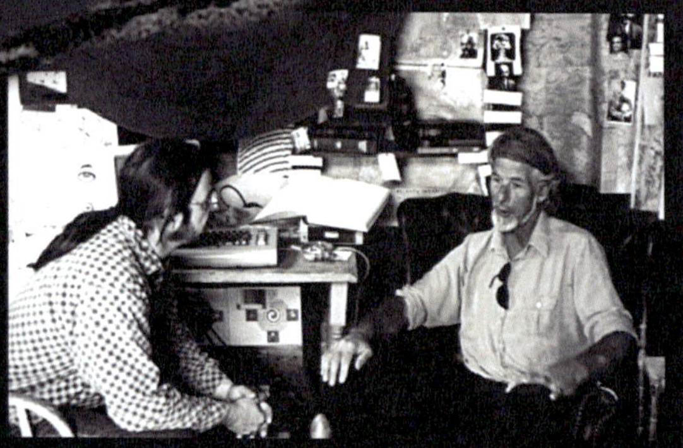

"Herr Dockter," I asked.

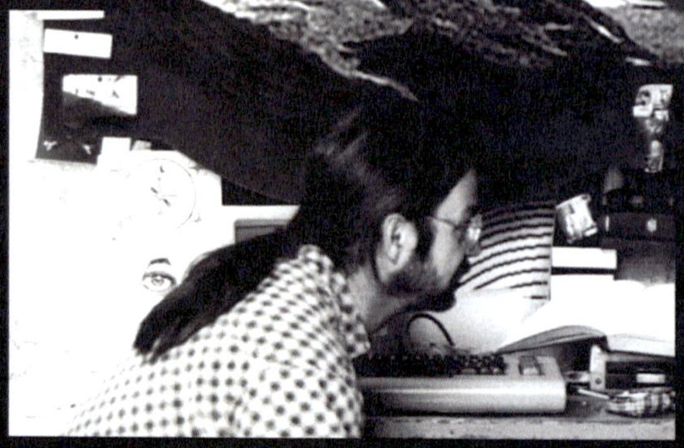

"Earlier you said we held a belief in common."

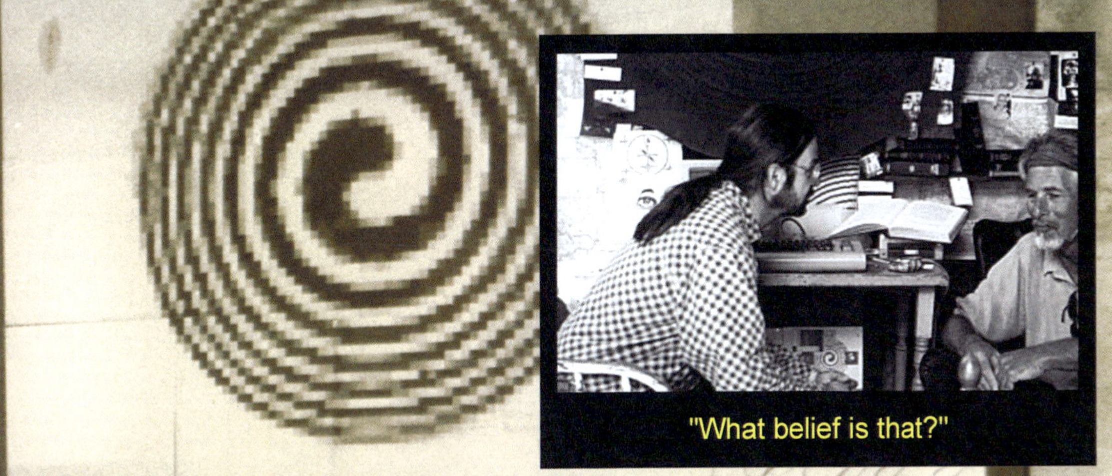

"What belief is that?"

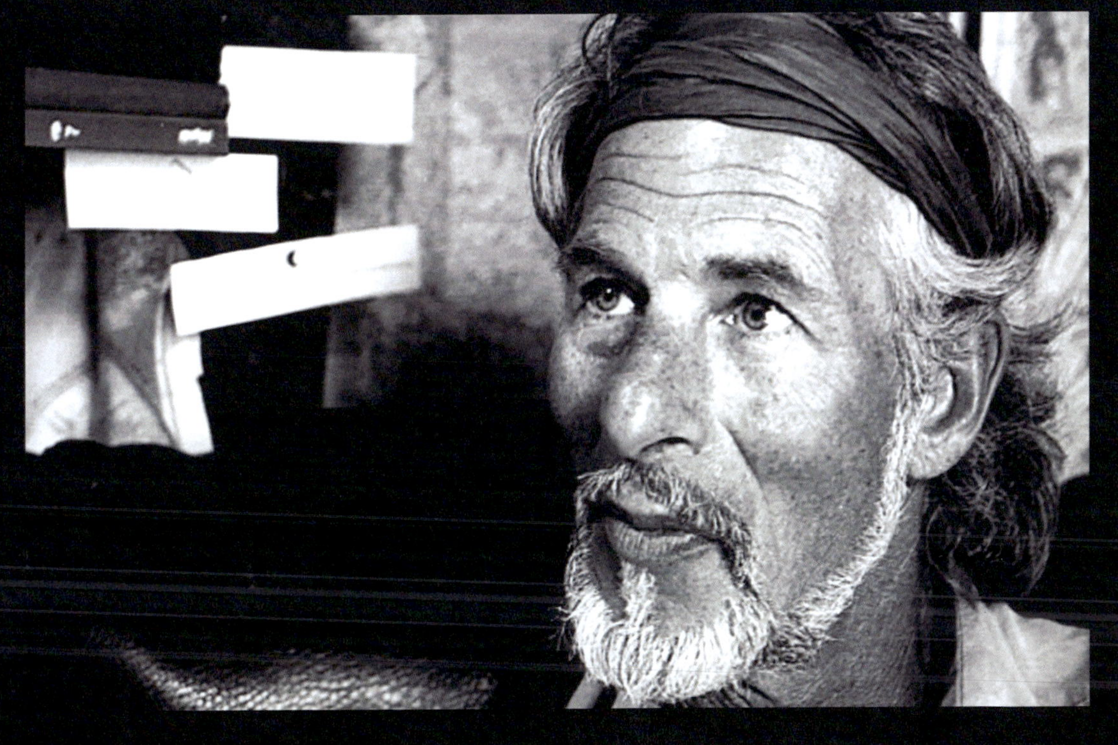

"Why – we both believe in hopelessness," he replied.
"In the ability of hopelessness to reveal great truths."

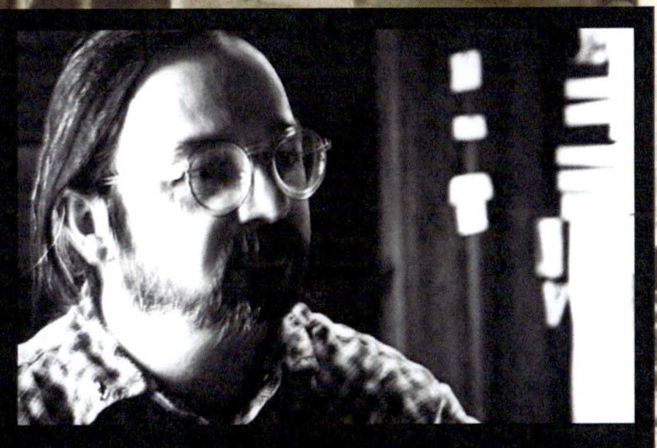

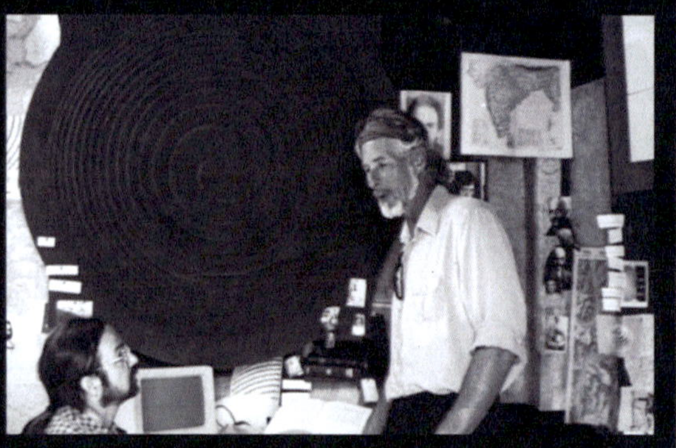
He rose and began an animated discourse on the physical sciences.

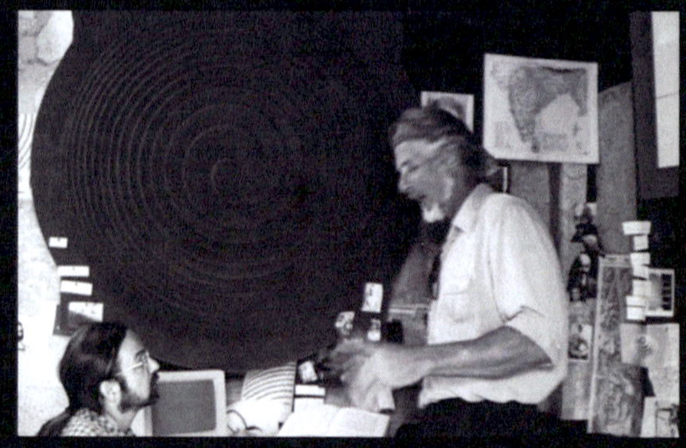
"Now, you are, no doubt, aware of new discoveries in quantum mechanics,

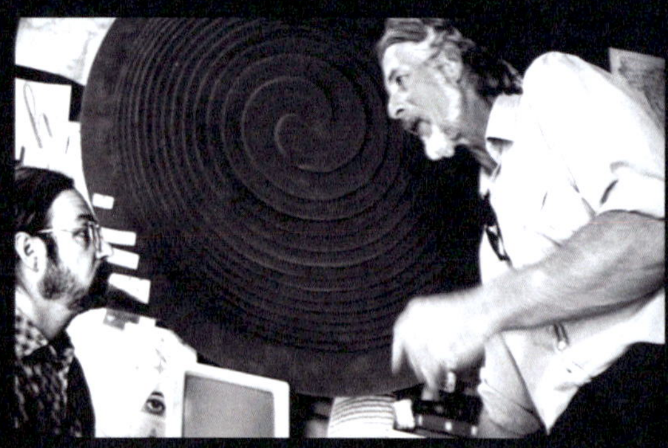
the behavior of sub-atomic particles, nano-technology, superstring theory.

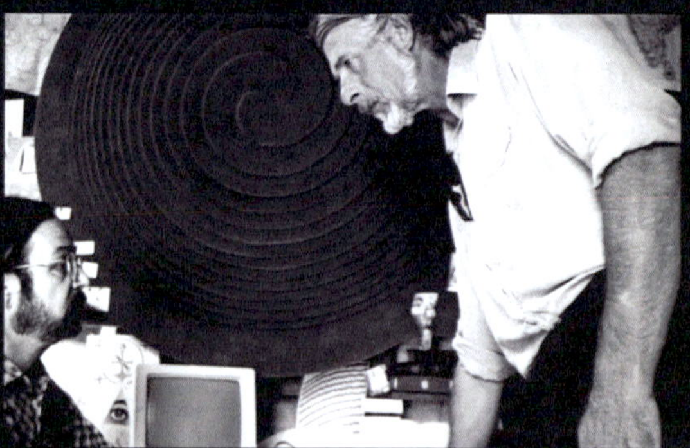
The reality-shifting research emerging concerning the idea of a multiverse.

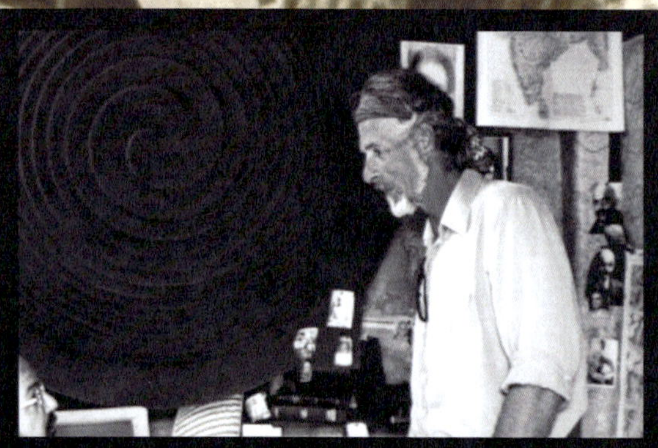
Science, pure accredited science, is now poised to converge

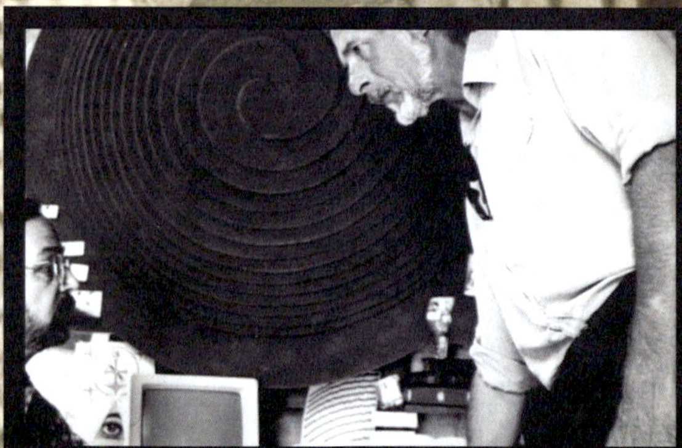
with more esoteric and ancient ways of perception!

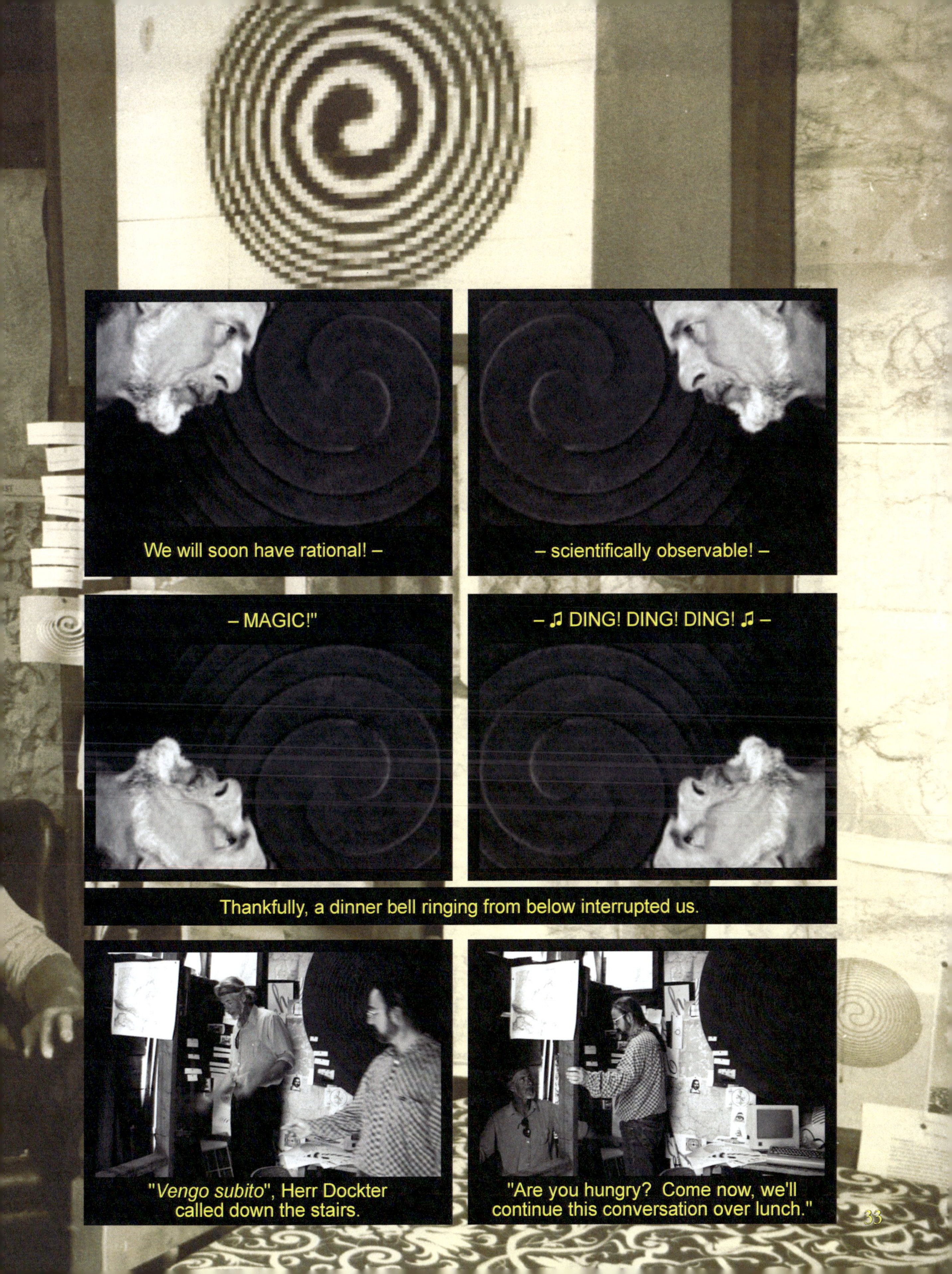

We will soon have rational! –

– scientifically observable! –

– MAGIC!"

– ♫ DING! DING! DING! ♫ –

Thankfully, a dinner bell ringing from below interrupted us.

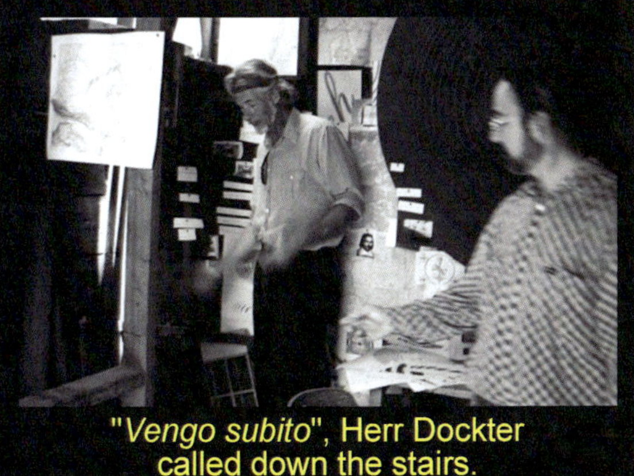

"*Vengo subito*", Herr Dockter
called down the stairs.

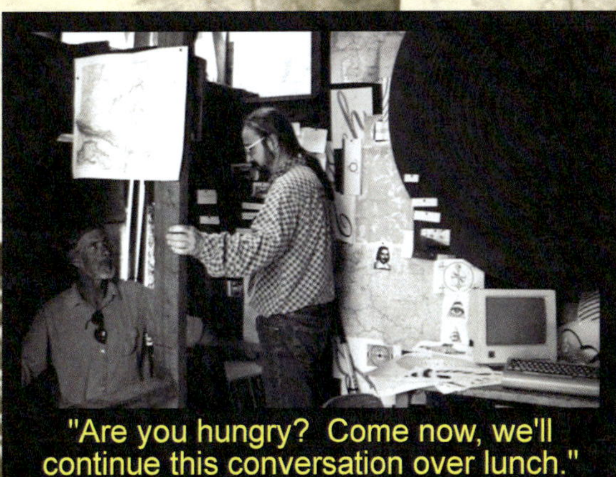

"Are you hungry? Come now, we'll
continue this conversation over lunch."

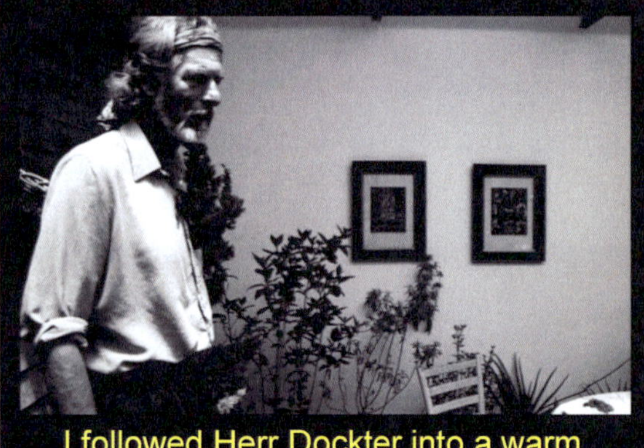

I followed Herr Dockter into a warm
and bright first floor room.

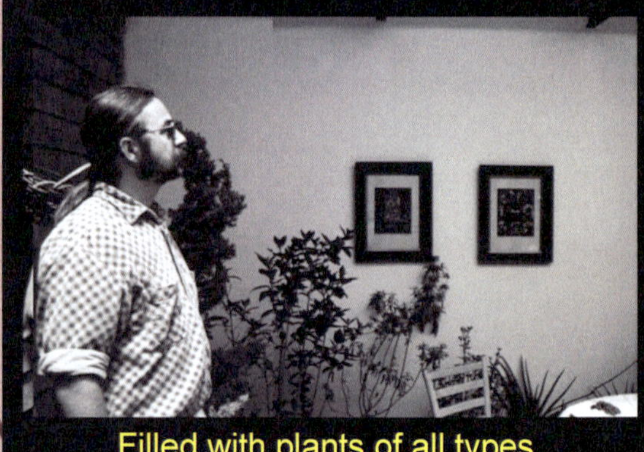

Filled with plants of all types,
it seemed more a conservatory.

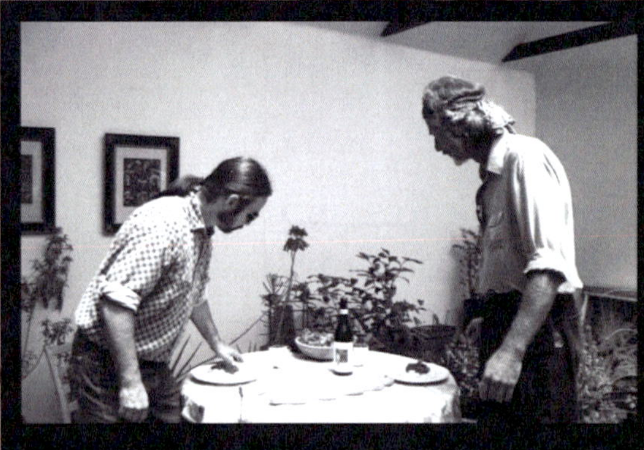

We seated ourselves at a small,

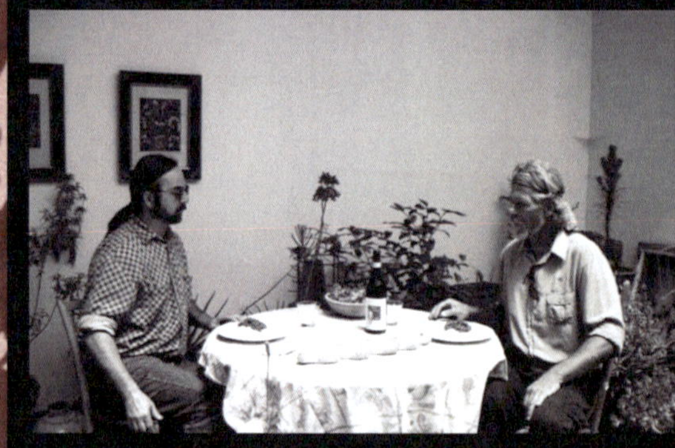

round table in the room's center

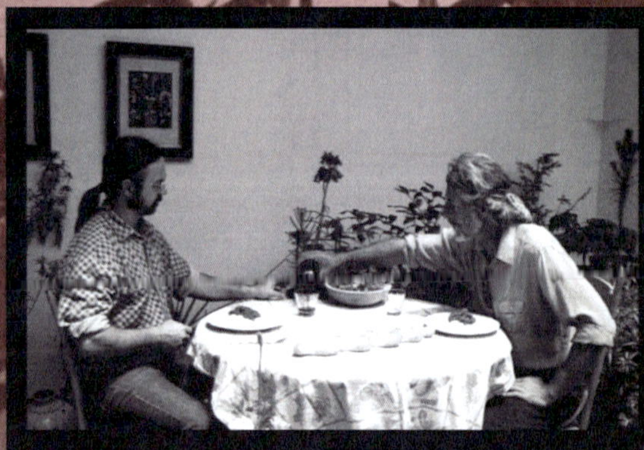

and he filled both our glasses.

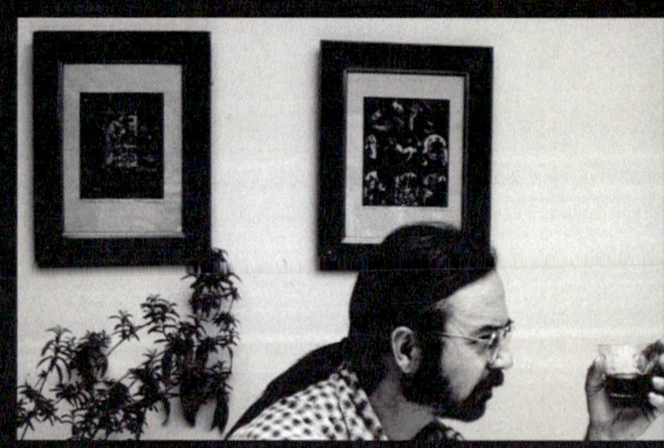

Behind me, the only works of art in the
room: Two German-Expressionist

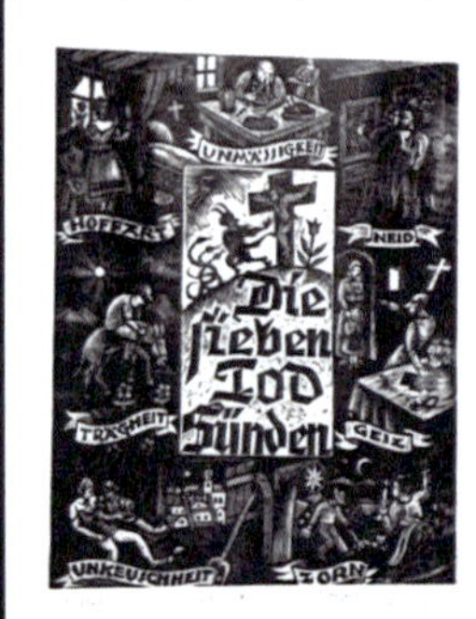
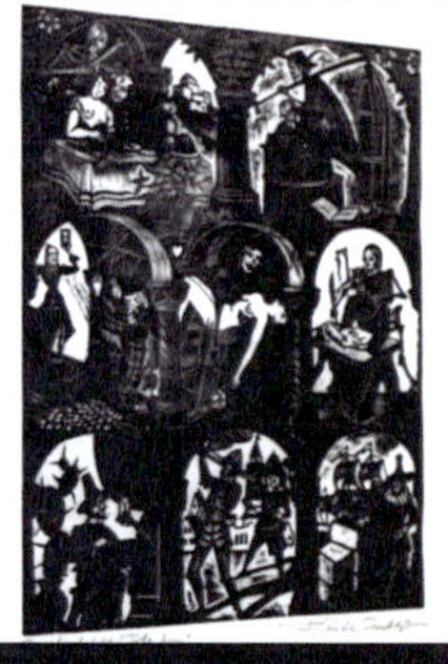

woodcut prints, *The Seven Deadly Sins*
and *The Totentanz*.

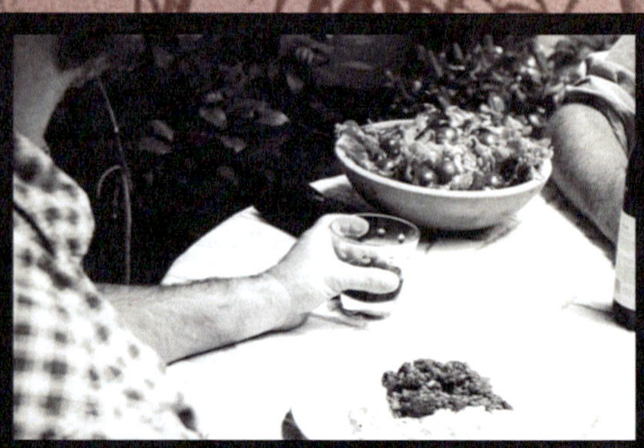

"Now here, at last, something real,"
Herr Dockter began.

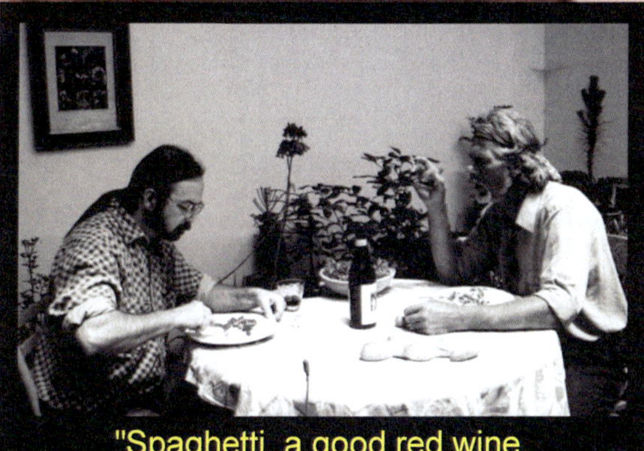

"Spaghetti, a good red wine.
My housekeeper, an Italian woman,

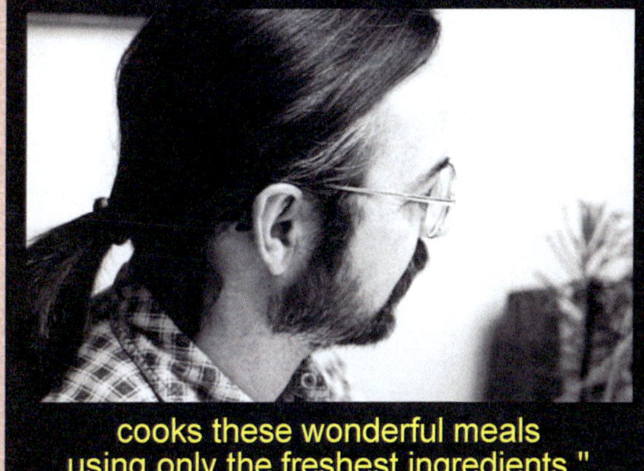

cooks these wonderful meals
using only the freshest ingredients."

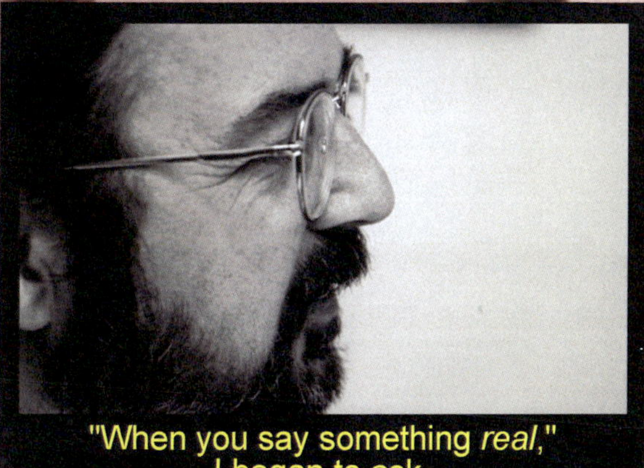

"When you say something *real*,"
I began to ask.

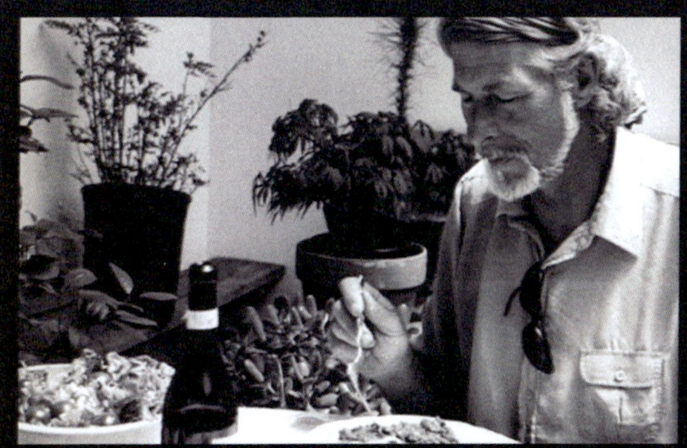

"In comparison to our discussion upstairs,"
he replied.

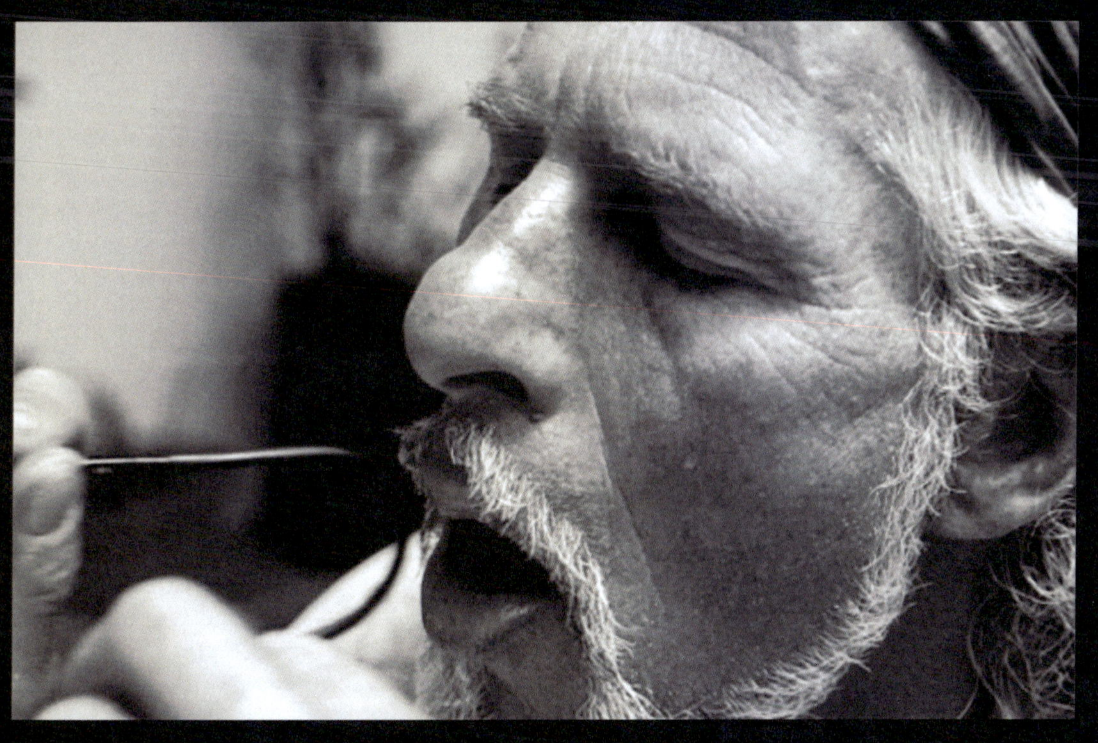

"I mean a real pasta is worth more than any philosophy.
Tell me," he said quietly. "Have you ever had a near-death experience?"

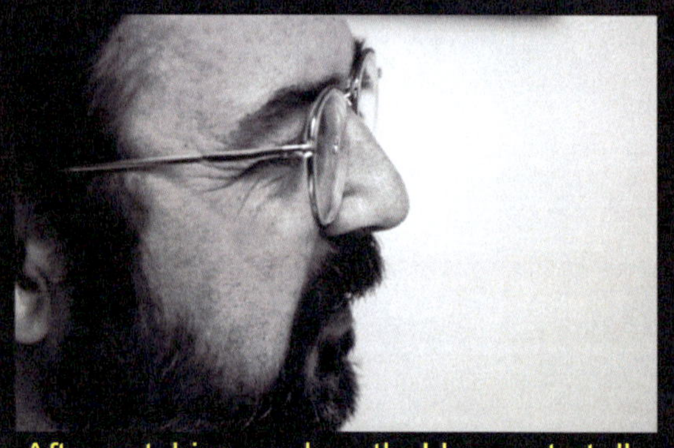

After catching my breath, I began to tell
Herr Dockter of my time at sea.

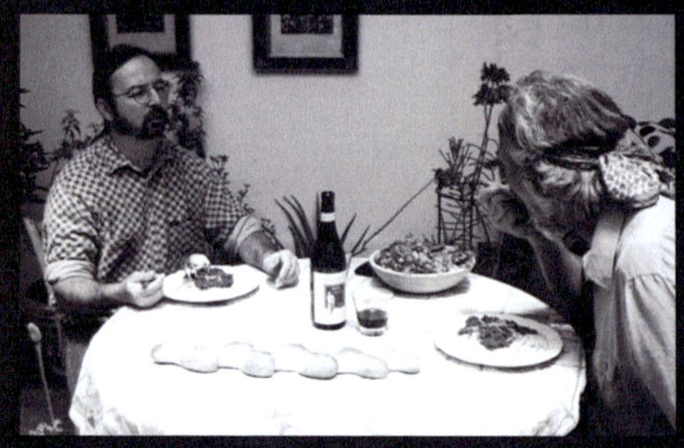

"On Christmas Eve, 30 years ago, the crab
boat I was working on was capsized by a

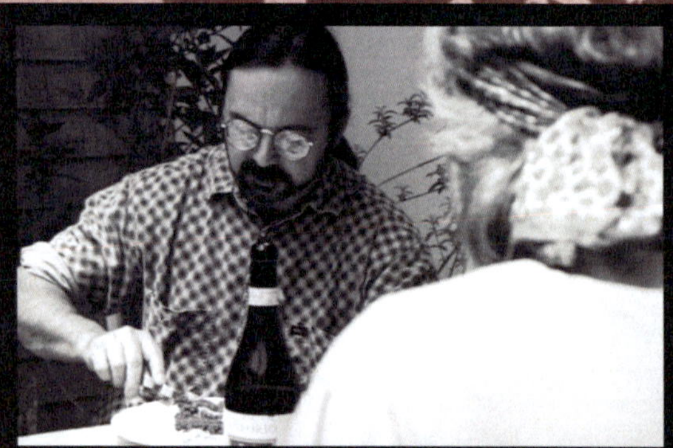

15 meter wave while crossing the bar.
The skipper and I were trapped

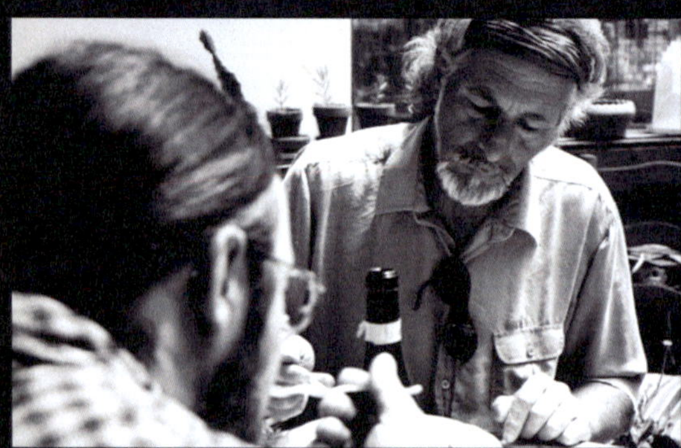

together in a tiny, dark, airspace.
There seemed nothing to do but wait

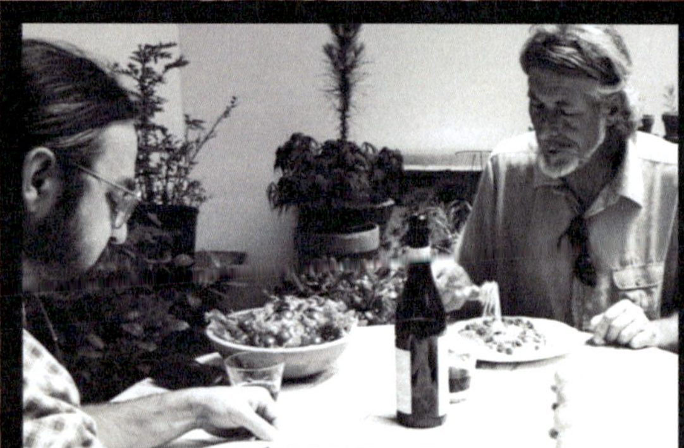

for the death that was sure to come when
the ship broke up and sank completely."

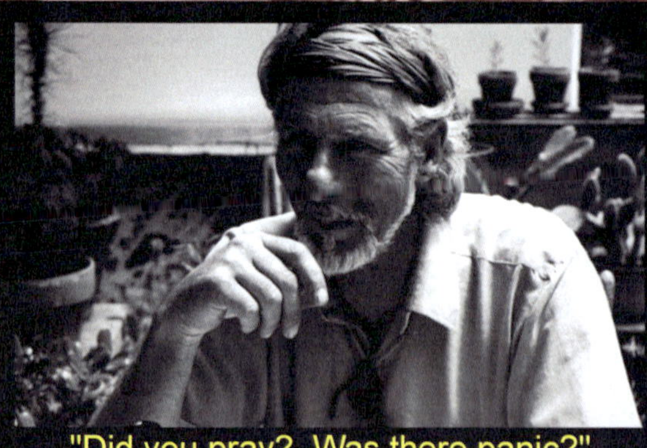

"Did you pray? Was there panic?"
Herr Dockter asked.

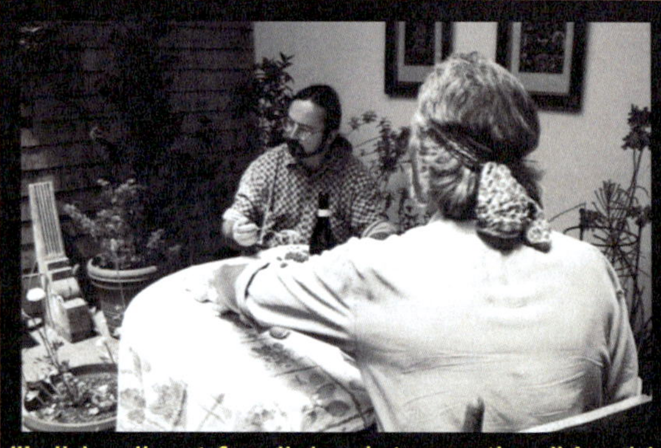

"I did call out for divine intervention," I said.
"I thought that if ever there was a time."

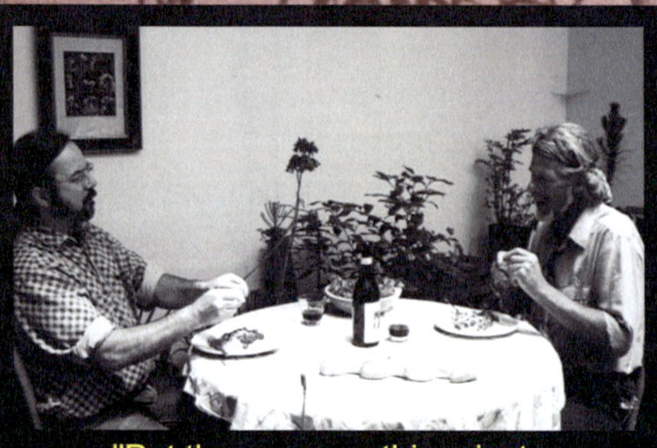

"But there was nothing, just
a pure clarity and calmness."

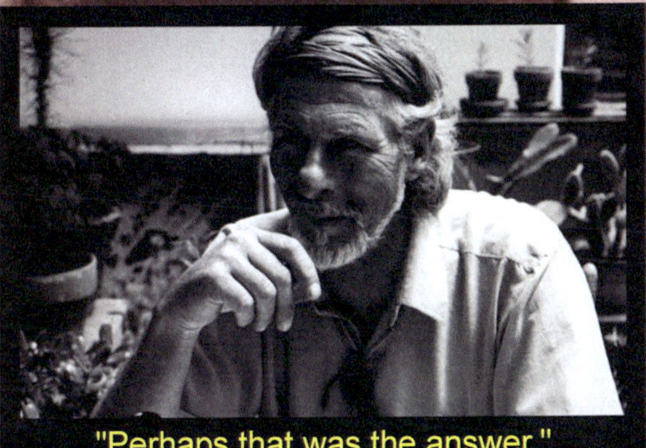

"Perhaps that was the answer."
Herr Dockter said.

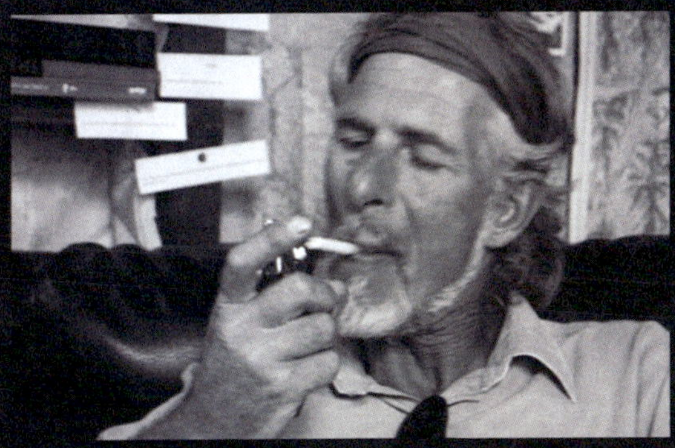

After lunch, we returned to the upstairs room, where Herr Dockter lit a cigarette.

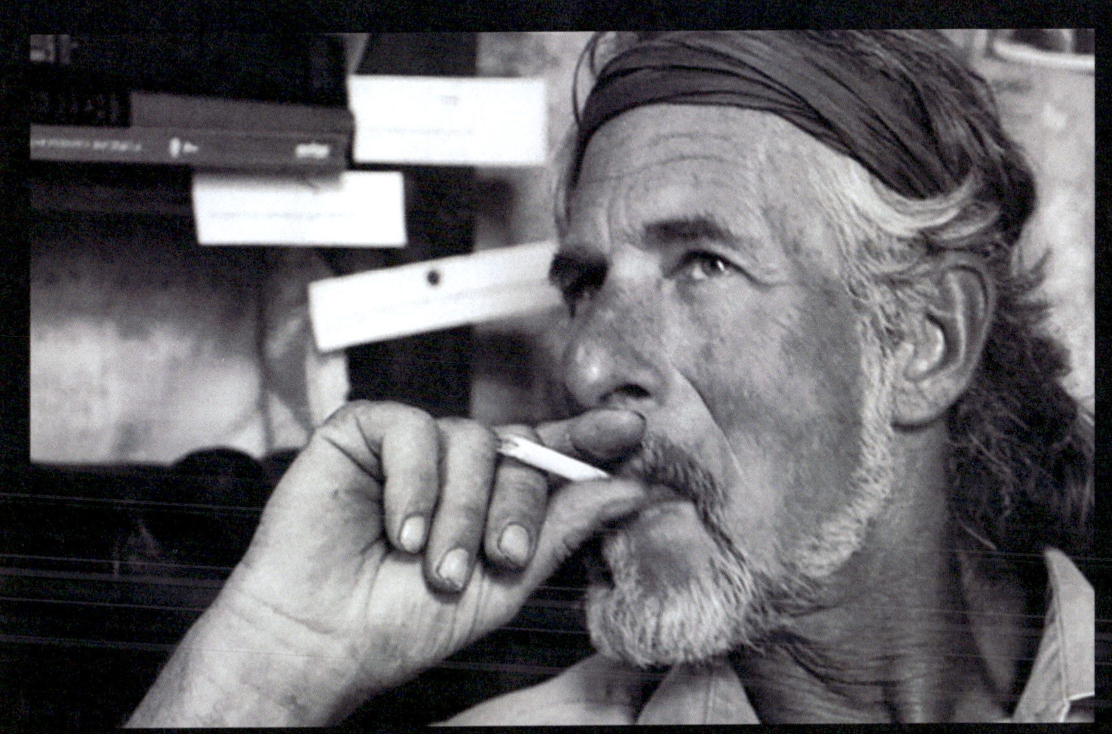

"We'll meet again next week", he said.   "I know several people I would like to include in such an expedition.   You may also know of someone.   Next week I'll explain more of my theories, and answer any lingering questions you may have."

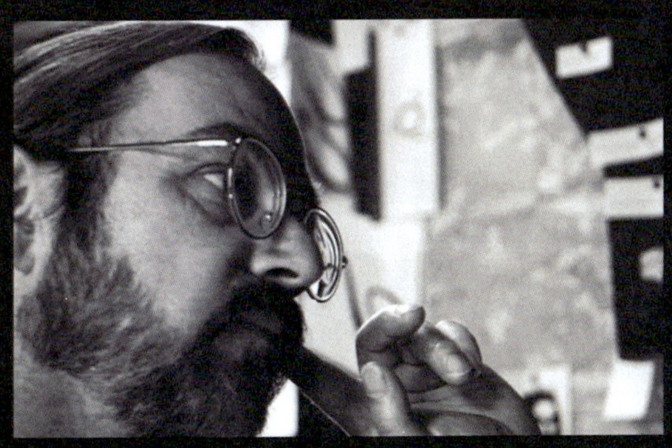

Herr Dockter laughed and closed his eyes.

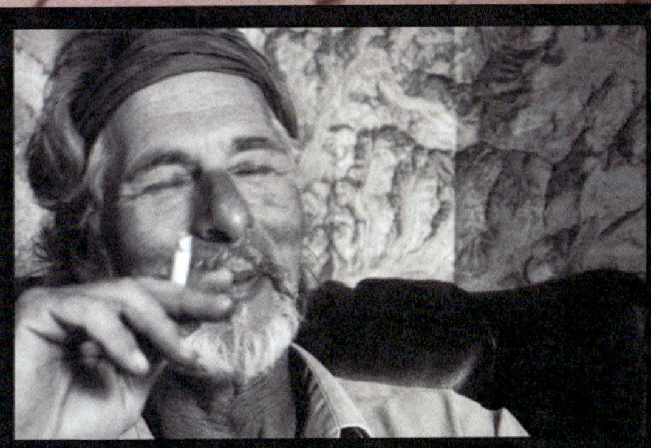

I sensed our first meeting was at an end.

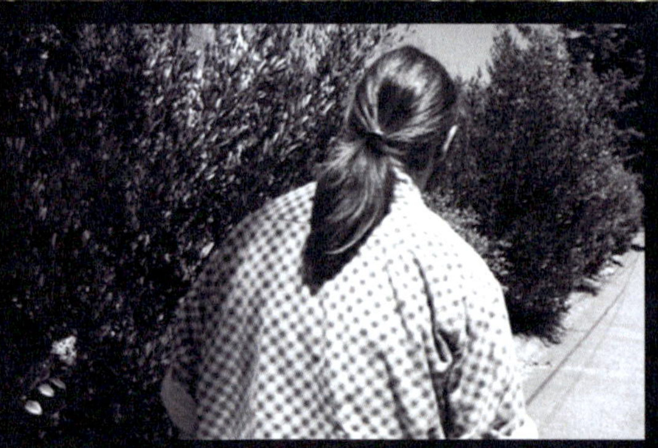

I walked home trying to put Herr Dockter's information in perspective.

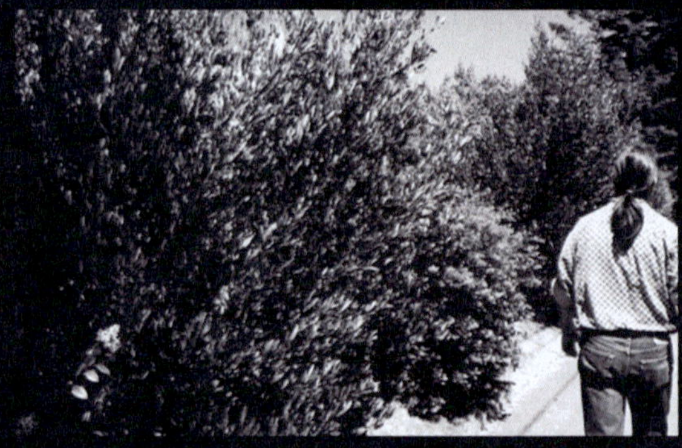

My wife, with feet firmly on the ground,

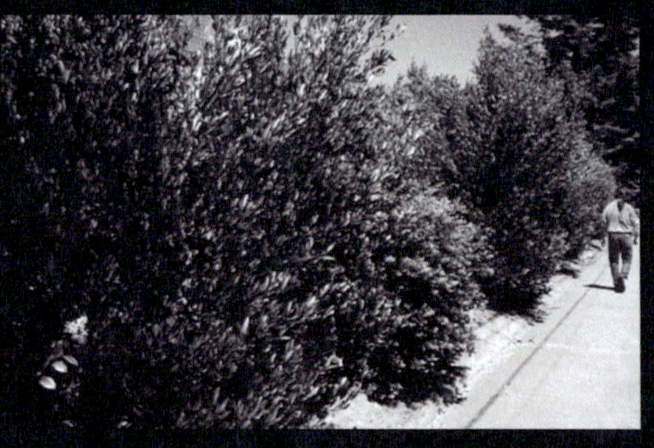

would have good advice,

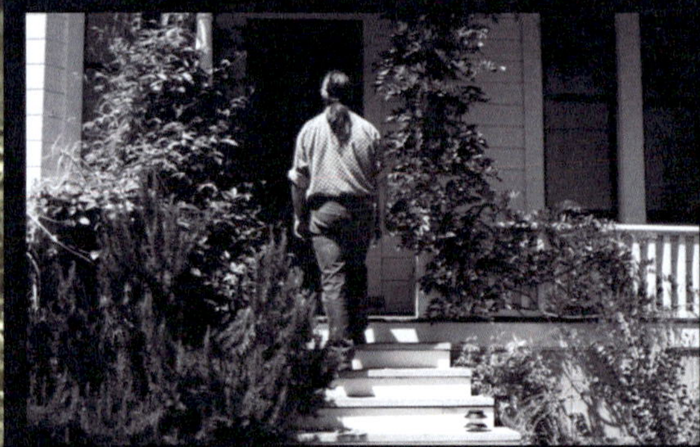

and I thought about how best to explain it all to her.

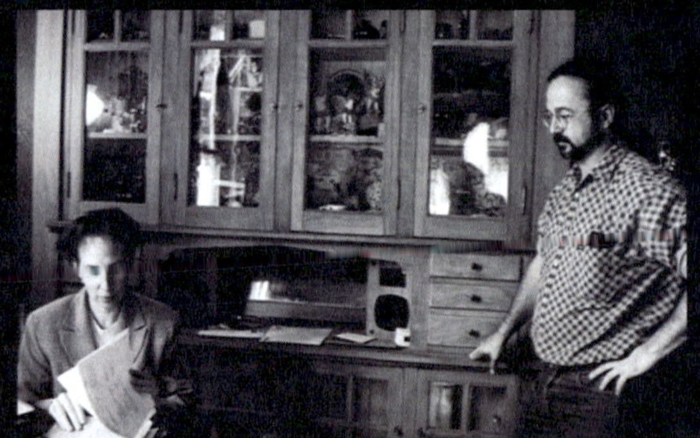

I told my wife as concisely as I could the details of Herr Dockter's strange ideas.

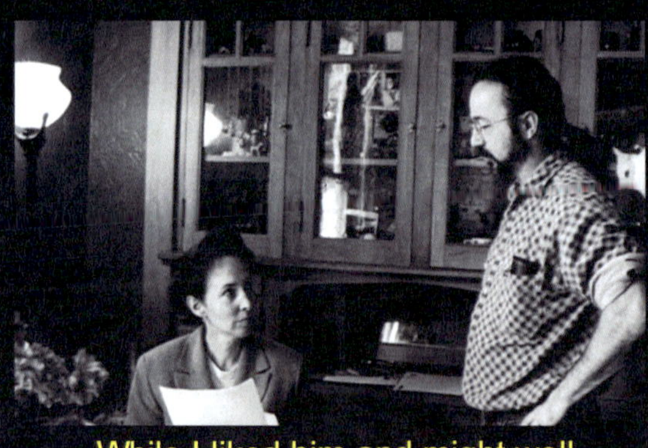

While I liked him, and might well accompany him on this quest,

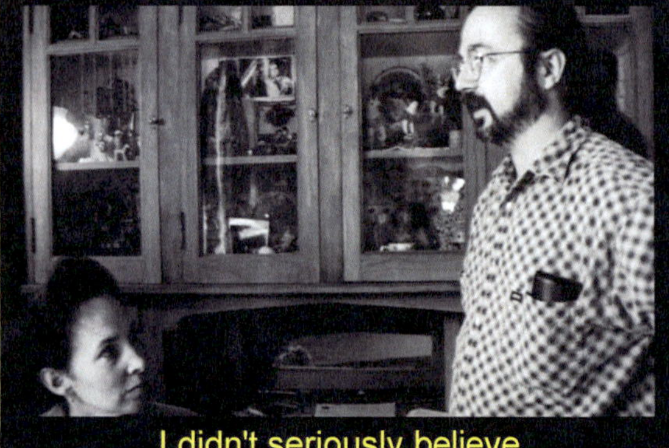

I didn't seriously believe any of what he had told me.

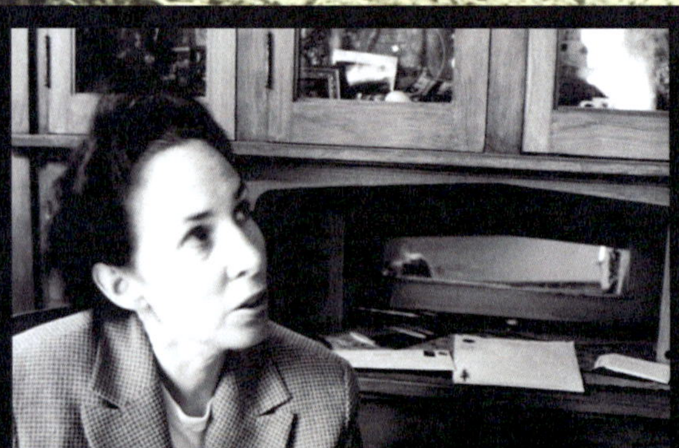

"It's the most fascinating idea I've heard in years." she said. "I'm going with you."

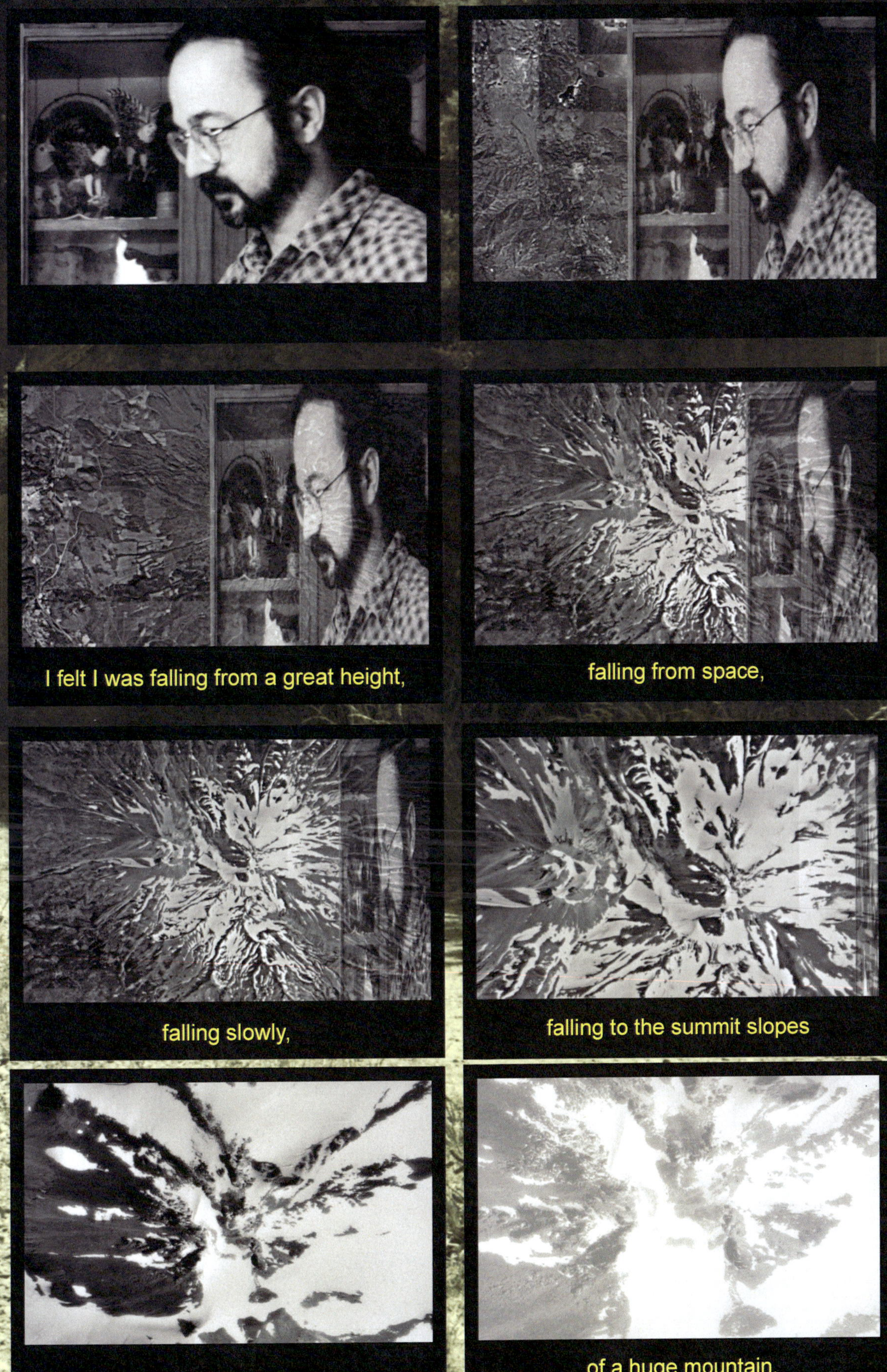
I felt I was falling from a great height,
falling from space,
falling slowly,
falling to the summit slopes
of a huge mountain.

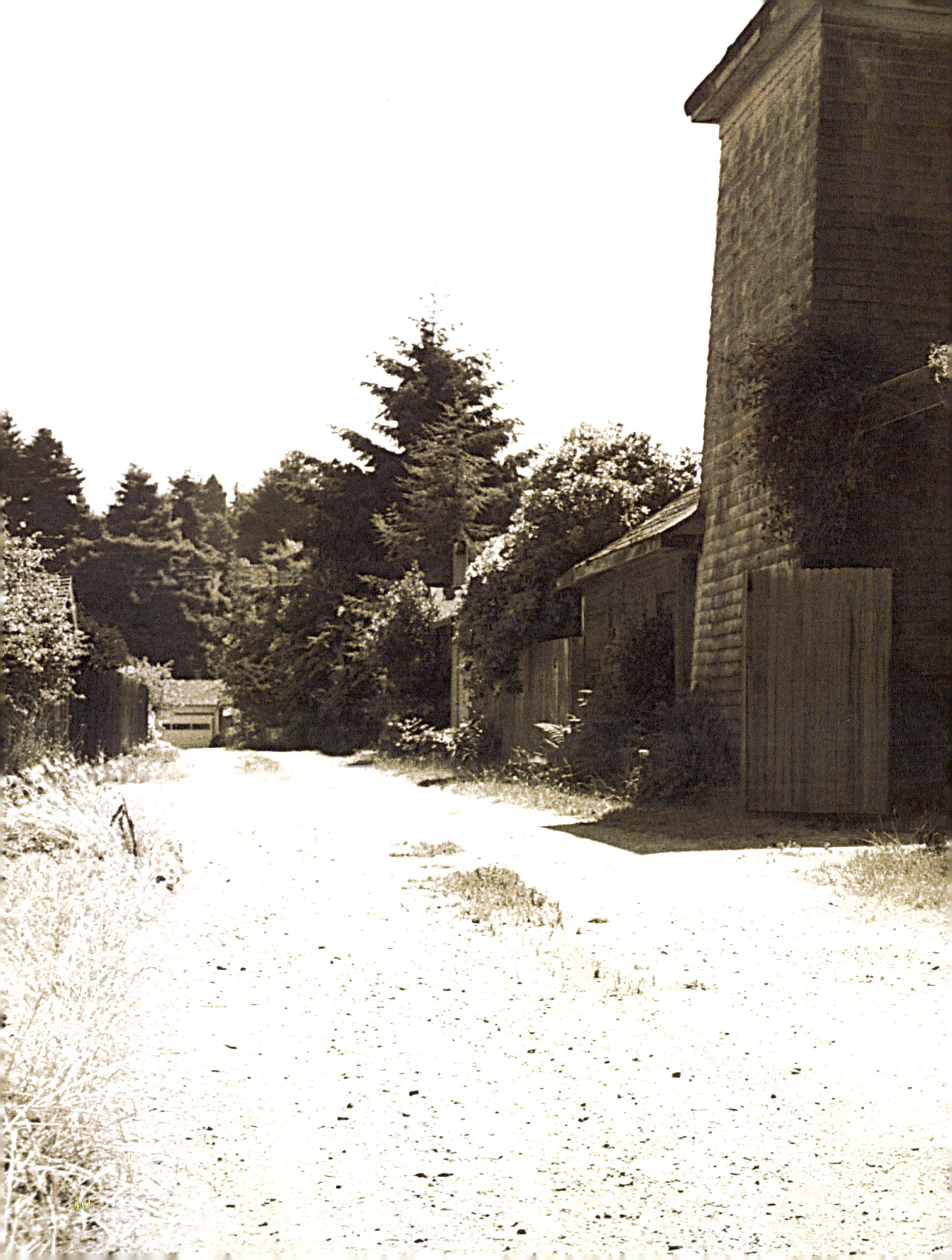

△

Chapter Three
- The Group is Formed -
- A Cloud Story - A Magnificent Failure -

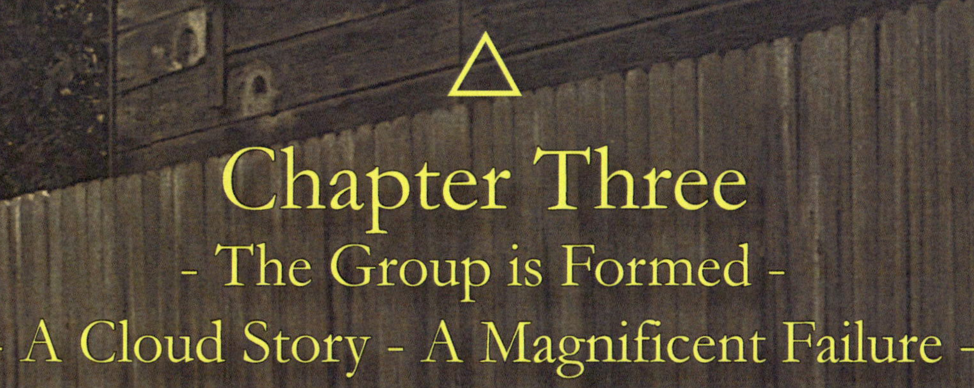

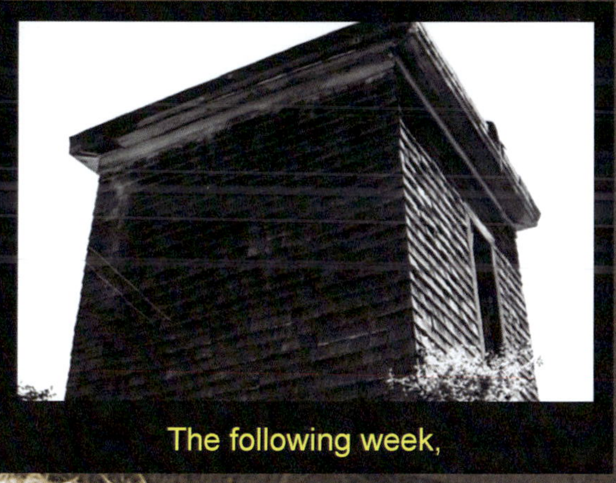

The following week,

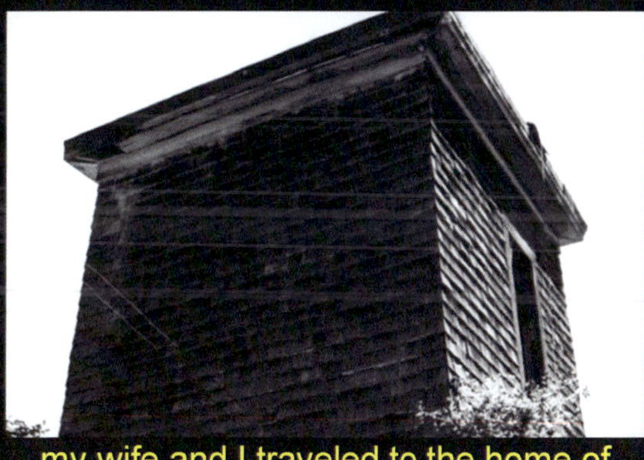

my wife and I traveled to the home of Herr Dockter for the scheduled meeting.

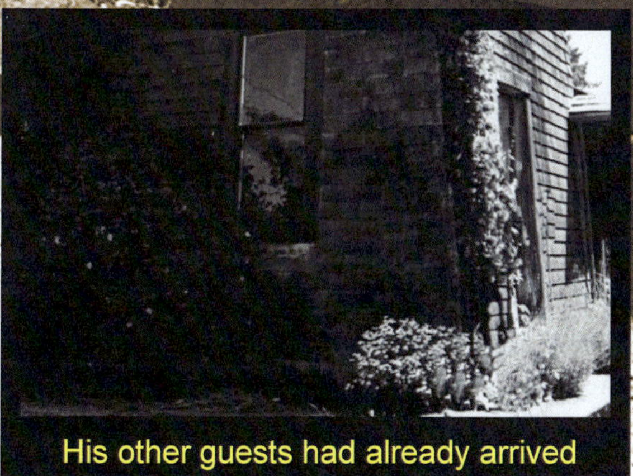

His other guests had already arrived

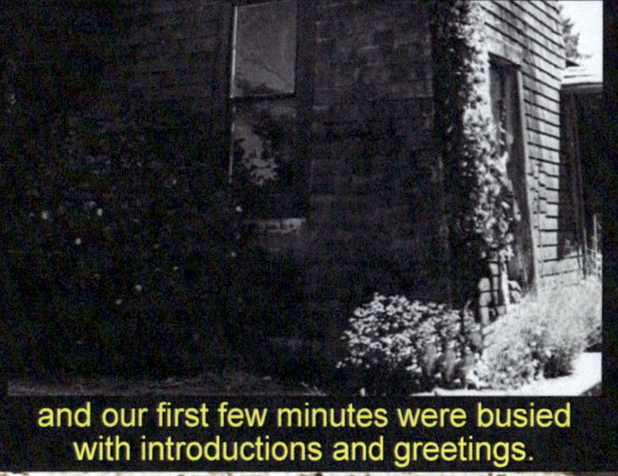

and our first few minutes were busied with introductions and greetings.

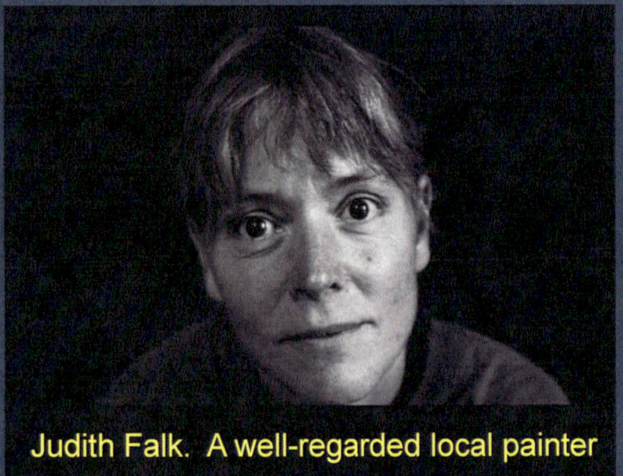

Judith Falk. A well-regarded local painter

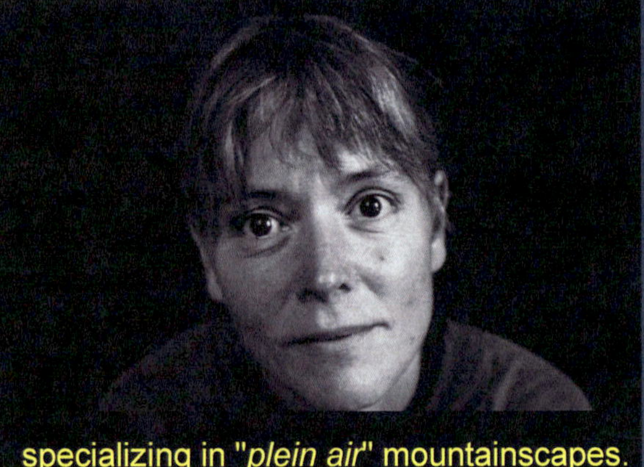

specializing in "*plein air*" mountainscapes.

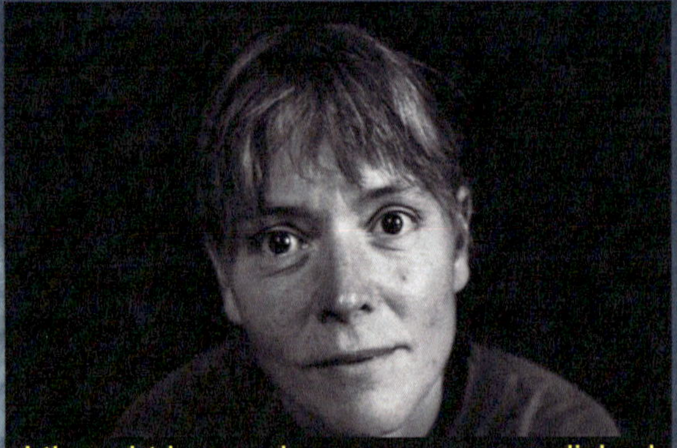

I thought her work was very accomplished and would sell well if not for the tiny,

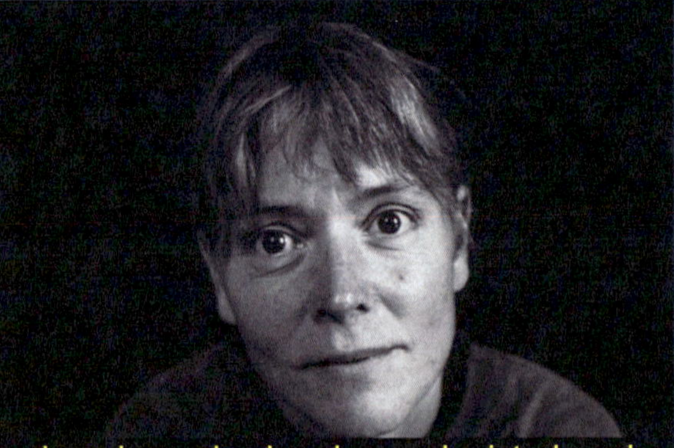

winged people she always depicted peeking out of crevices or from behind rocks.

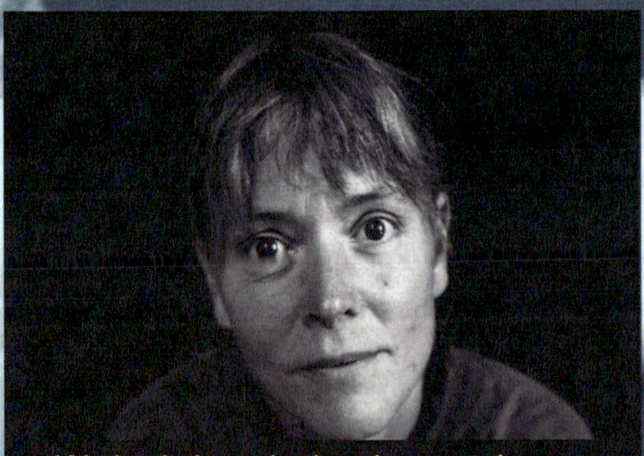

We had shared a laugh several years

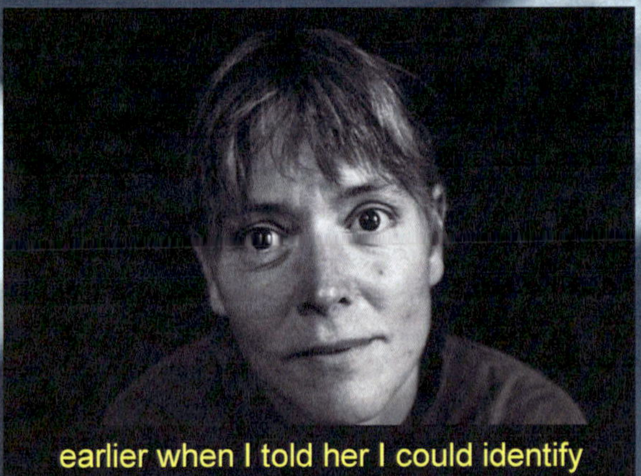

earlier when I told her I could identify

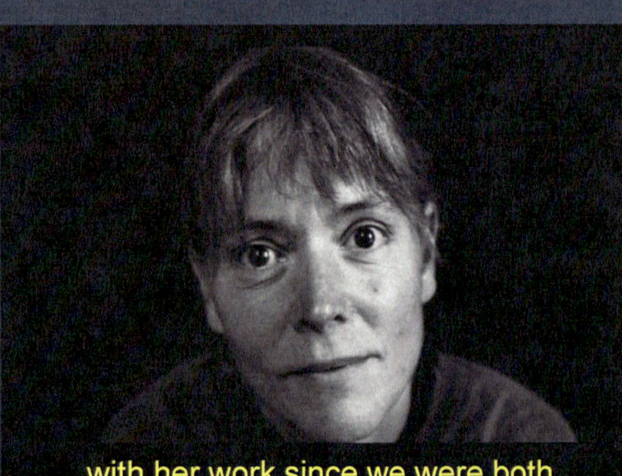

with her work since we were both

so concerned with "pixels".

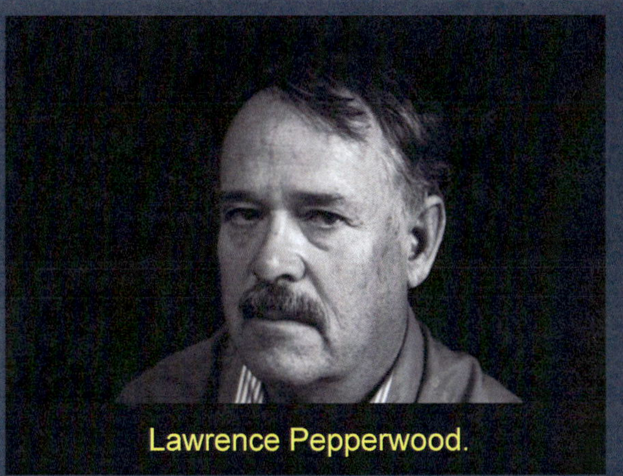

Lawrence Pepperwood.

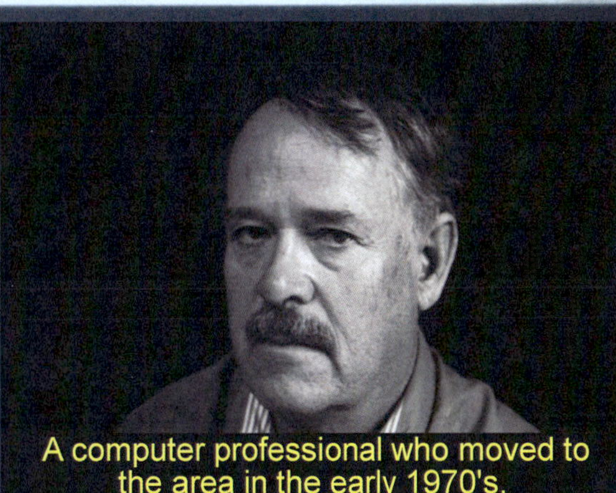

A computer professional who moved to the area in the early 1970's.

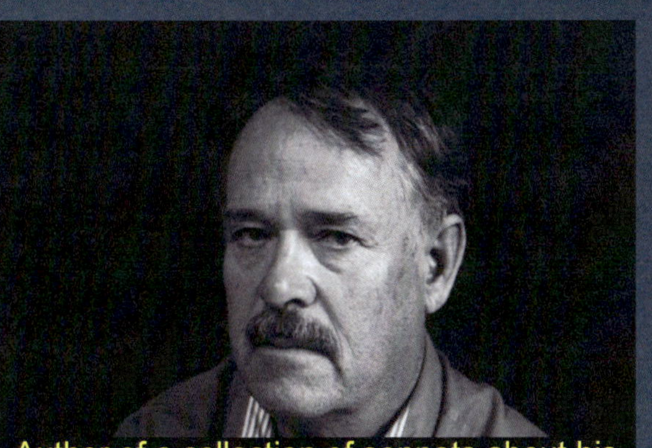

Author of a collection of sonnets about his Vietnam experience, he was host of a

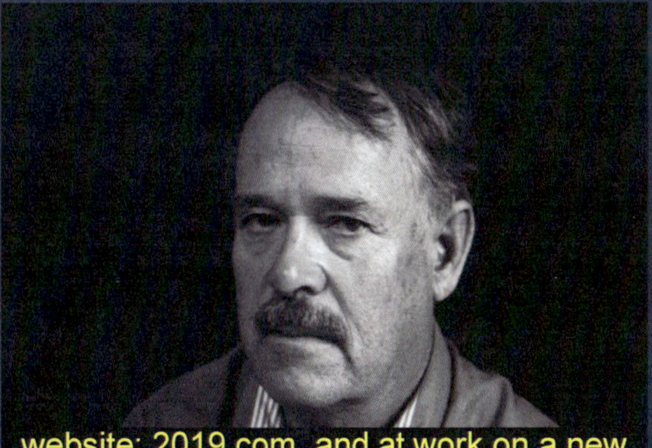

website: 2019.com, and at work on a new book concerning The Singularity.

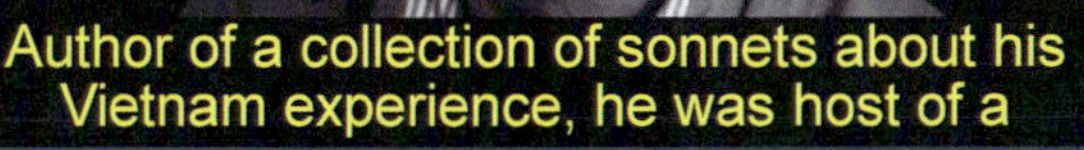

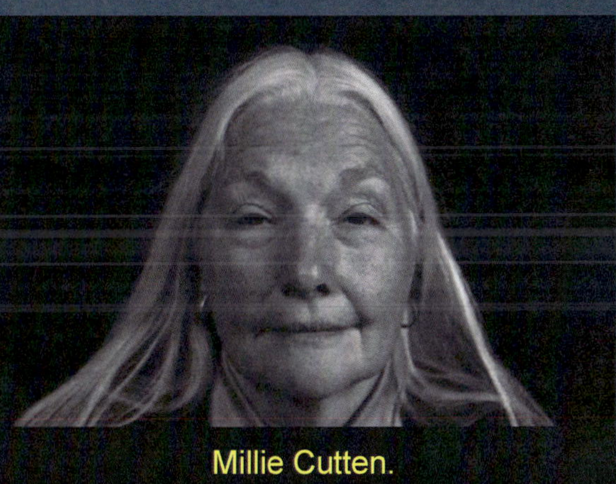

Millie Cutten.

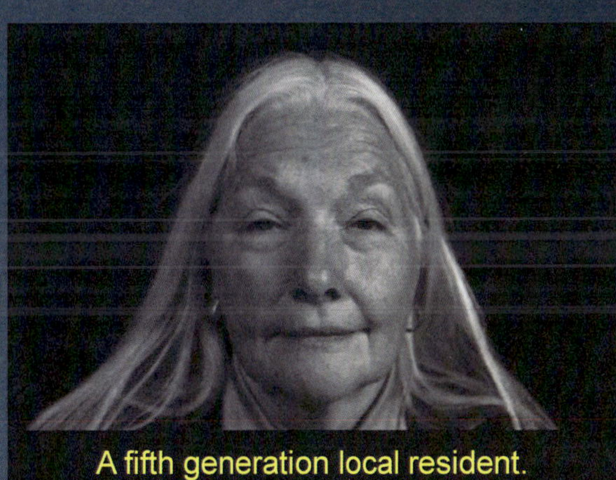

A fifth generation local resident.

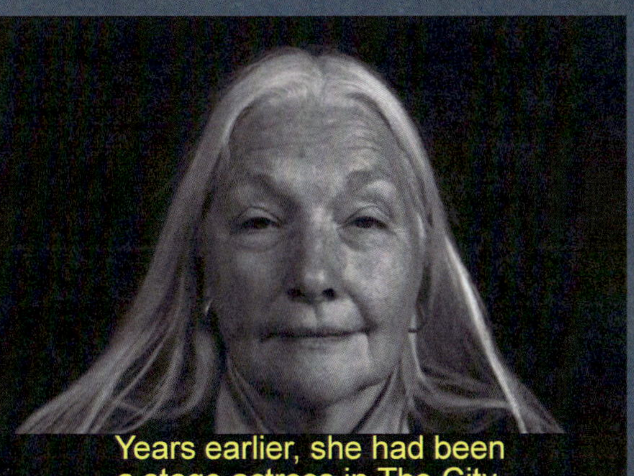

Years earlier, she had been a stage actress in The City.

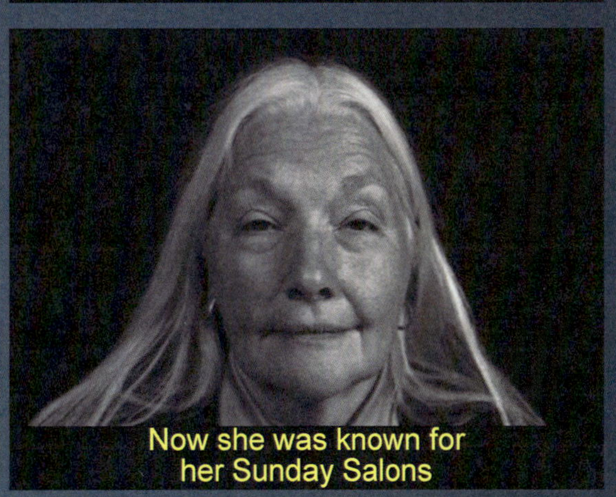

Now she was known for her Sunday Salons

43

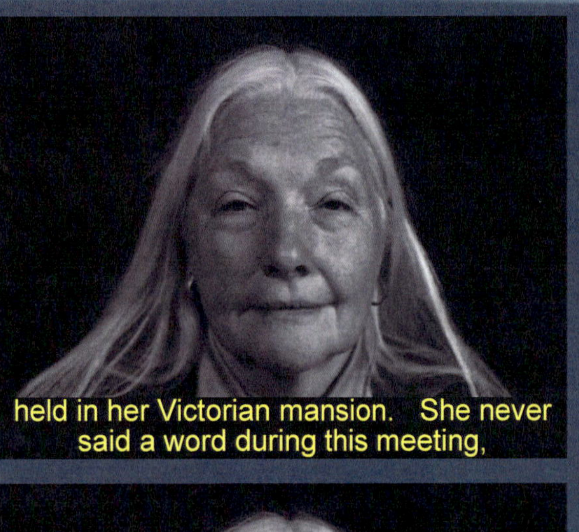
held in her Victorian mansion.   She never
said a word during this meeting,

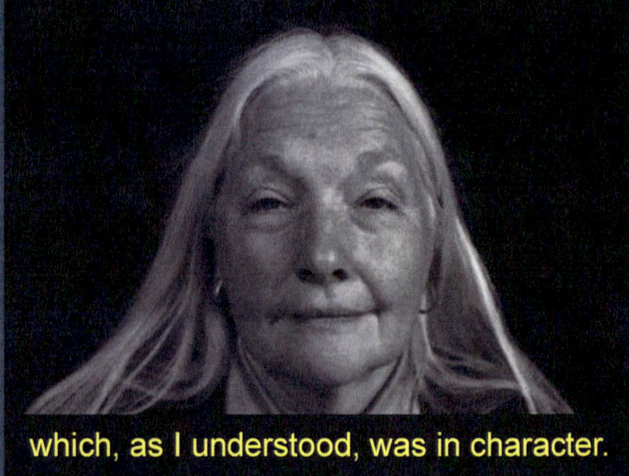
which, as I understood, was in character.

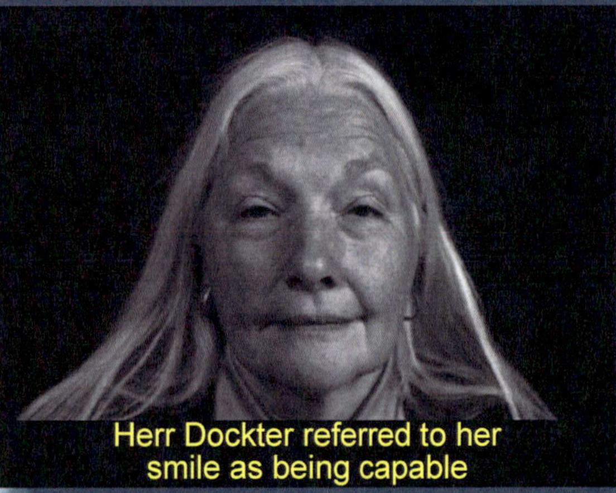
Herr Dockter referred to her
smile as being capable

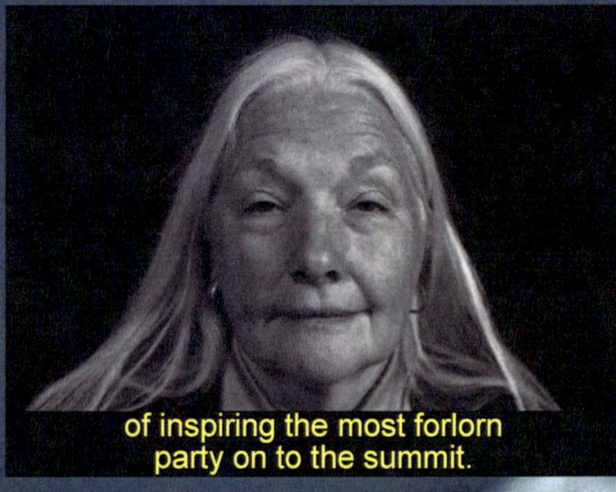
of inspiring the most forlorn
party on to the summit.

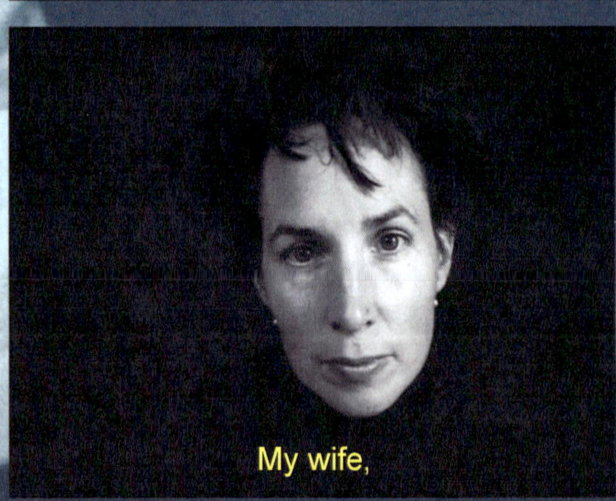
My wife,

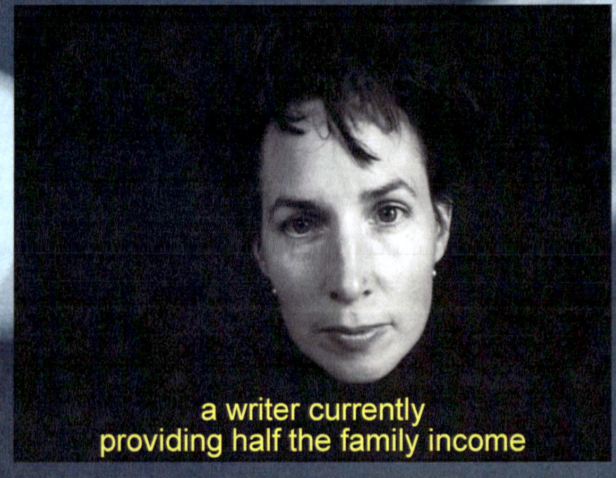
a writer currently
providing half the family income

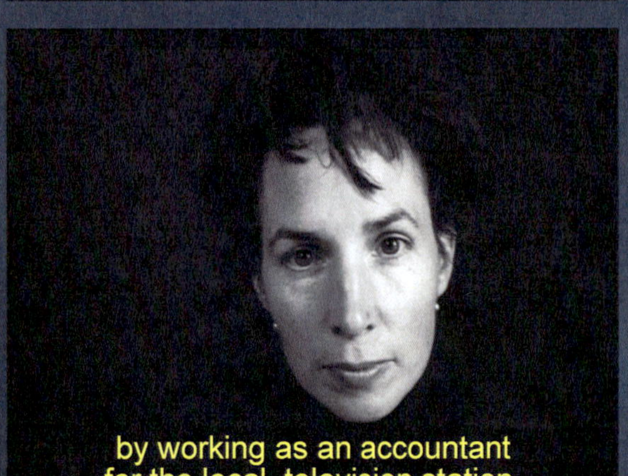
by working as an accountant
for the local television station.

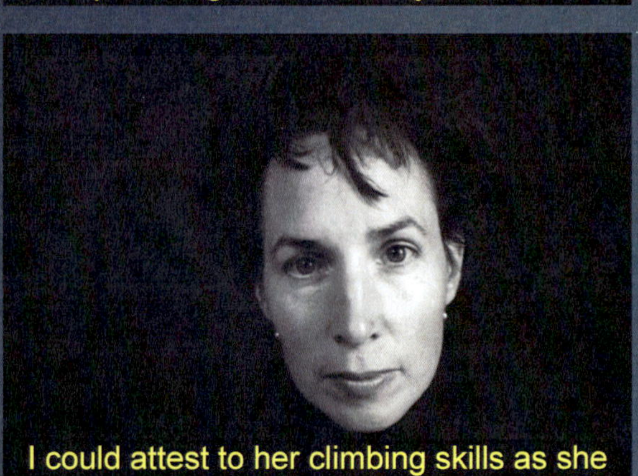
I could attest to her climbing skills as she
had continued on alone to the summit

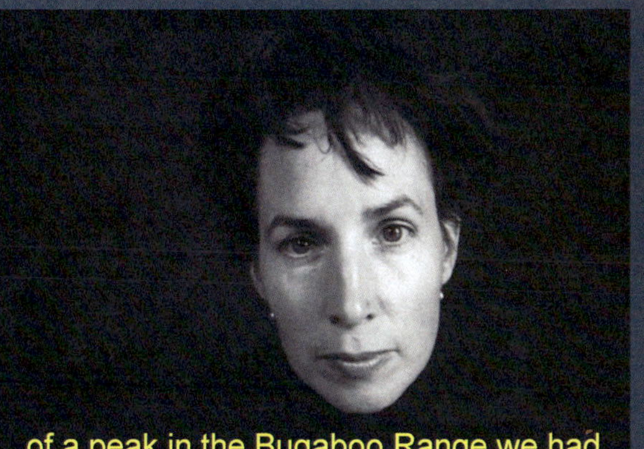

of a peak in the Bugaboo Range we had
chosen to climb on our honeymoon,

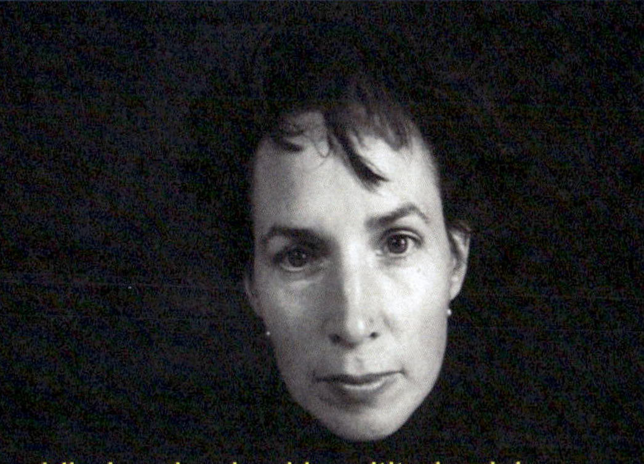

while I, pulverized by altitude sickness,
remained in the tent.

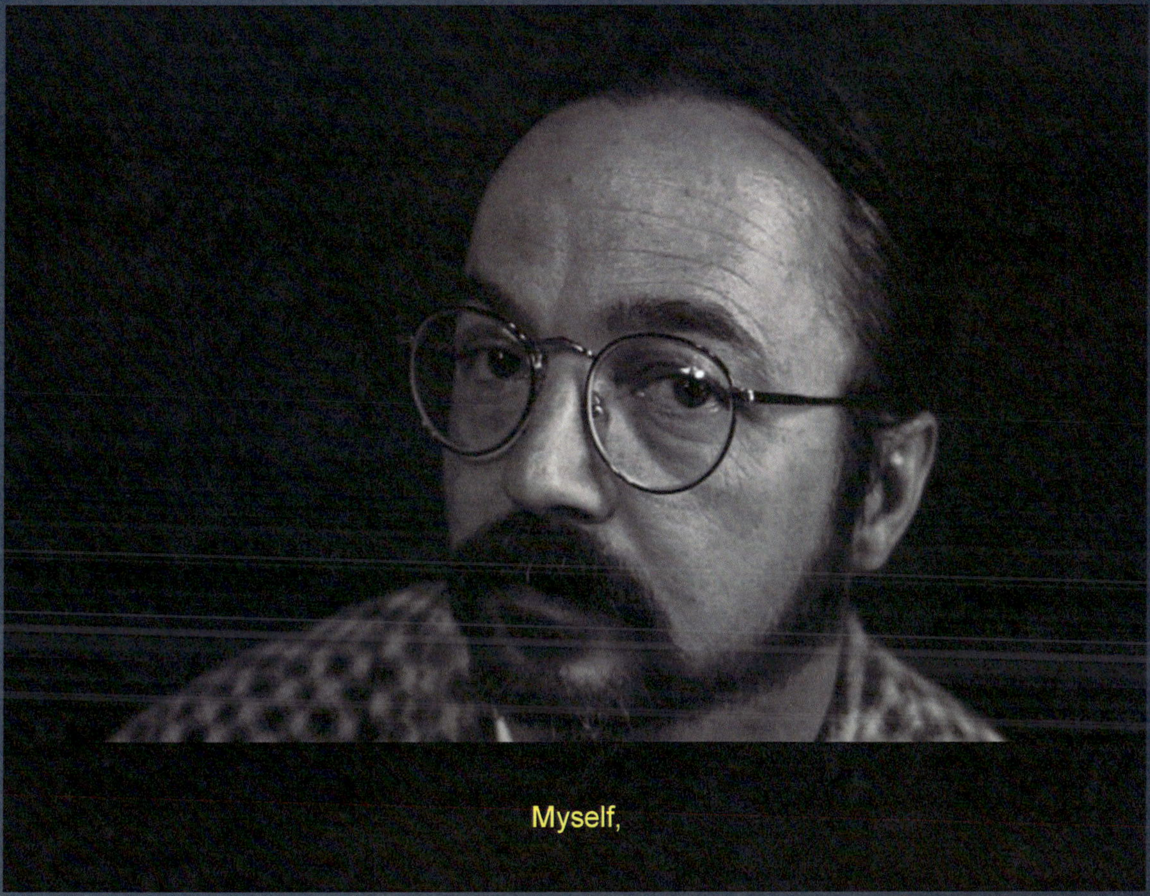

Myself,

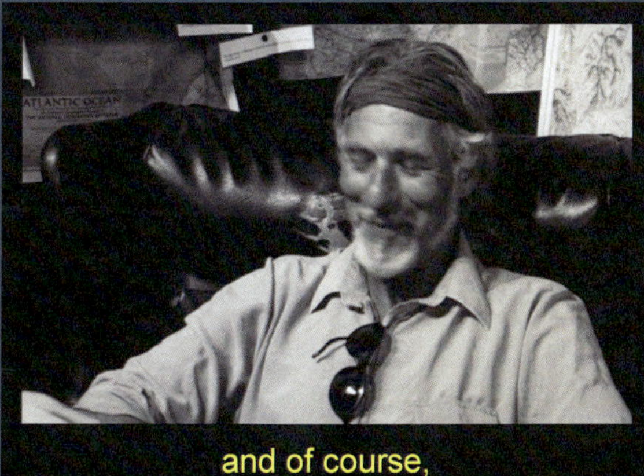

and of course,

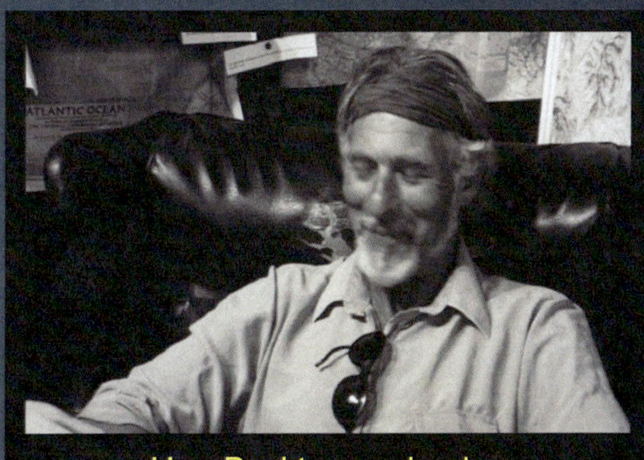

Herr Dockter, our leader.

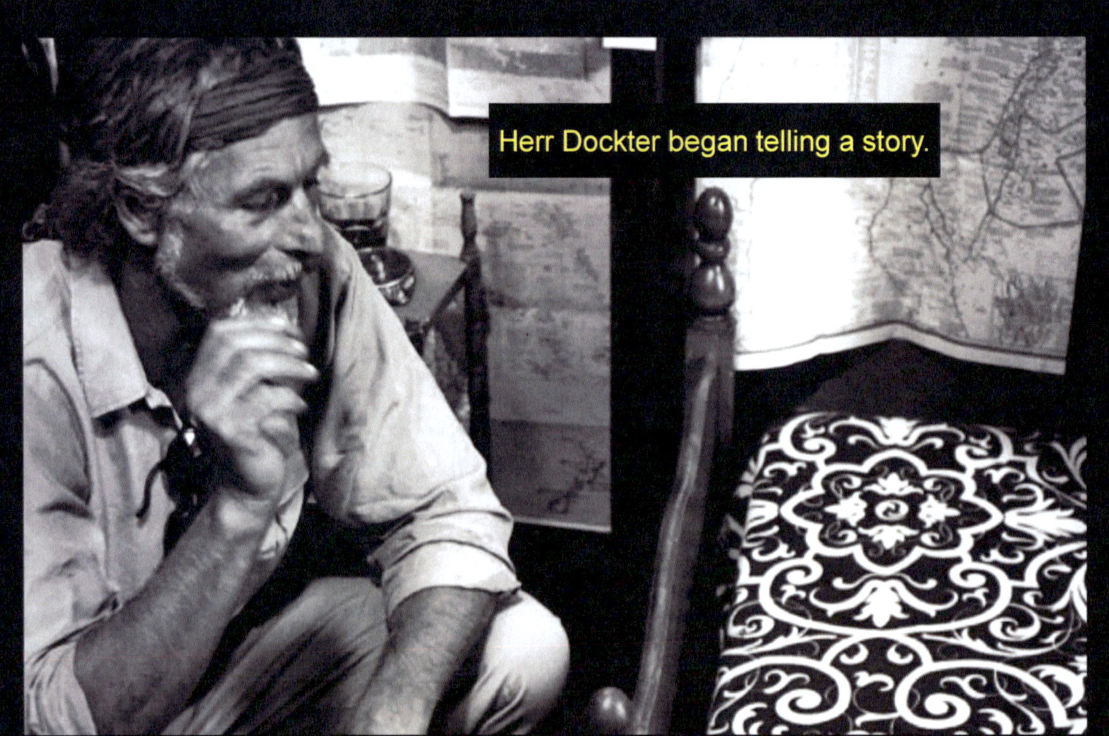

"In the fall of 1881, local hunter, scout and Civil War veteran, Lewis Quimson,
was leading a small group of homesteaders from Sacramento
into the Scott Valley region, west of Mount Shasta.
All proceeded well as the travelers made their way up the Central Valley

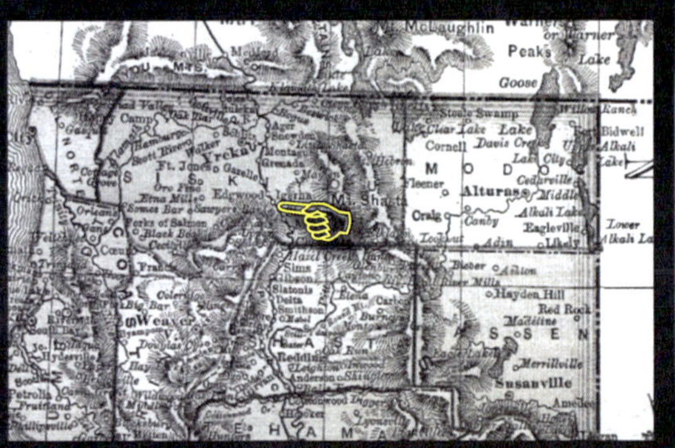

until the point when the mountain domi-
nates the horizon. In a statement made

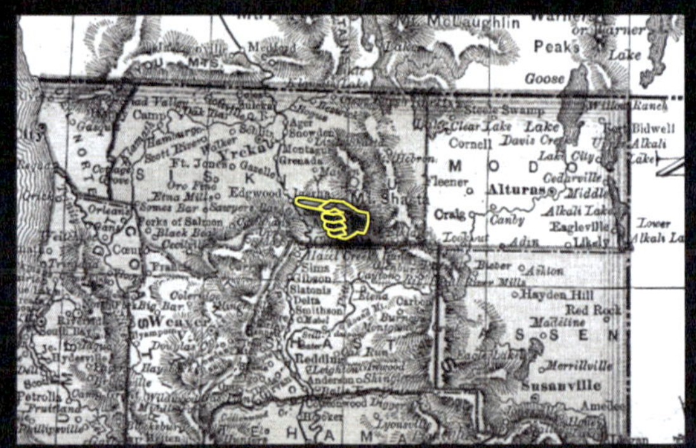

to authorities after the incident, Watson, a
sheep rancher with the group, recalled:

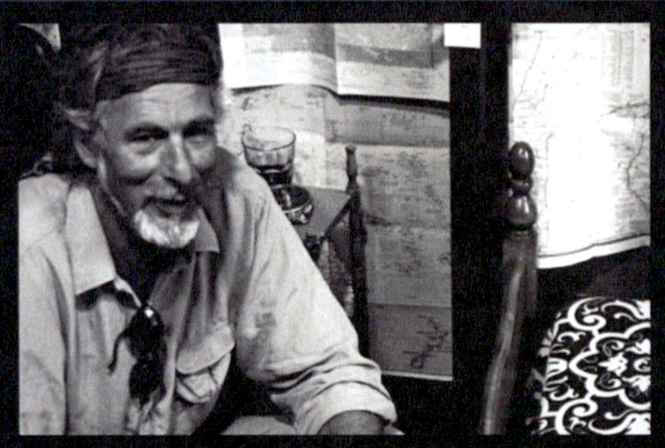

'Mr. Quimson began acting most
erratically, with pacing,

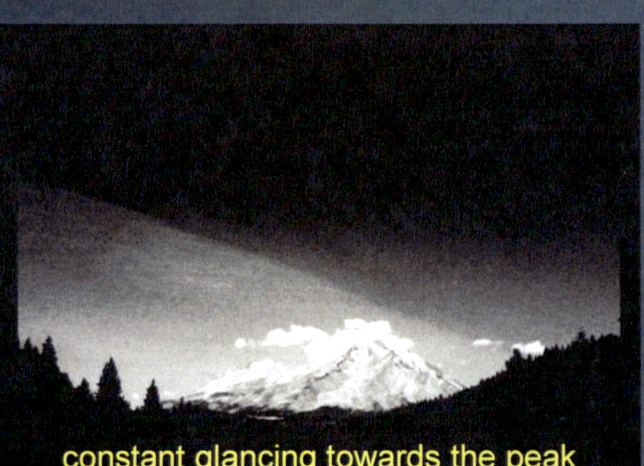

constant glancing towards the peak
and whispering to himself.'

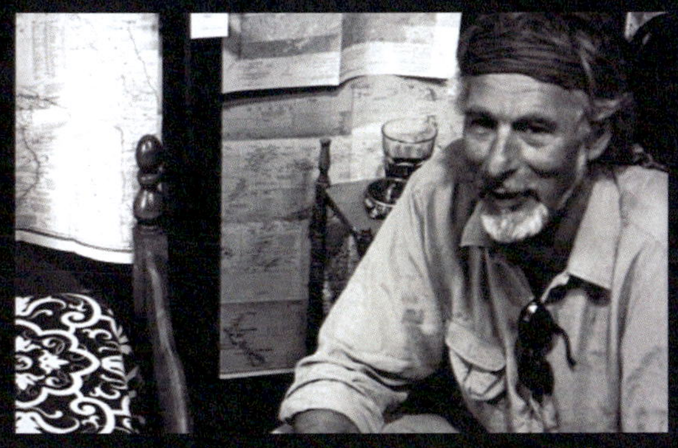

Although their guide had a reputation as a temperate man,

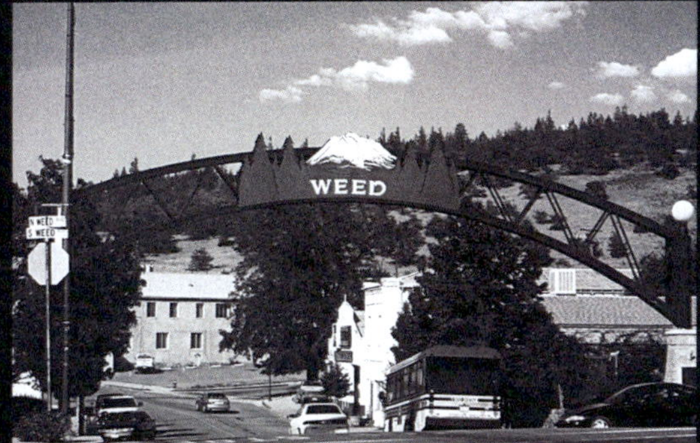

several of the women felt he had taken to the bottle.

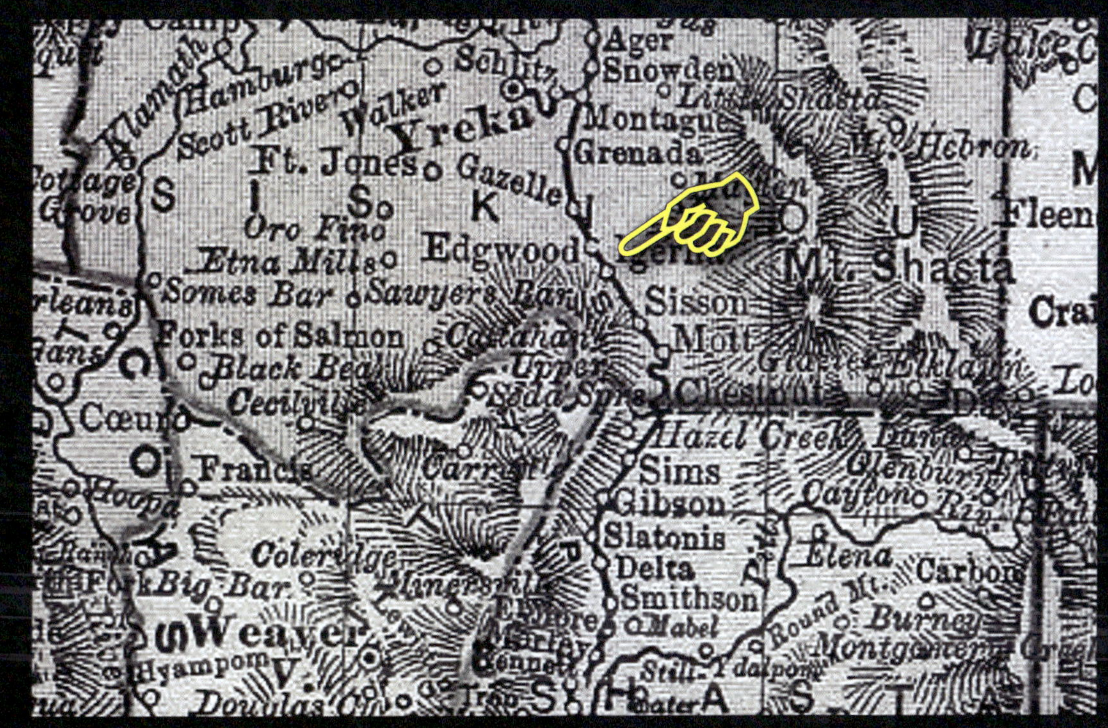

Quimson's odd behavior culminated at a stop near the present location of the city of Weed, when witnesses reported that between bouts of crying, laughing and 'muttering in tongues', he scrawled directions for the homesteaders on a map,

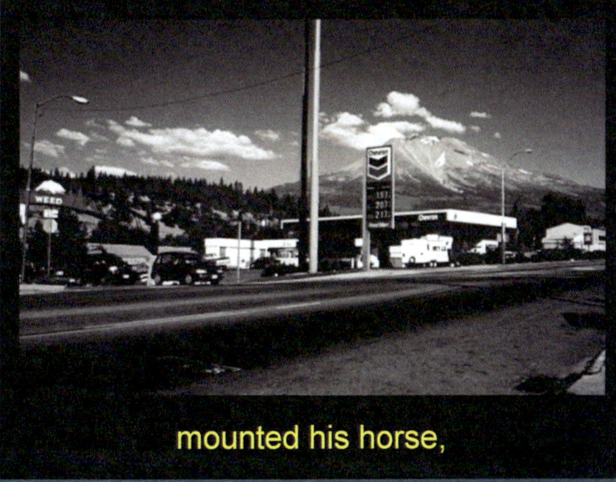

mounted his horse,

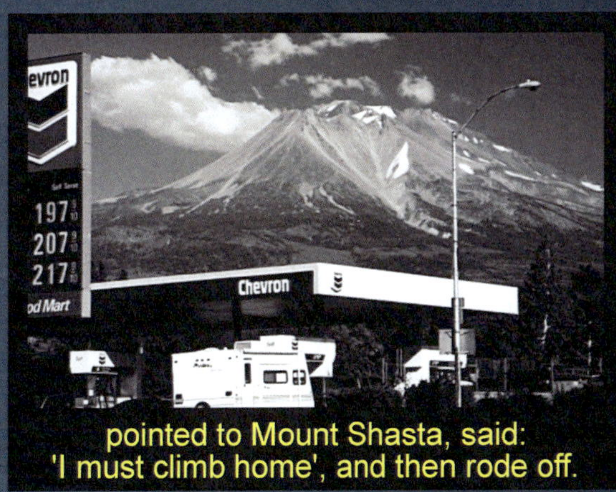

pointed to Mount Shasta, said: 'I must climb home', and then rode off.

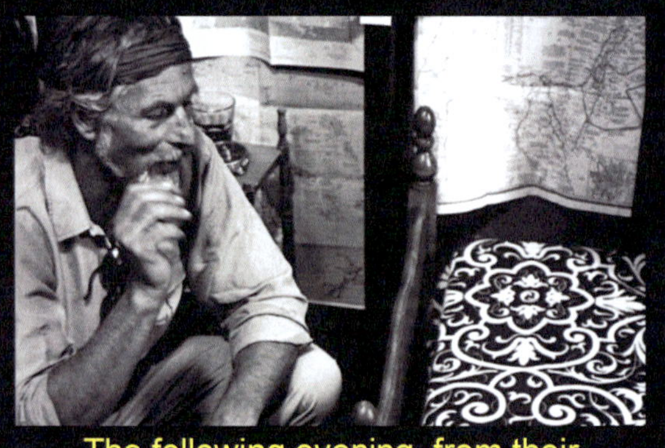
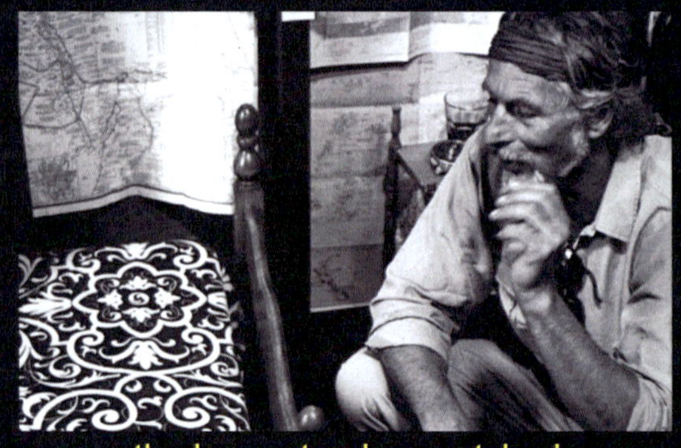

The following evening, from their campsite above Stewart Springs,

the homesteaders watched a huge cloud form above a

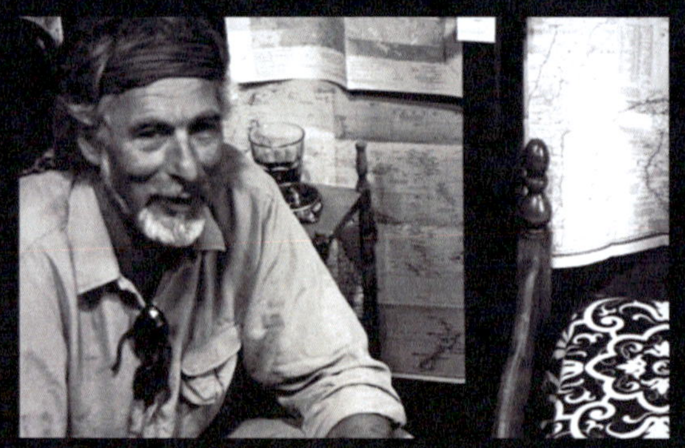
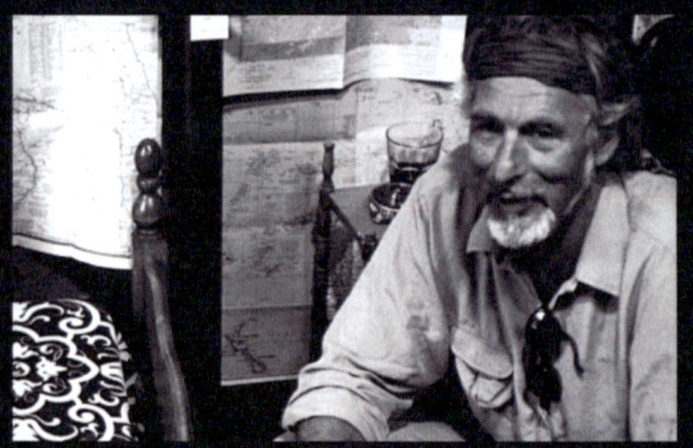

Mount Shasta bathed in the rich glow of sunset.

Quoting from Rancher Watson's statement again:

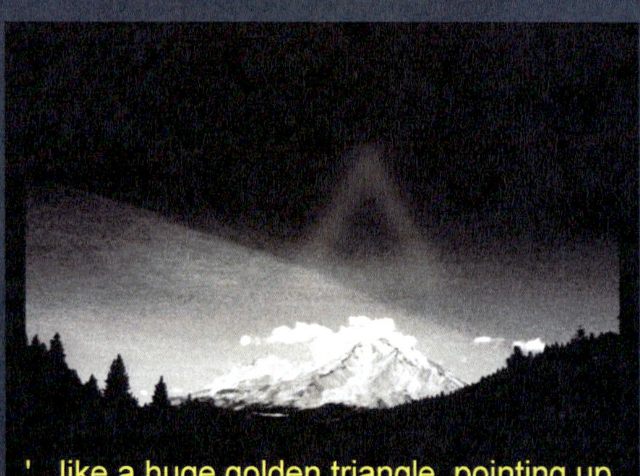

'...like a huge golden triangle, pointing up,

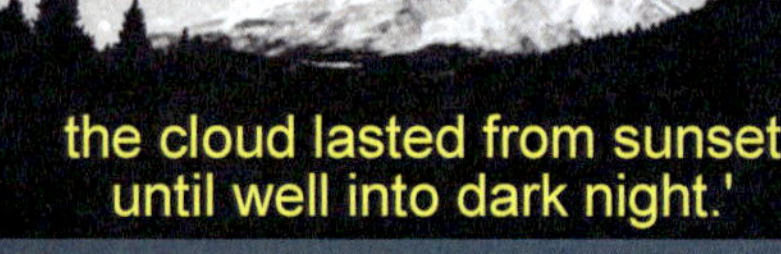

the cloud lasted from sunset until well into dark night.'

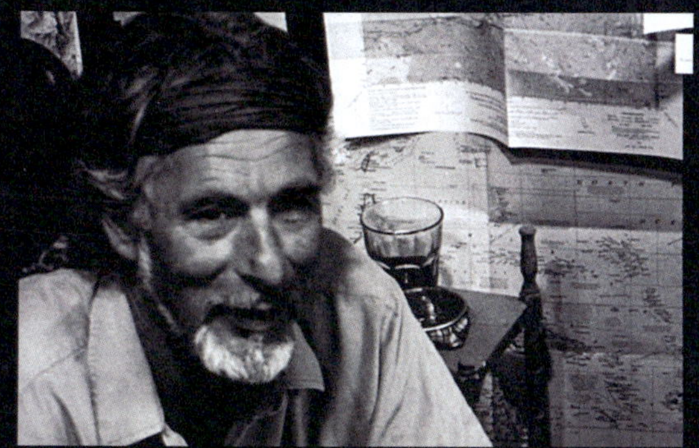

The lenticular clouds of Mount Shasta are well documented," Herr Dockter said,

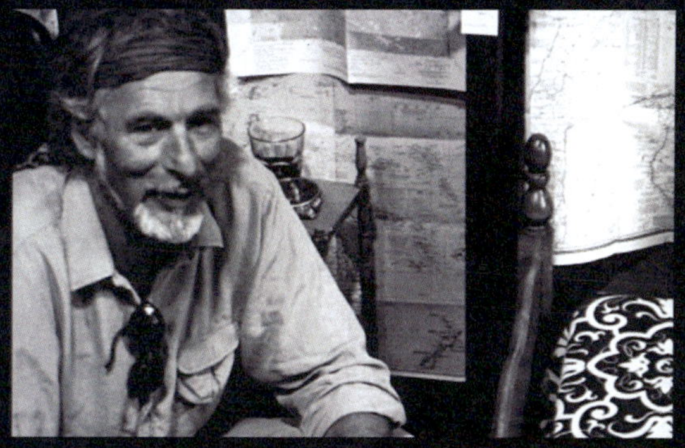

bringing us back from his story.

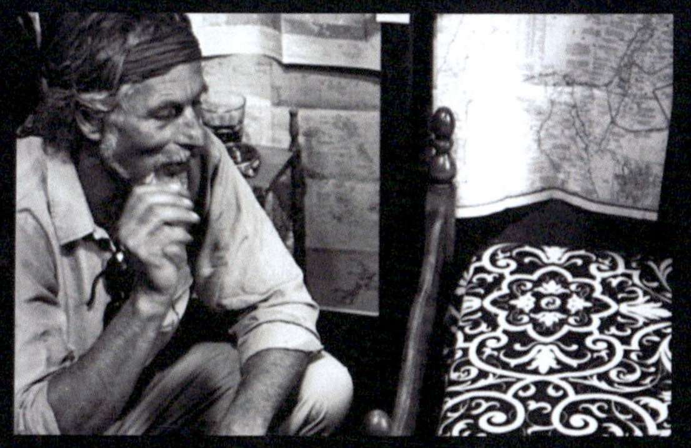

"Let me show you some photographs."

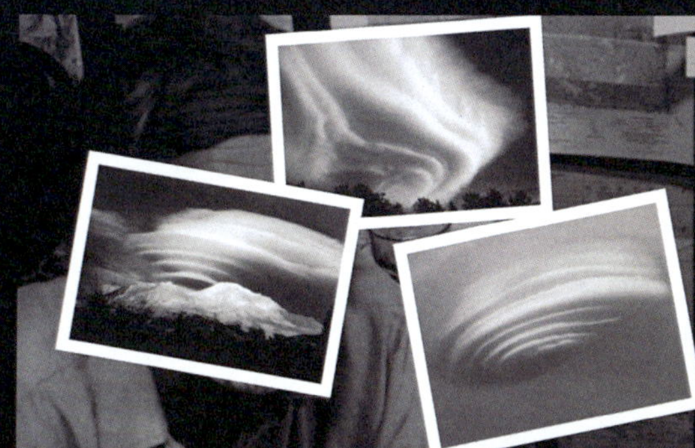

He passed a set of small prints around the group.

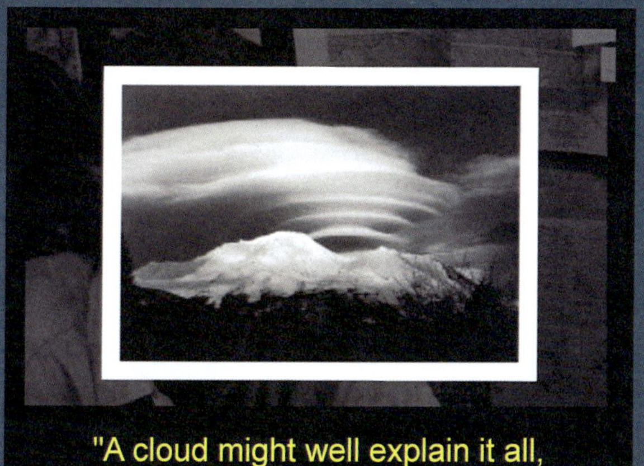

"A cloud might well explain it all,

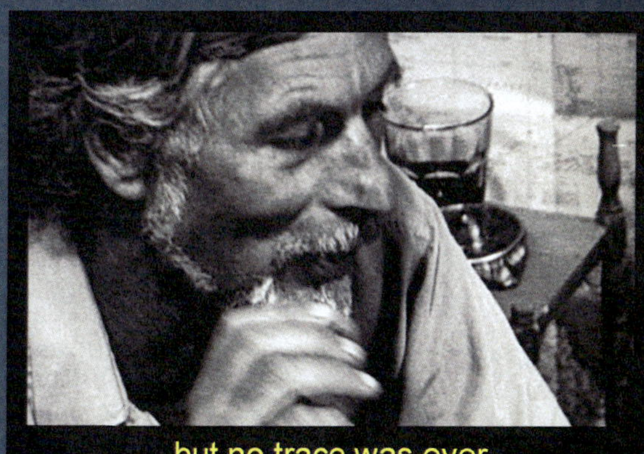

but no trace was ever found of Mr. Quimson."

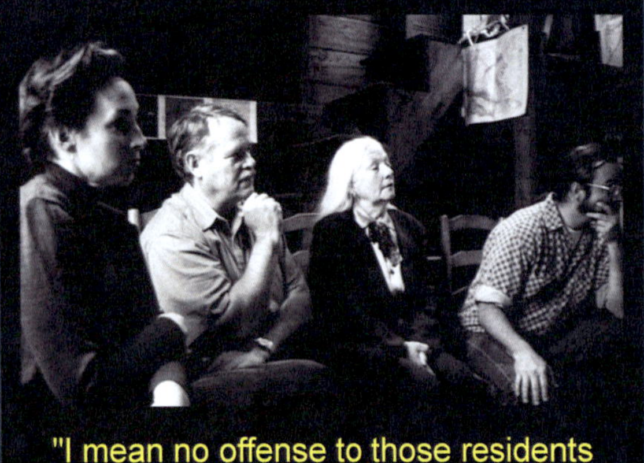

"I mean no offense to those residents

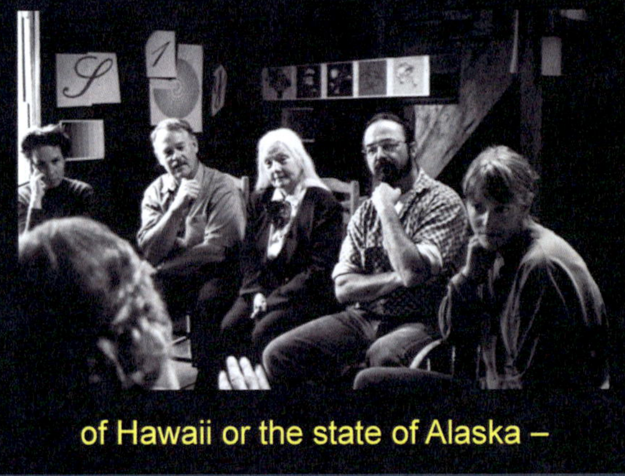

of Hawaii or the state of Alaska –

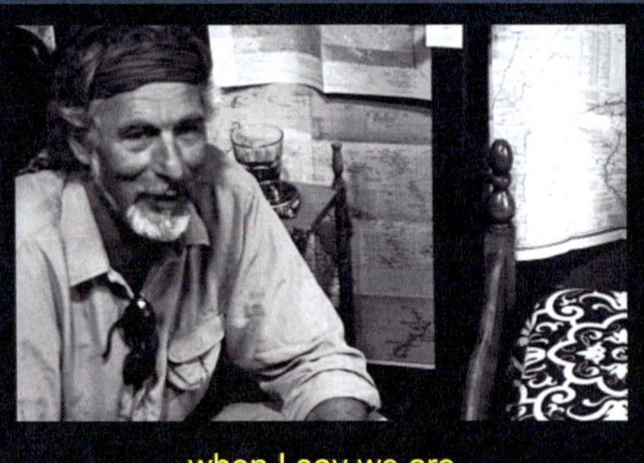

when I say we are

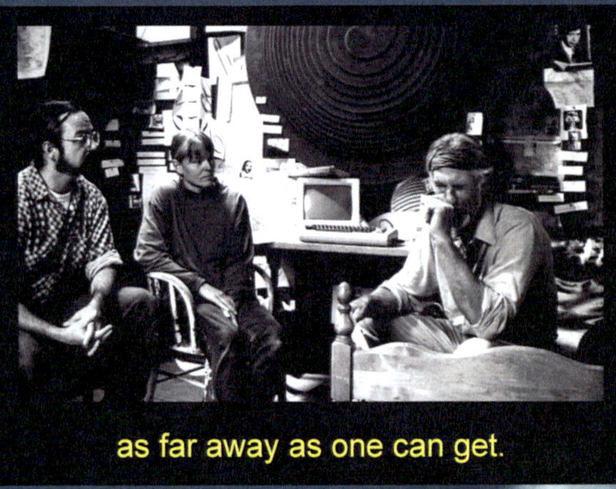

as far away as one can get.

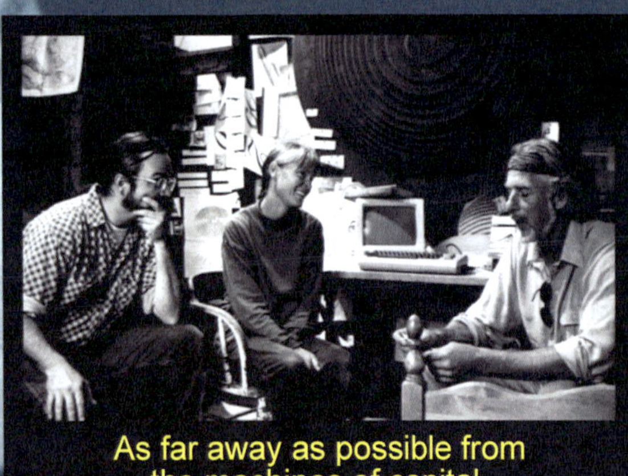

As far away as possible from
the machines of capital,

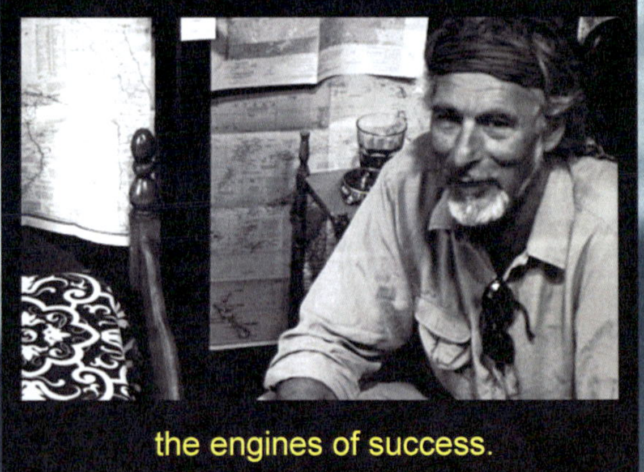

the engines of success.

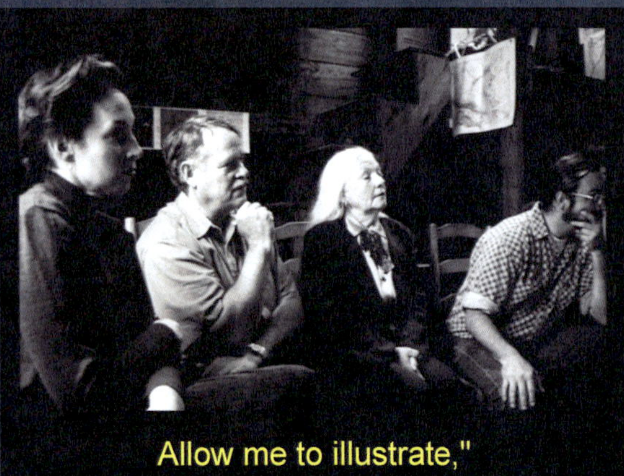

Allow me to illustrate,"

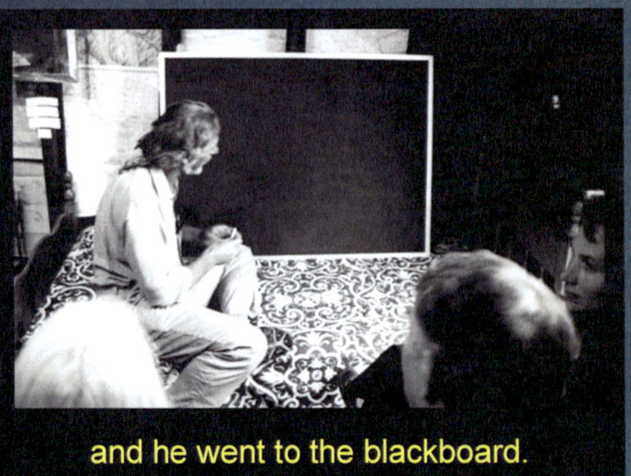

and he went to the blackboard.

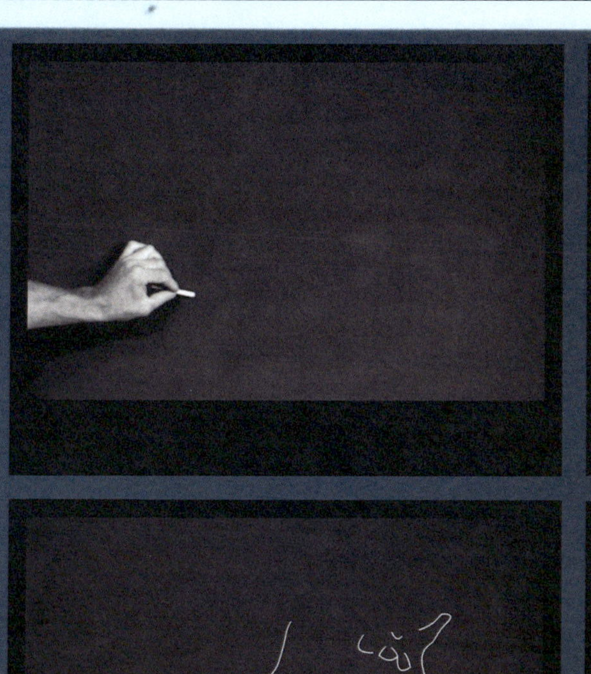

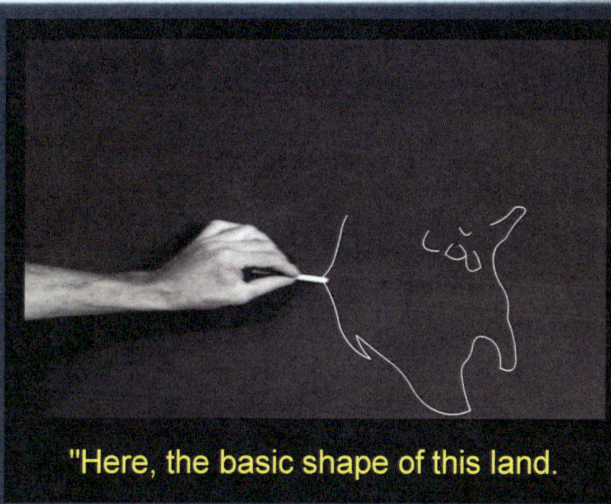
"Here, the basic shape of this land.

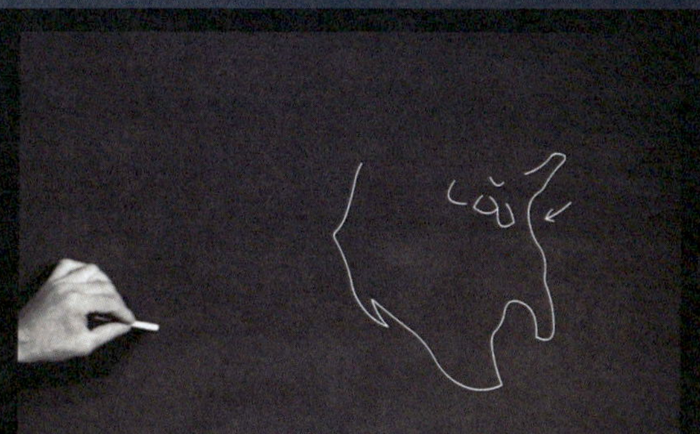
By immigrants, refugees – By those
seeking to get away, by those seeking.

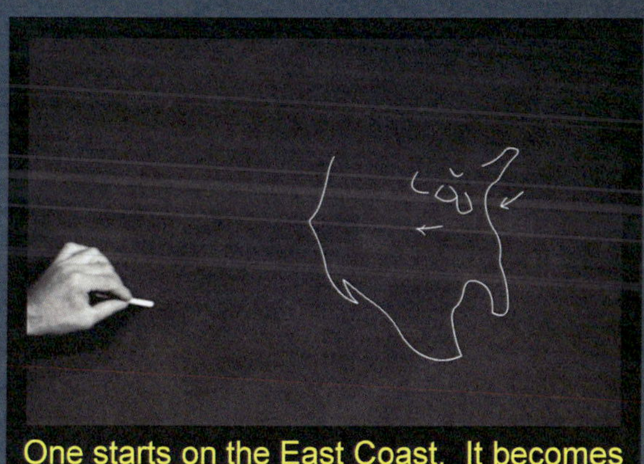
A country formed by those unable
to succeed in Europe.

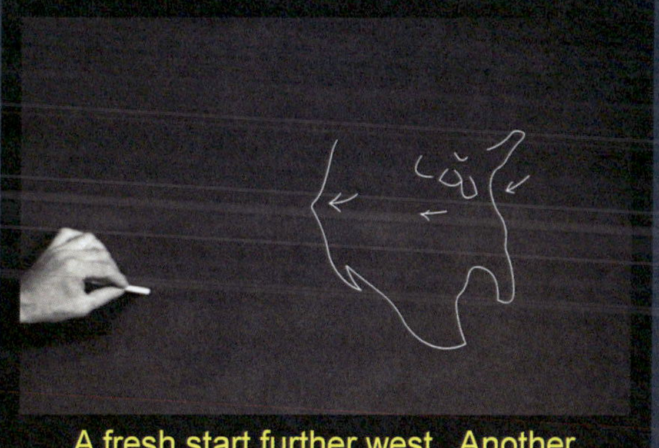
One starts on the East Coast. It becomes
too much like what came before.

A fresh start further west. Another
chance. Pushing on ever westward.

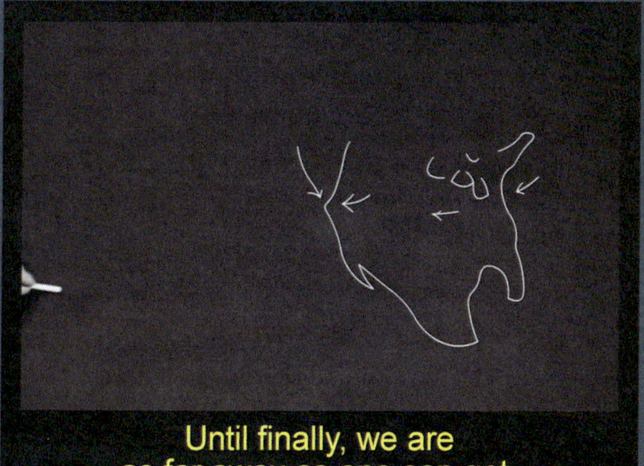
Until finally, we are
as far away as one can get.

What better place for a sacred mountain,
a link between earth and heaven."

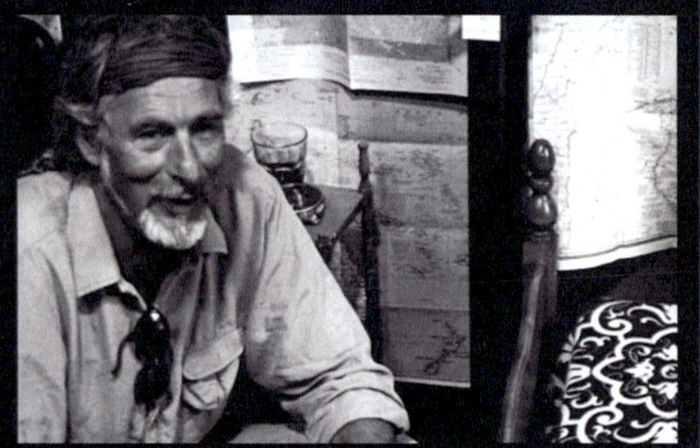

"I first heard tales about this peak
while bivouacking high

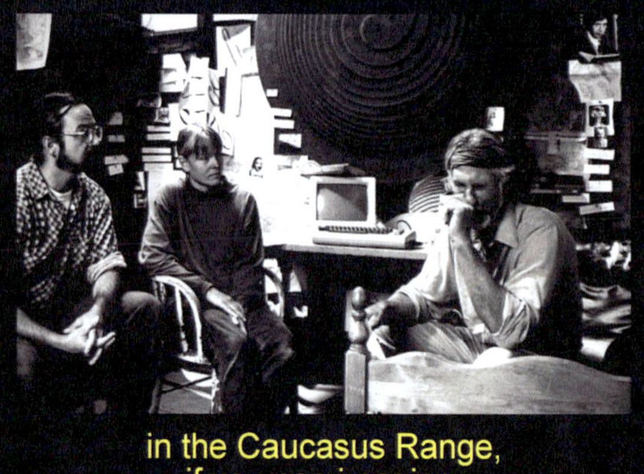

in the Caucasus Range,
if you can imagine.

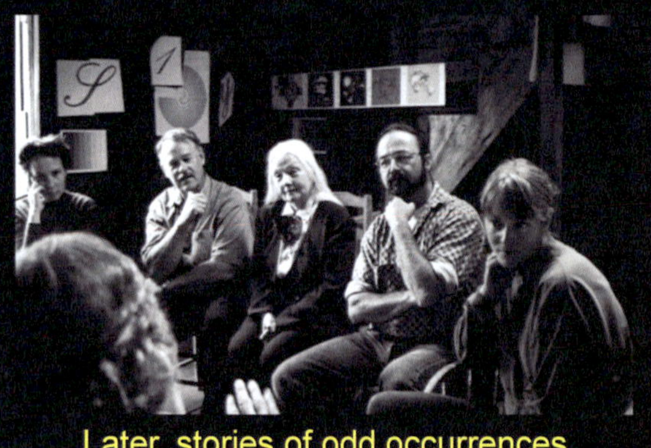

Later, stories of odd occurrences
on Mount Shasta's north side

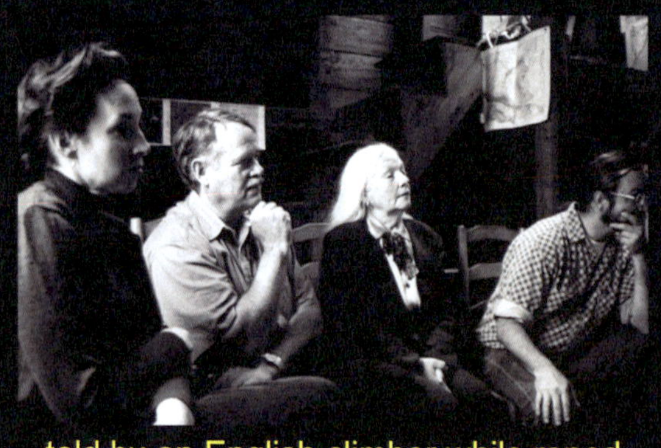

told by an English climber while roped
together on Mt. Robson,

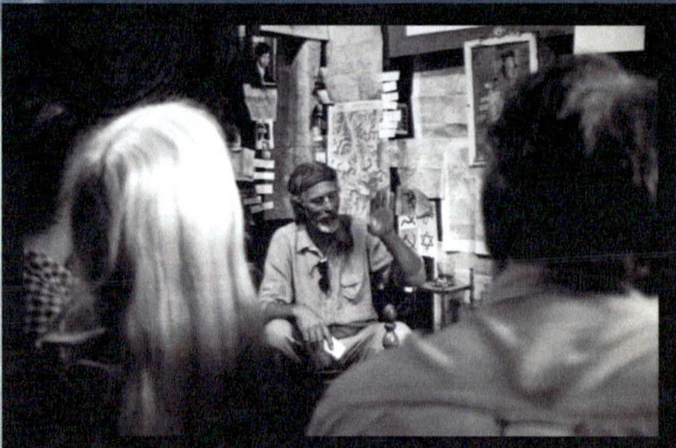

convinced me to move here, eke out a
living giving mountaineering lessons,

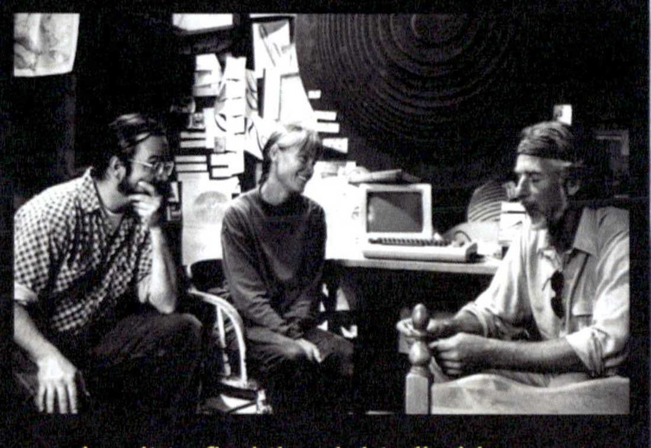

and wait to find the right climbing party.

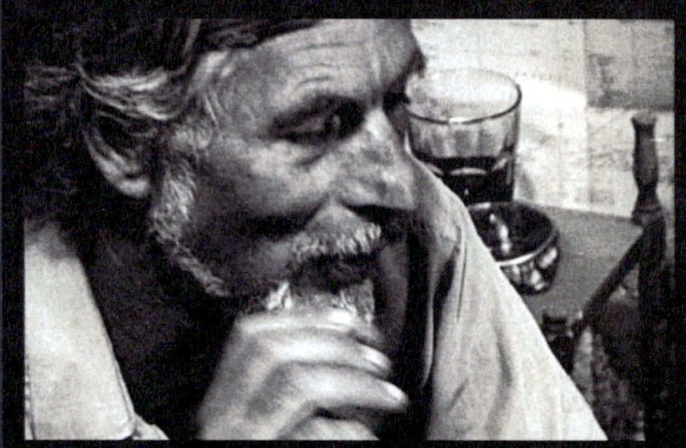

Now, after many years and
many ascents of that peak,

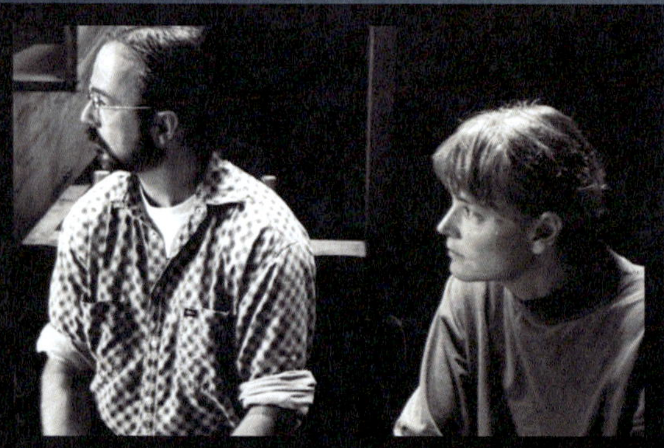

I am sure I know the right route and have
the right group of companions."

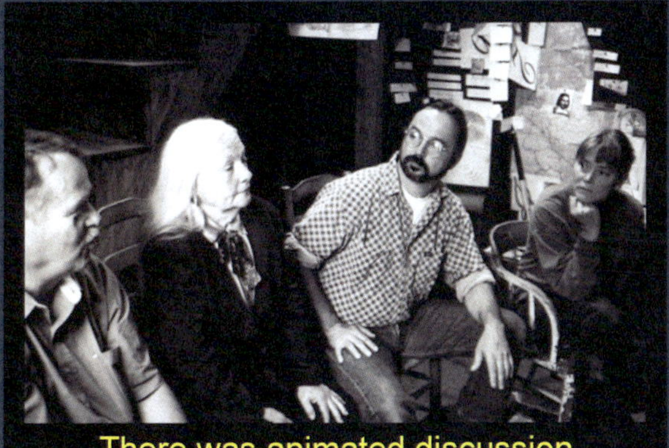

There was animated discussion amongst Herr Dockter's audience.

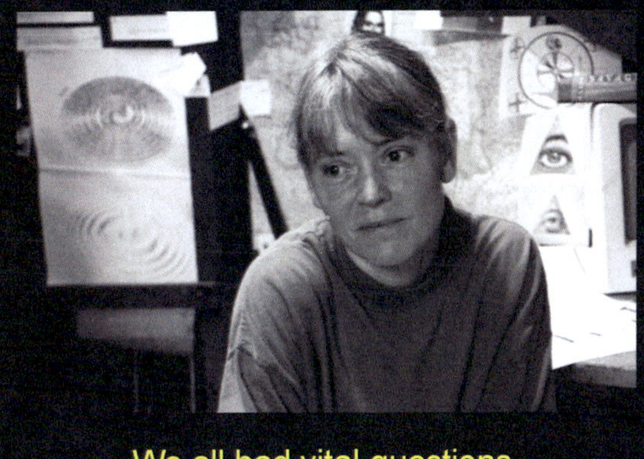

We all had vital questions.

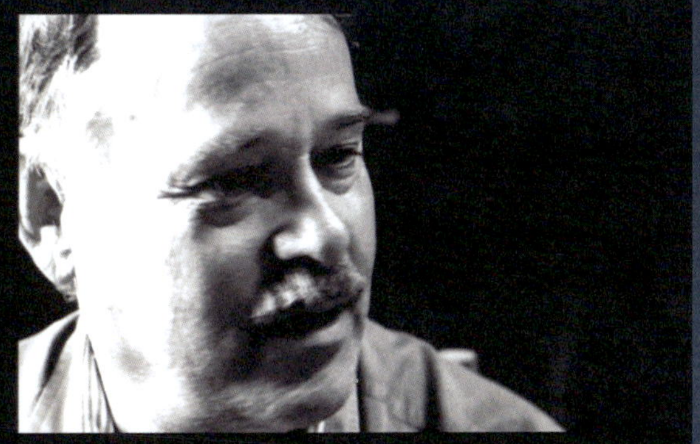

Mr. Pepperwood wished to know why we had each been selected.

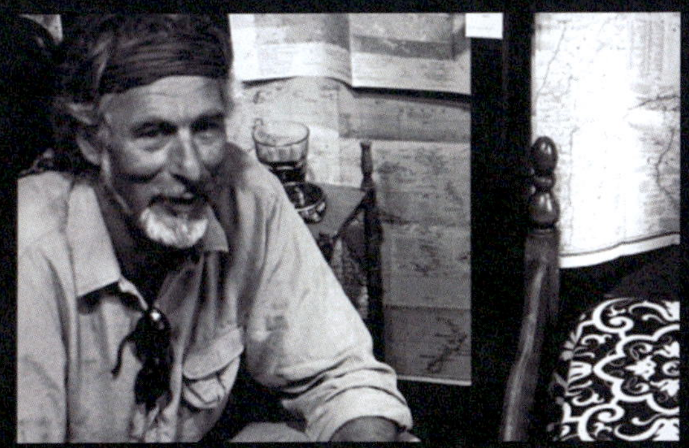

"I'll try to explain as well as possible," Herr Dockter replied.

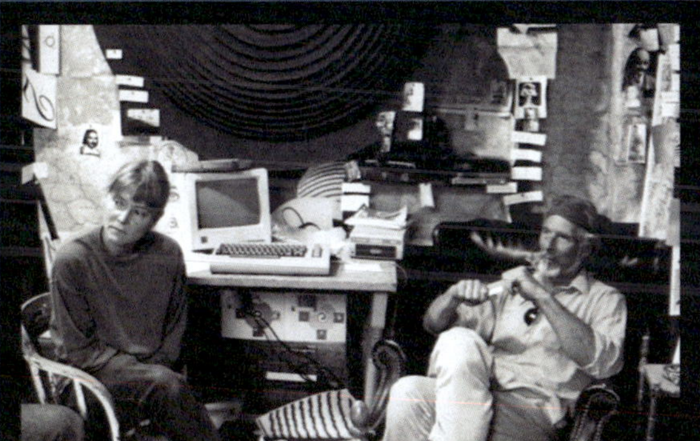

"Keep in mind that you have a reputation as a strong climber –

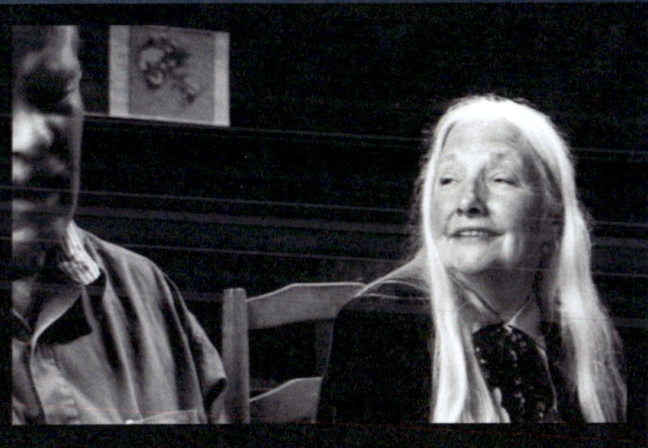

– tenacious on glacier ice.

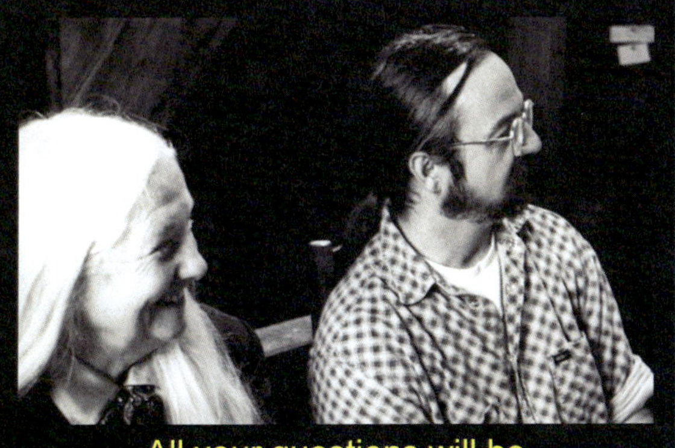
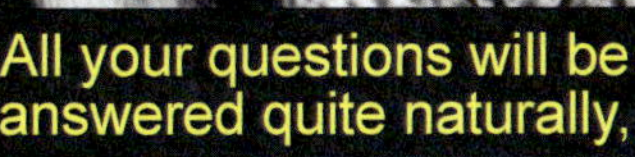

All your questions will be answered quite naturally,

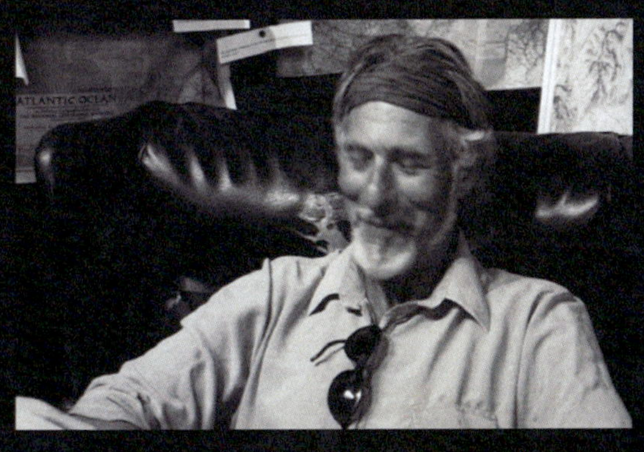

as our journey progresses."

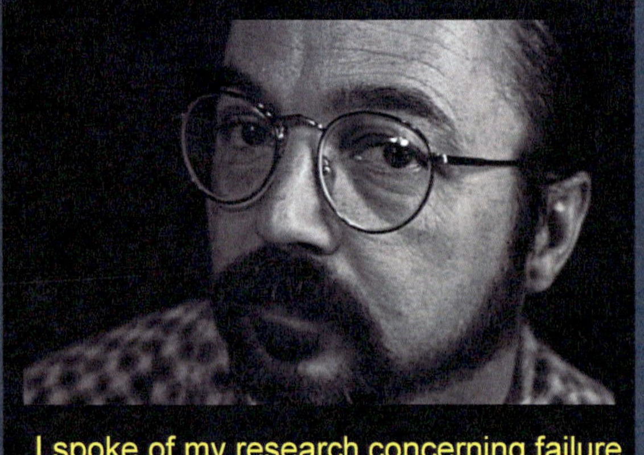

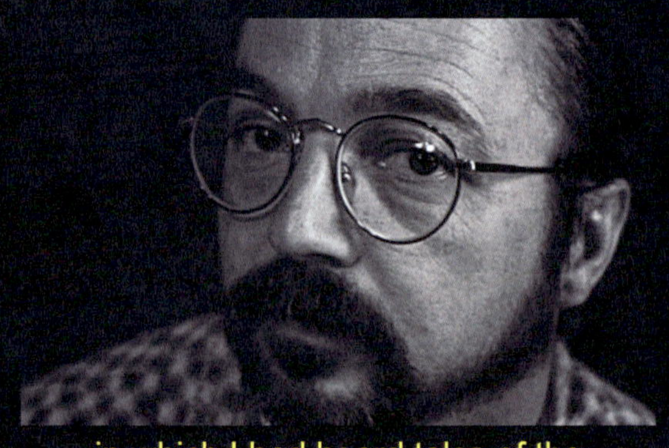

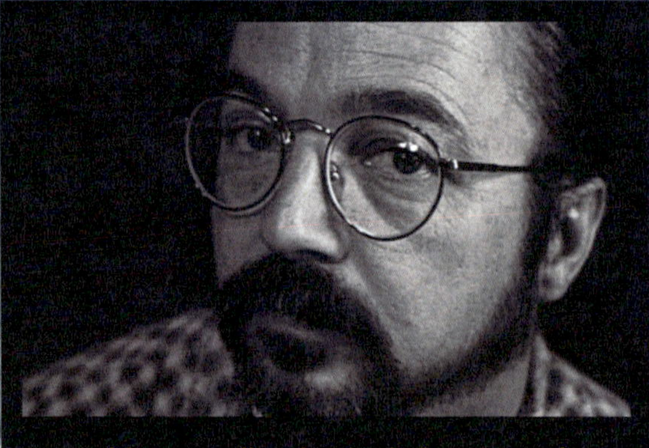

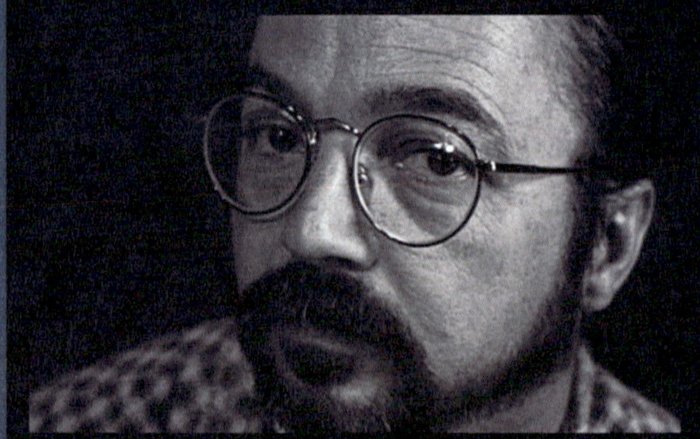

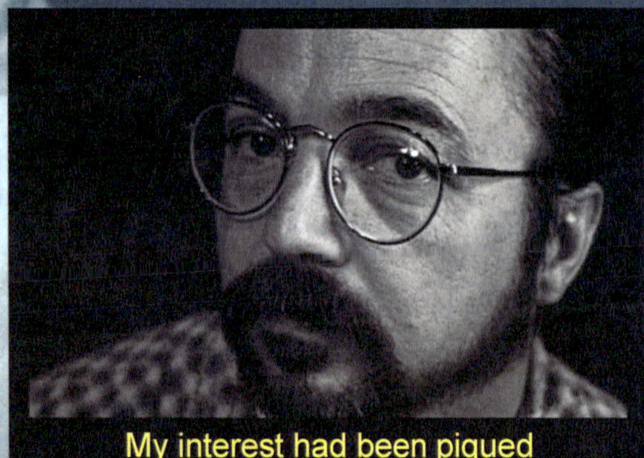

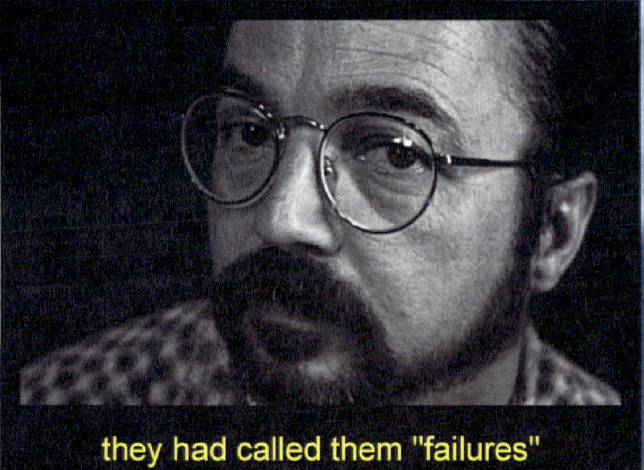

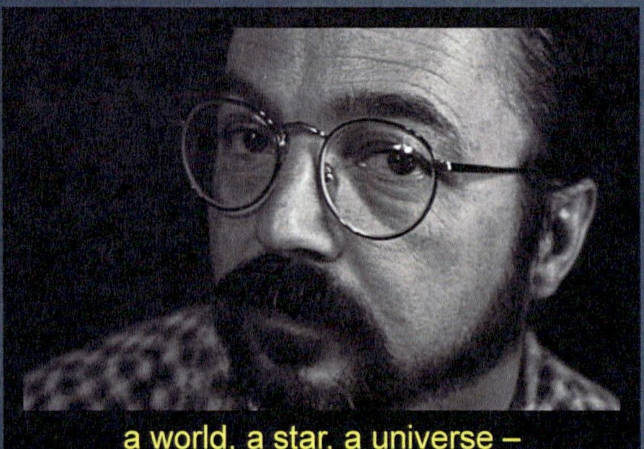

referring to a belief that upon completion,

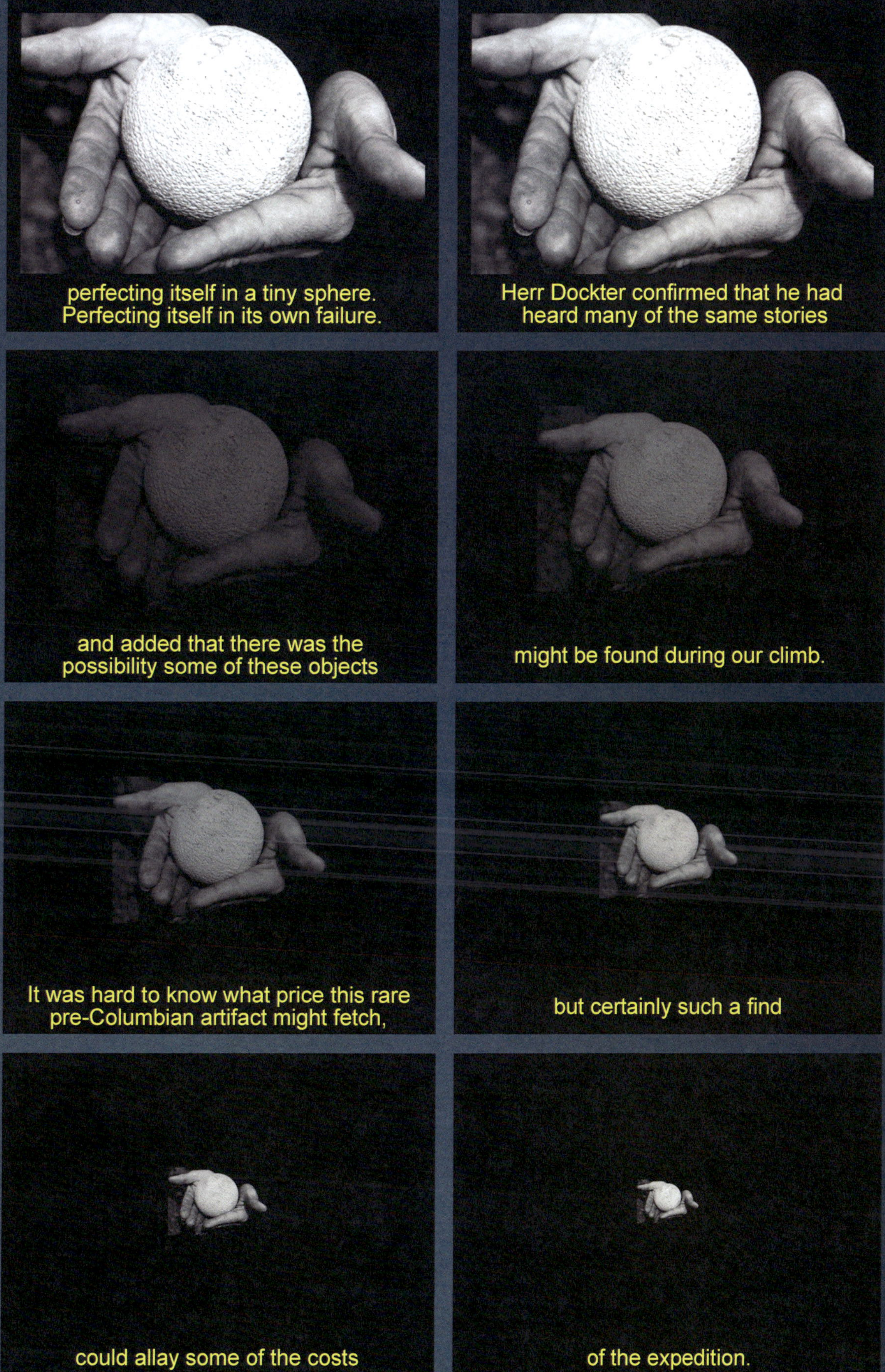
perfecting itself in a tiny sphere.
Perfecting itself in its own failure.

Herr Dockter confirmed that he had
heard many of the same stories

and added that there was the
possibility some of these objects

might be found during our climb.

It was hard to know what price this rare
pre-Columbian artifact might fetch,

but certainly such a find

could allay some of the costs

of the expedition.

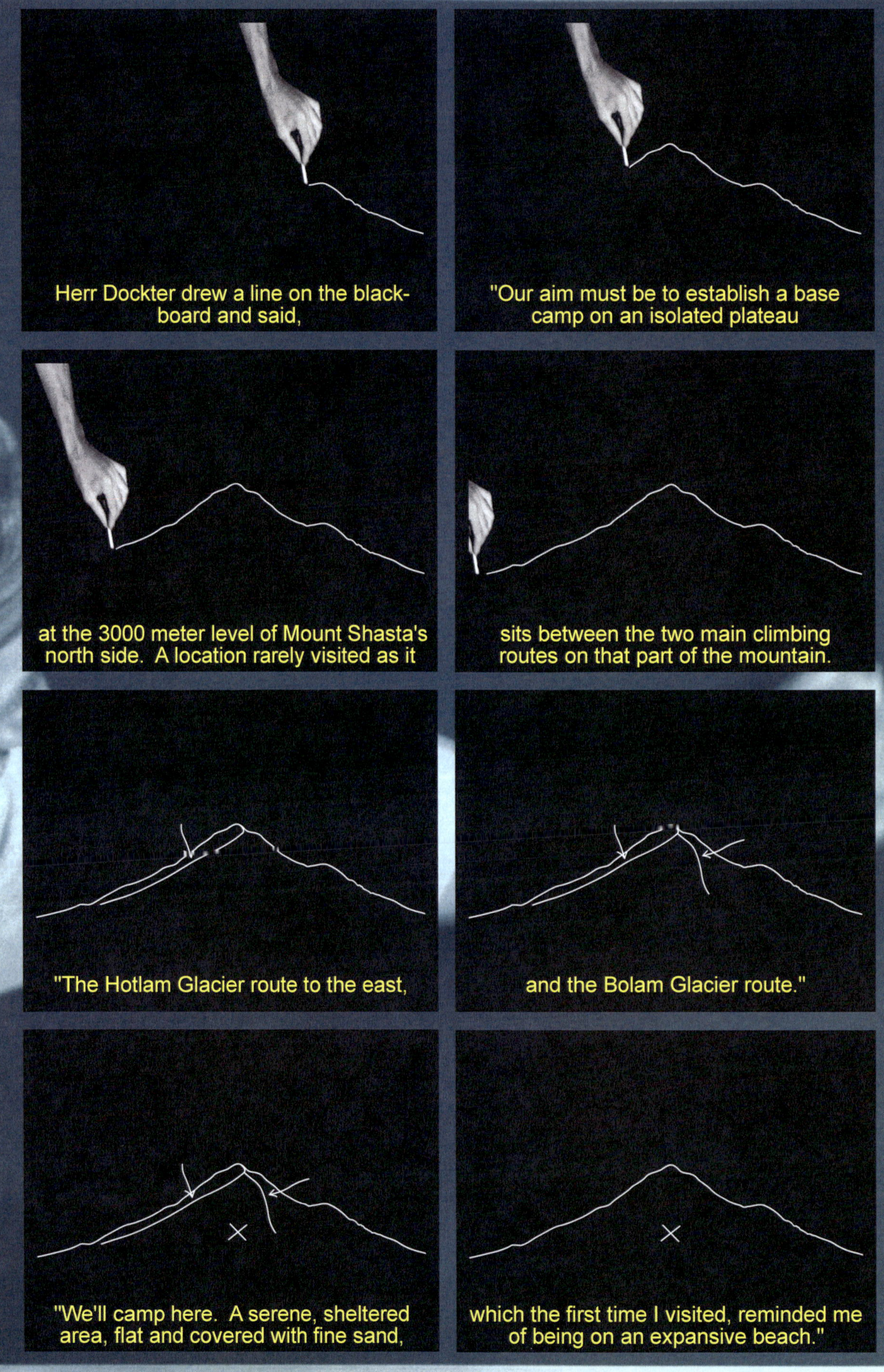

Herr Dockter drew a line on the blackboard and said,

"Our aim must be to establish a base
camp on an isolated plateau

at the 3000 meter level of Mount Shasta's
north side. A location rarely visited as it

sits between the two main climbing
routes on that part of the mountain.

"The Hotlam Glacier route to the east,

and the Bolam Glacier route."

"We'll camp here. A serene, sheltered
area, flat and covered with fine sand,

which the first time I visited, reminded me
of being on an expansive beach."

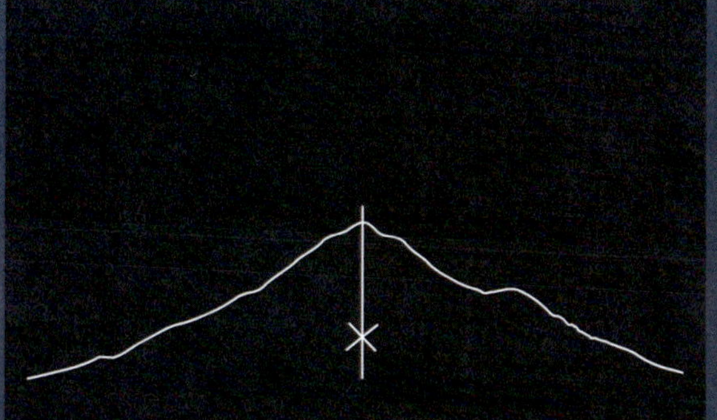

Herr Dockter glanced at me with a slight smile. "According to my calculations, this

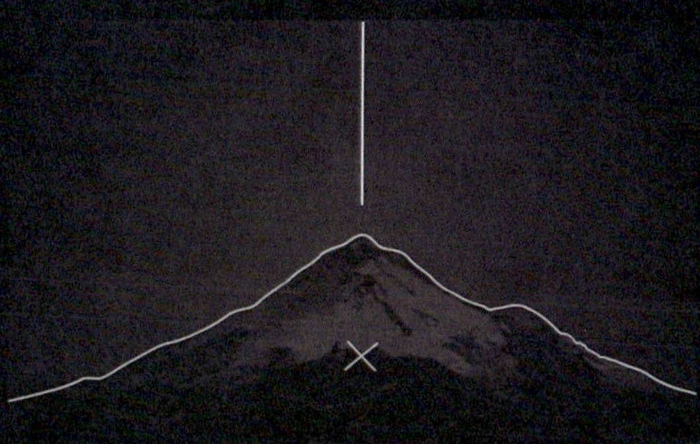

'beach' is exactly in the center of Mount Shasta when viewed from true north.

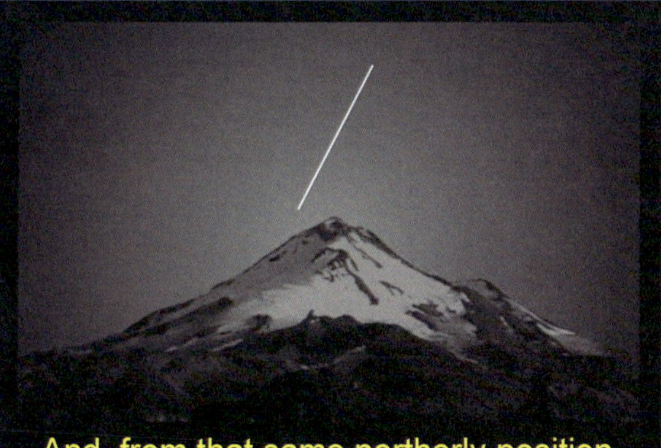

And, from that same northerly position, a line drawn vertically through

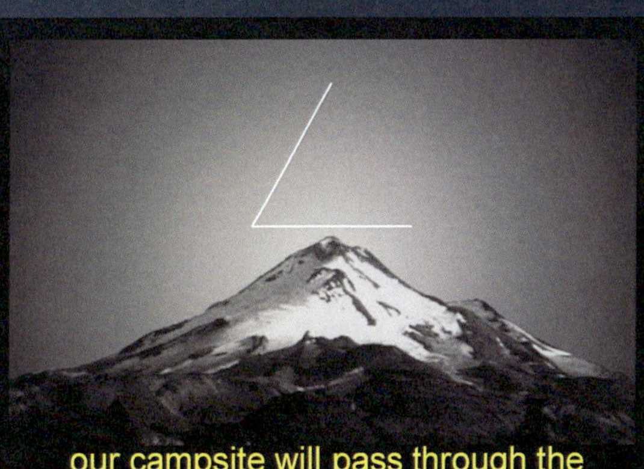

our campsite will pass through the highest point on the summit.

"We'll make our camp and plan on several days of acclimatization and careful scientific observation of natural phenomena as we await formation of the perfect cloud."

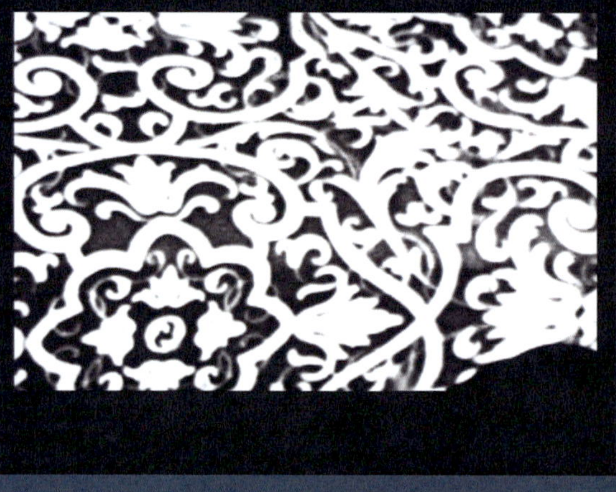

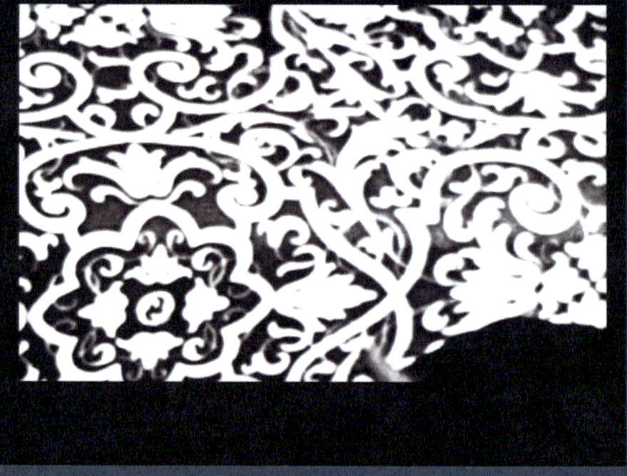

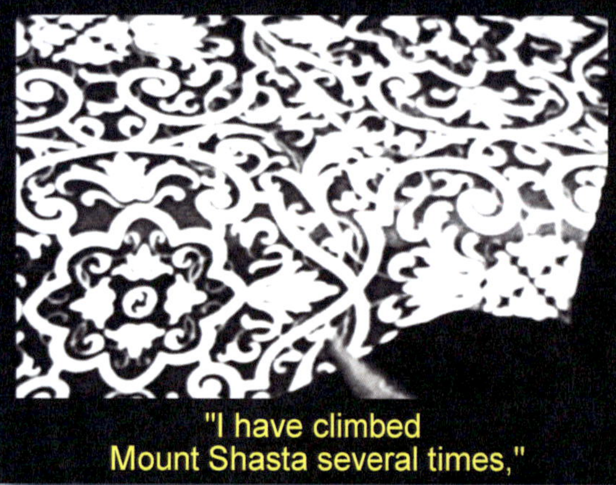
"I have climbed
Mount Shasta several times,"

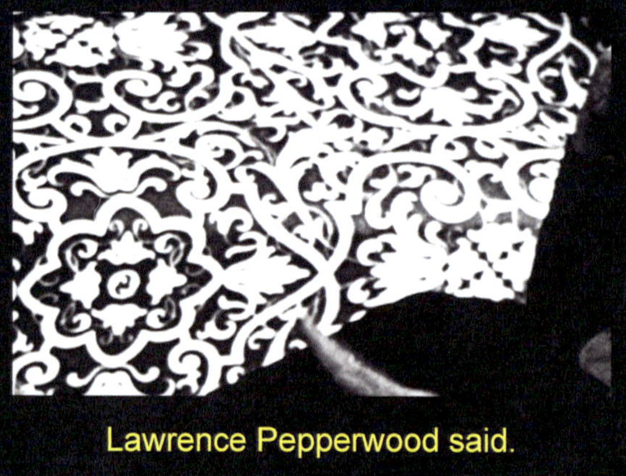
Lawrence Pepperwood said.

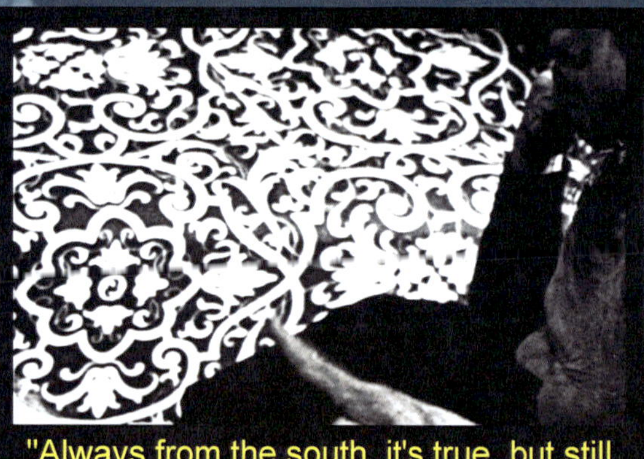
"Always from the south, it's true, but still
the same mountain.

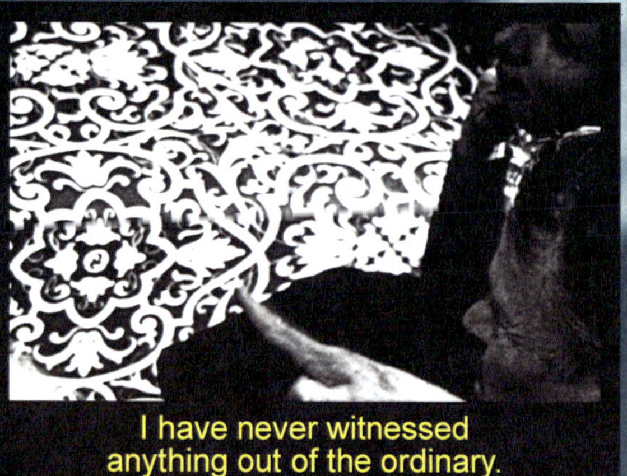
I have never witnessed
anything out of the ordinary.

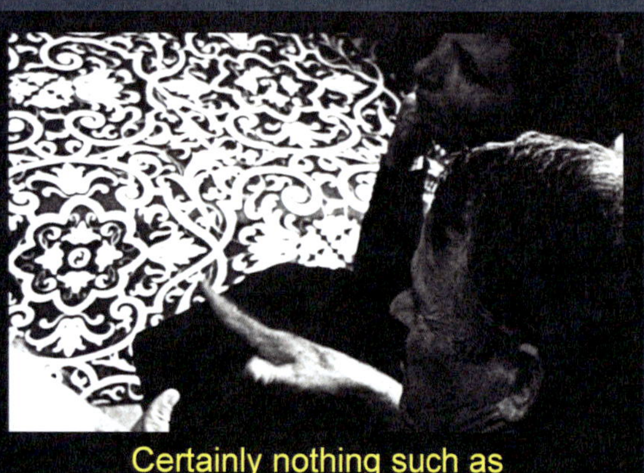
Certainly nothing such as
you are suggesting.

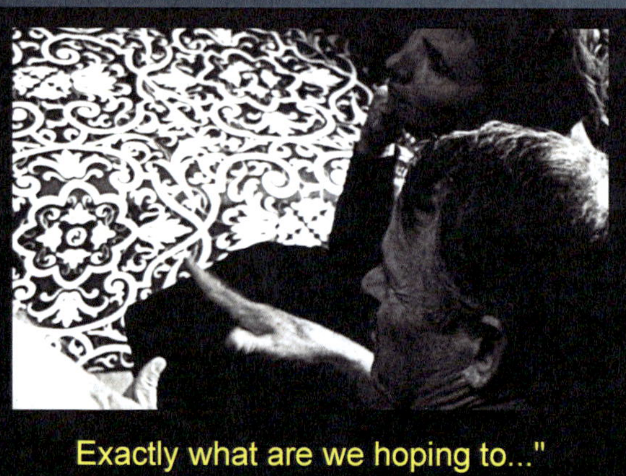
Exactly what are we hoping to..."

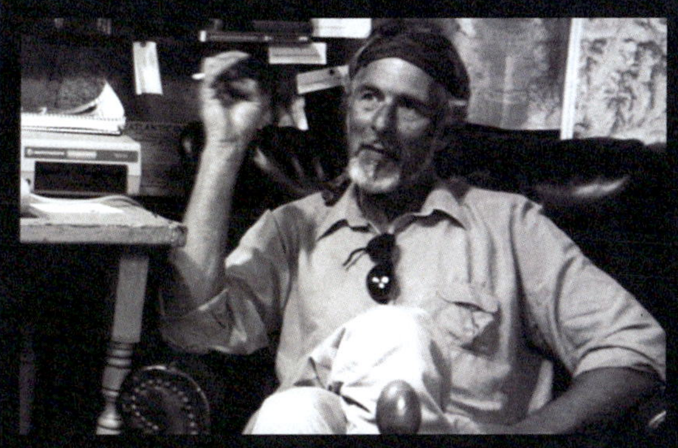

"No, not *'hope'*," Herr Dockter interrupted.

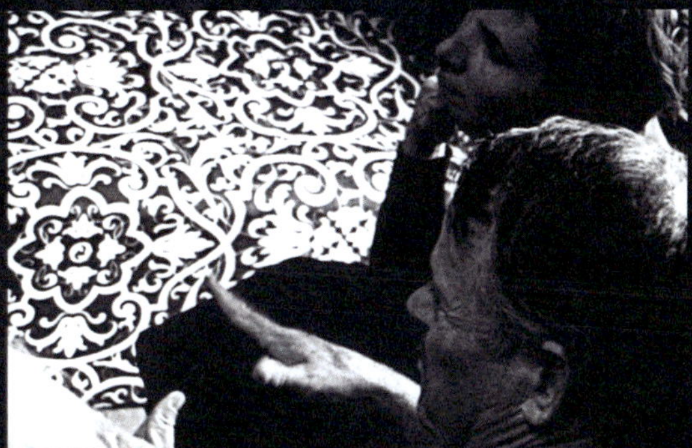

"*Hope*, with its preconceived visions, will only obscure. Our shared familiarity with

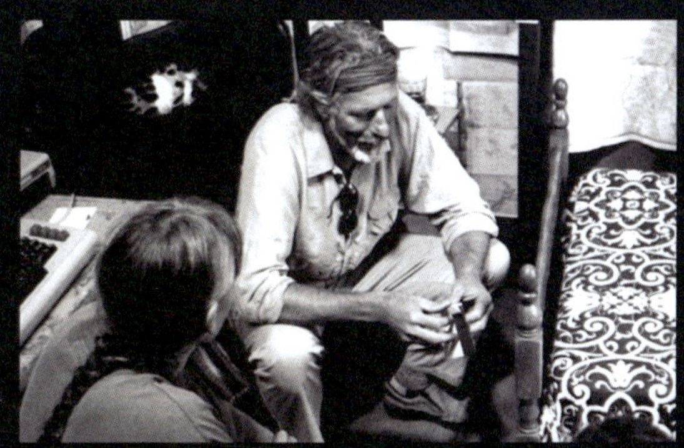

Failure will guide. Allowing us to see routes others have overlooked."

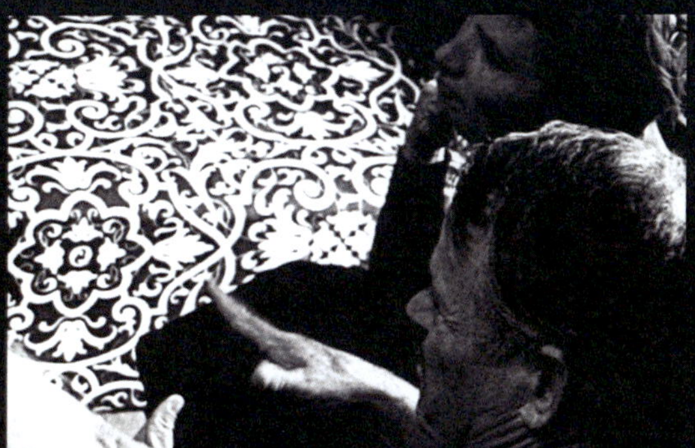

"Failure's no big achievement," said Pepperwood with a laugh.

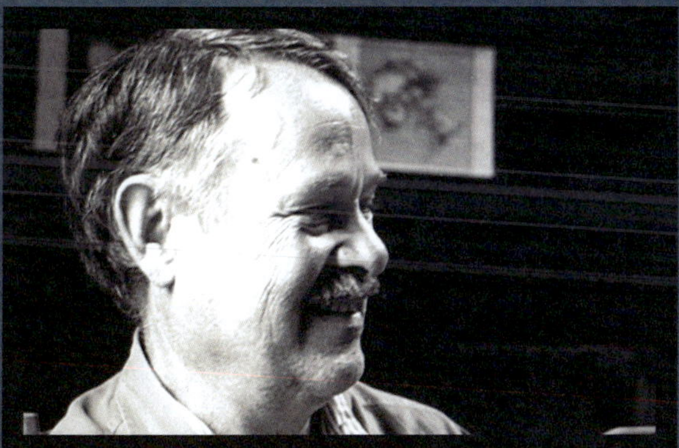

"I've accomplished it more than once."

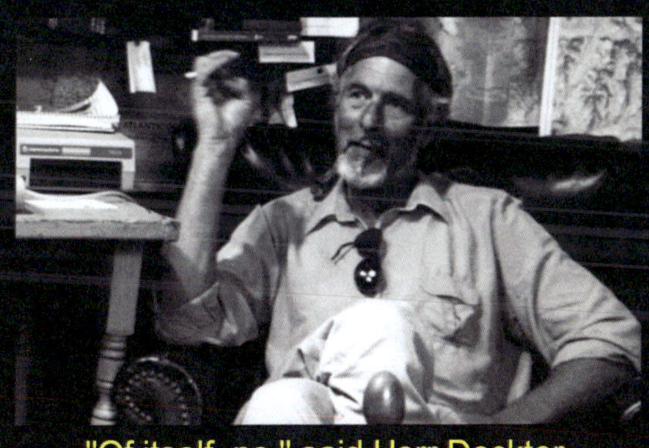

"Of itself, no," said Herr Dockter. "I agree."

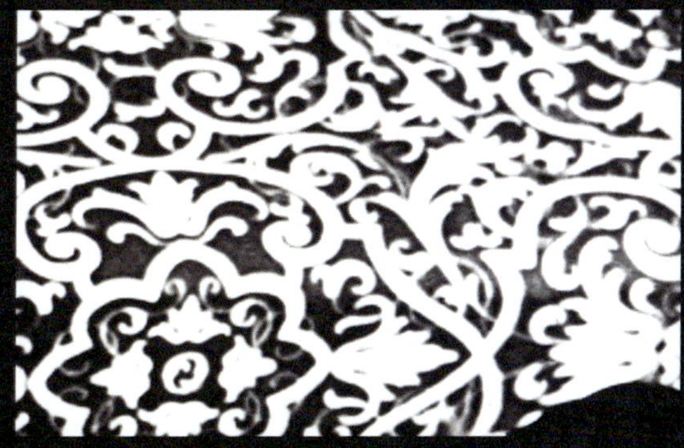

"But to continue on our climb with full understanding – that there is

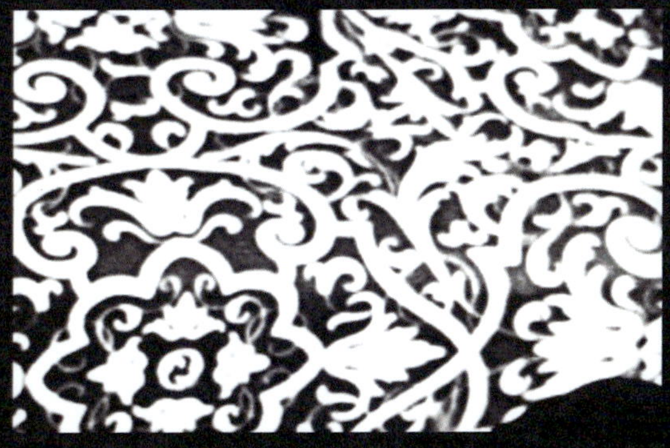

no hope of success – now – *that is something*."

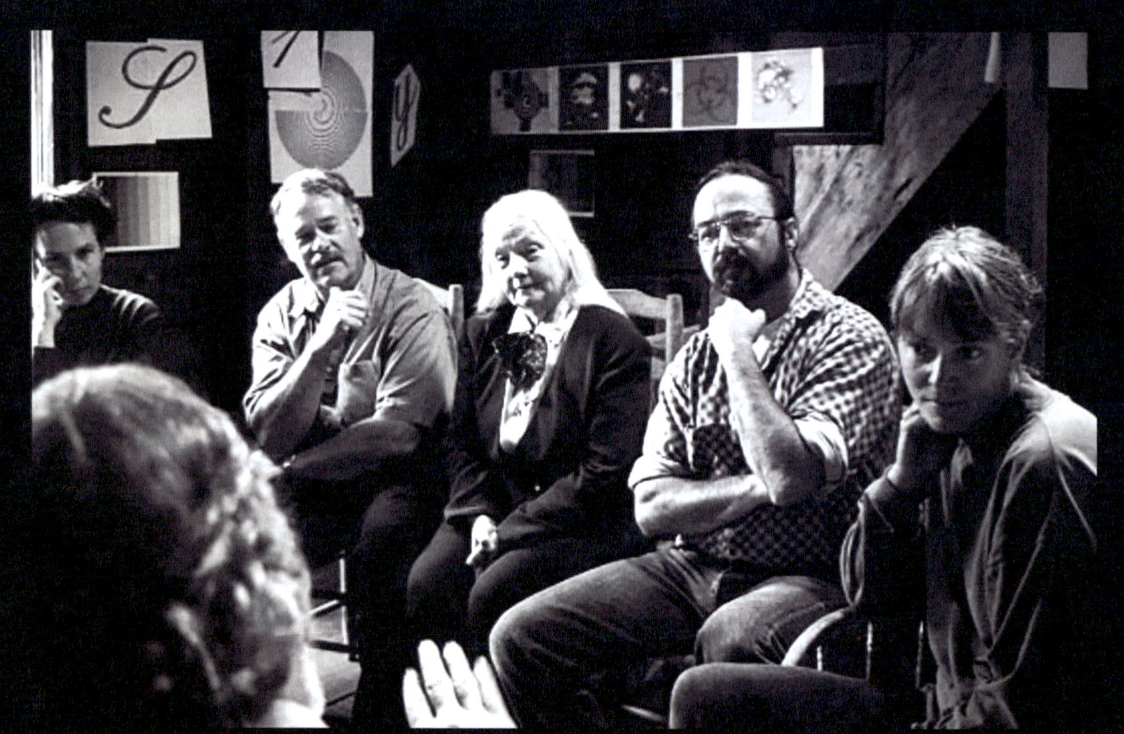

"I have made arrangements for transportation through an acquaintance of mine.
We'll all travel together.

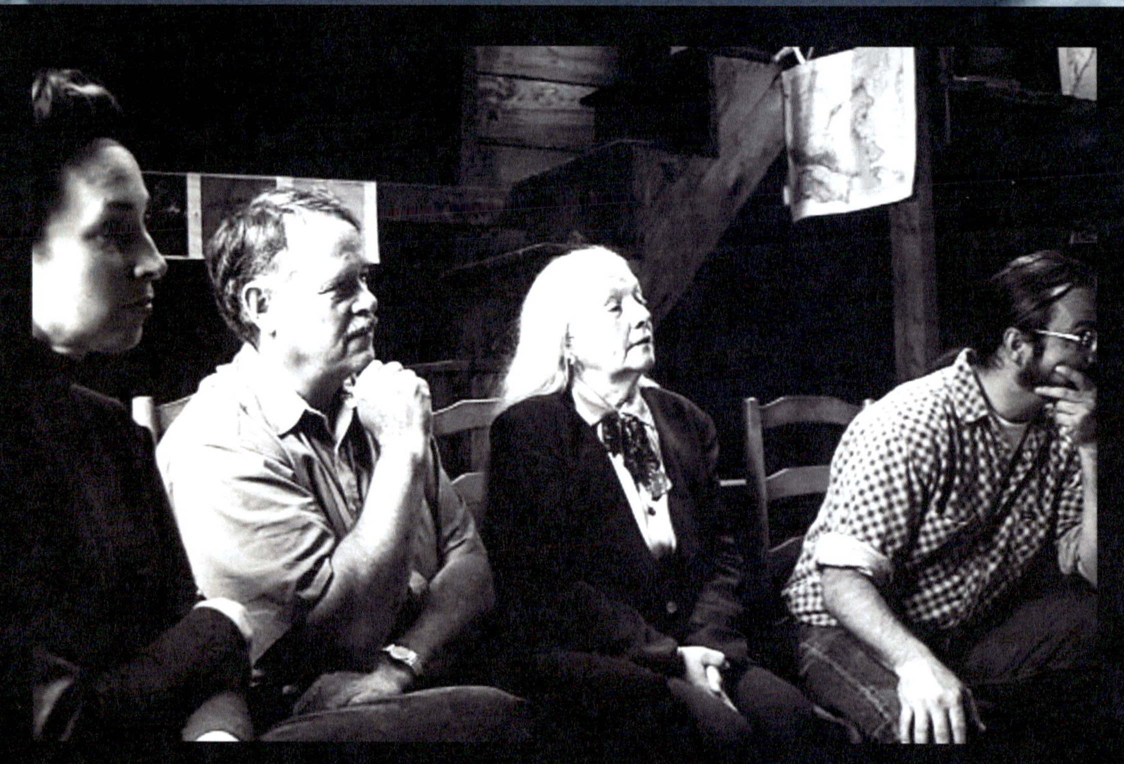

There's a full moon in two weeks time. Climbing conditions should be ideal
with the possibility of lenticular cloud formation at its height."

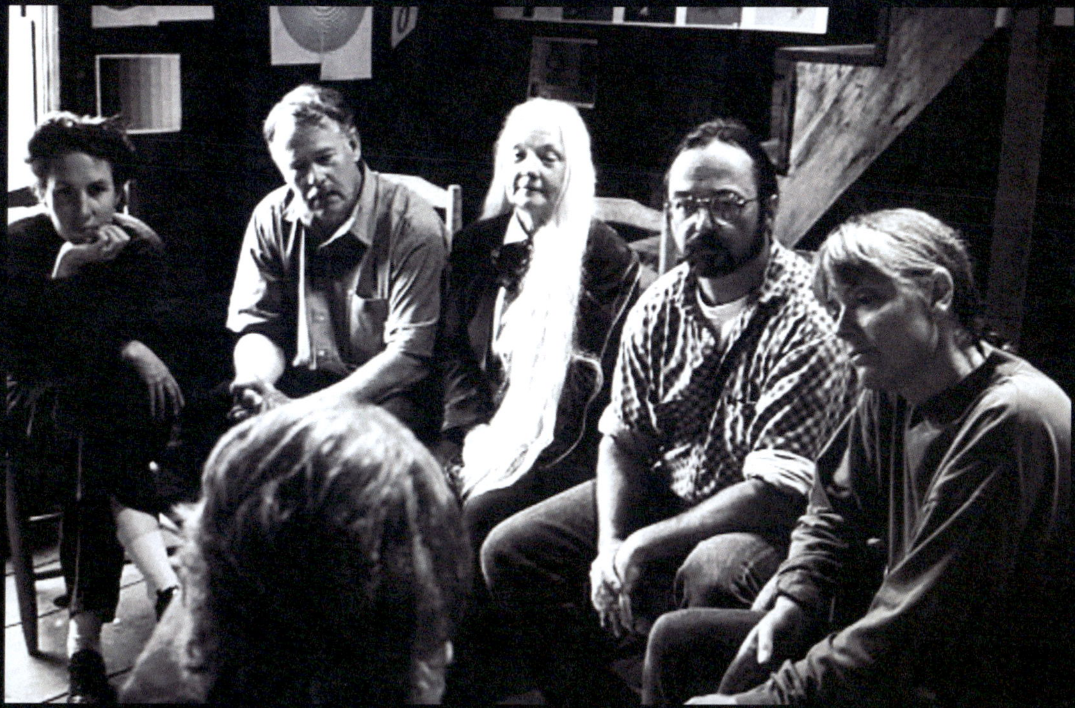

"So then, get your affairs in order,
gather your climbing equipment and personal supplies,

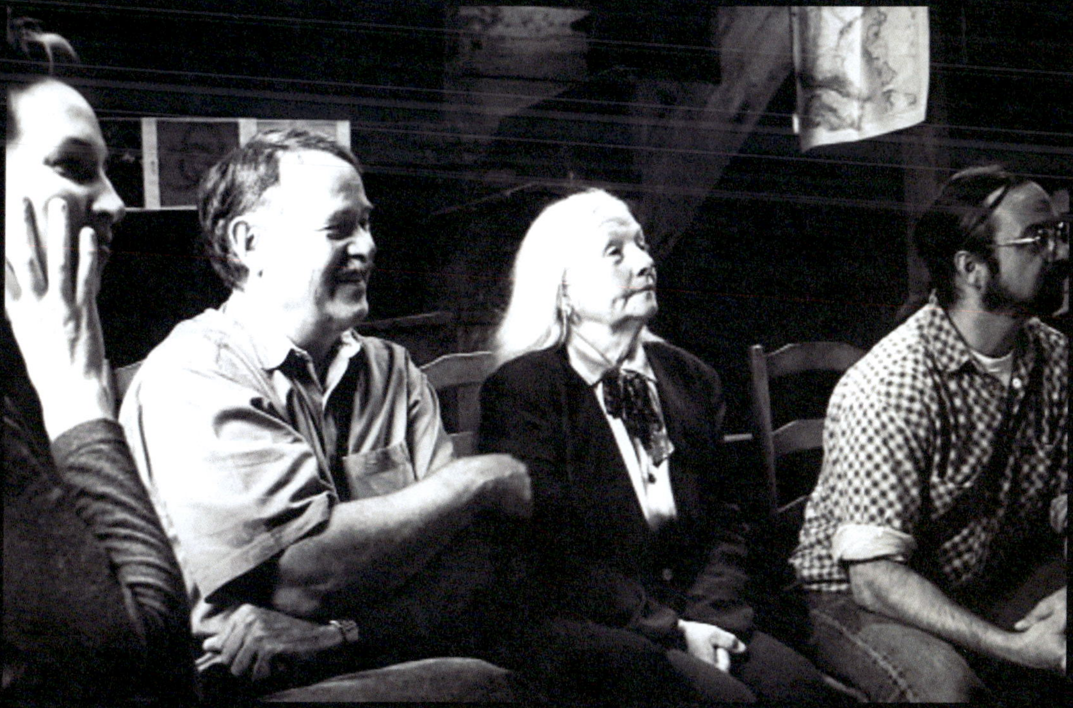

and we leave with the morning tide, a fortnight from now."

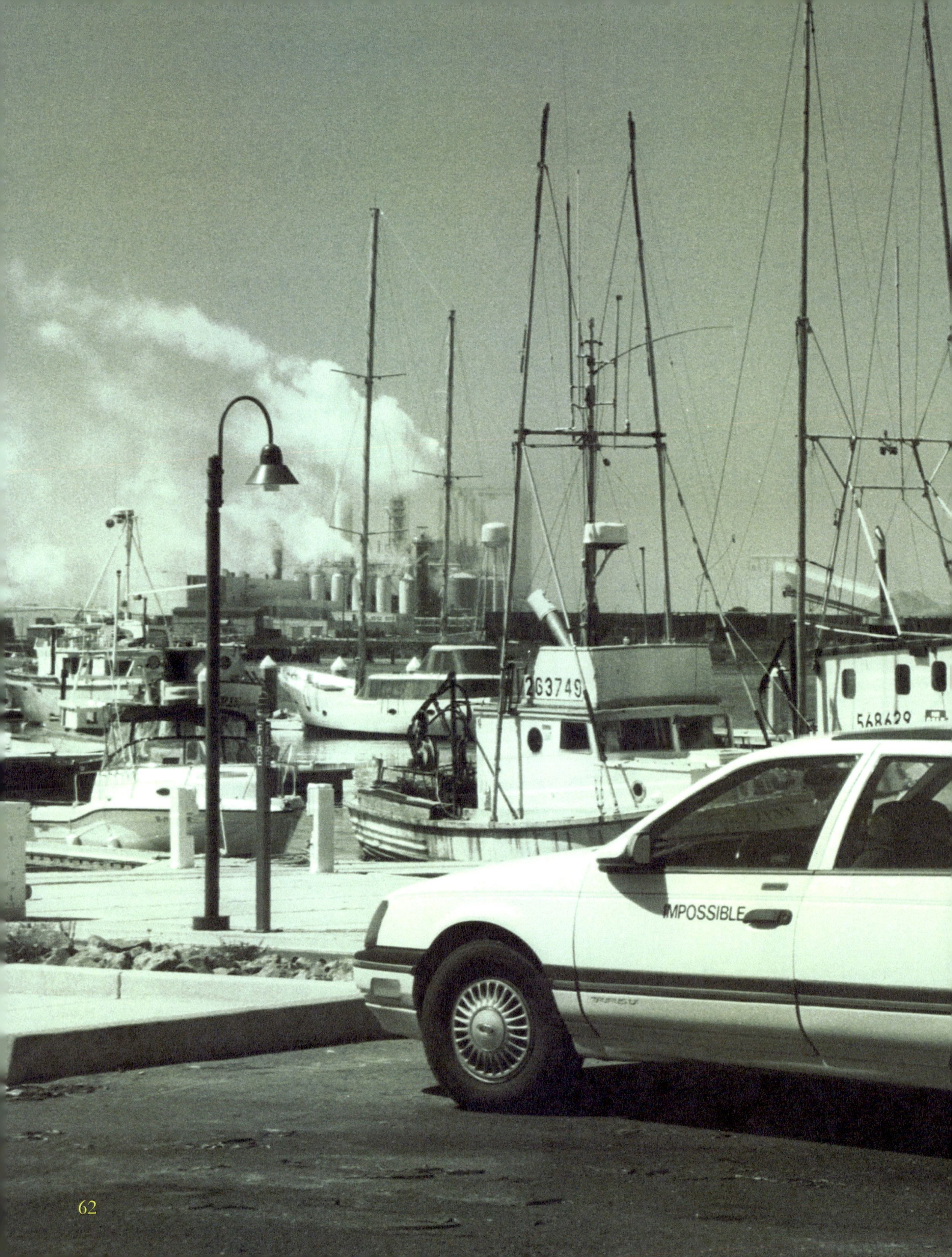
263749
568629
IMPOSSIBLE
FIRE

Chapter Four

- Which Concerns Our Travel to the Mountain -
- A Tale of the Lemurians -
- We Arrive at the Beginning -

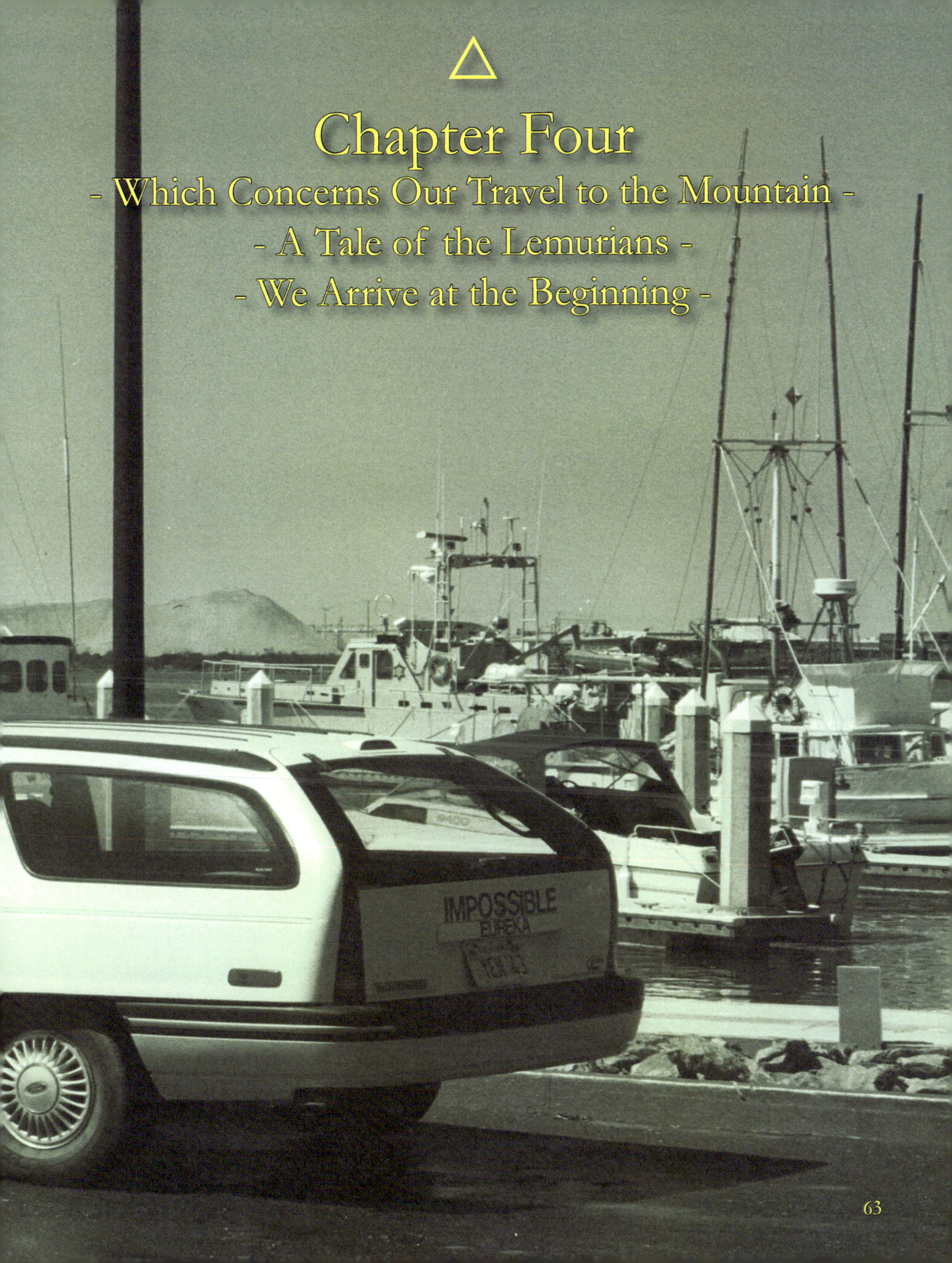

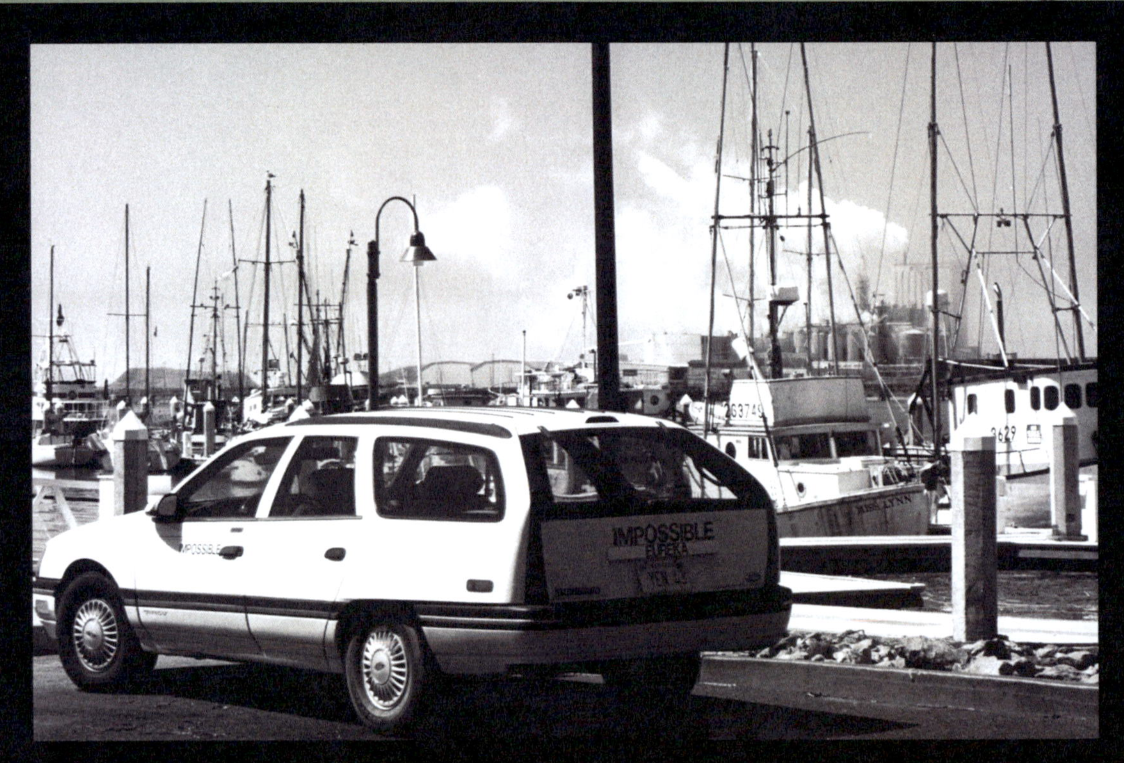

Herr Dockter had indeed secured transportation for the group.

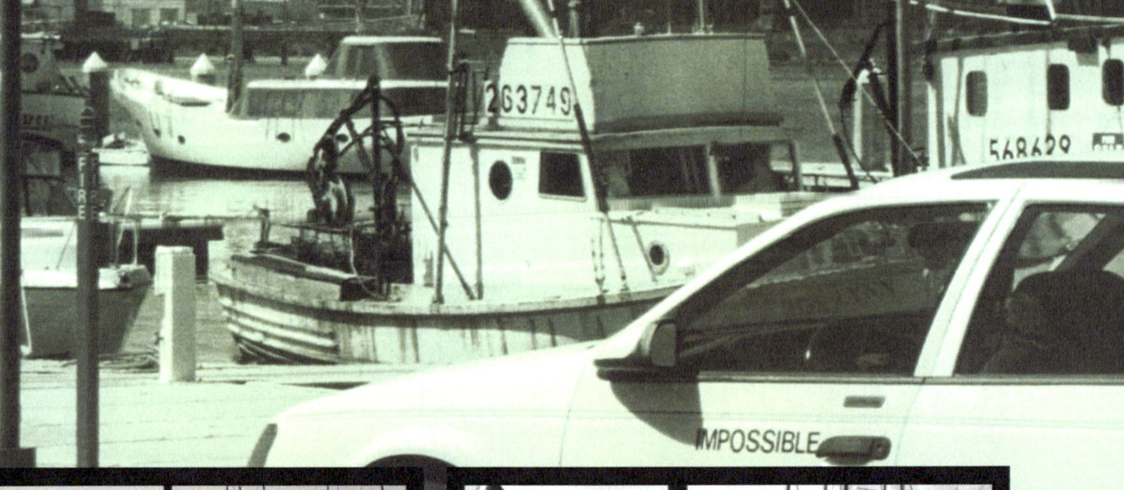

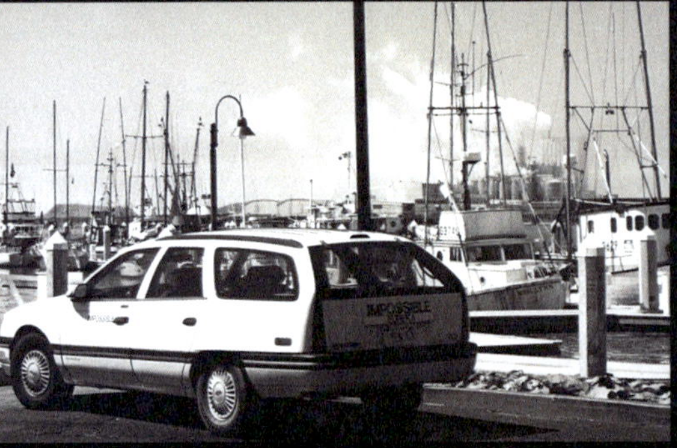

An older station wagon that appeared
to be the service vehicle for

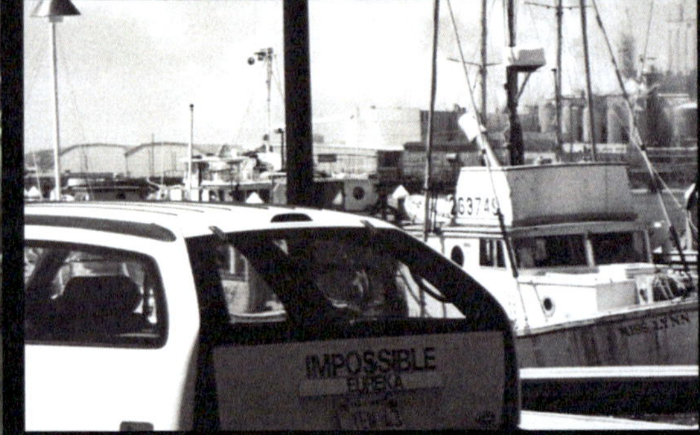

a commercial fishing vessel.

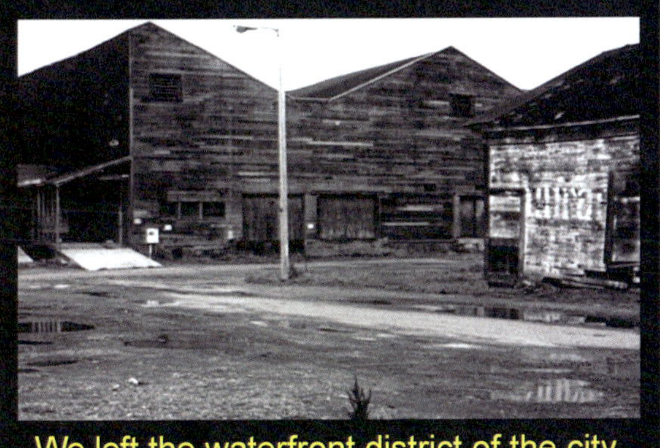

We left the waterfront district of the city,
and headed east.

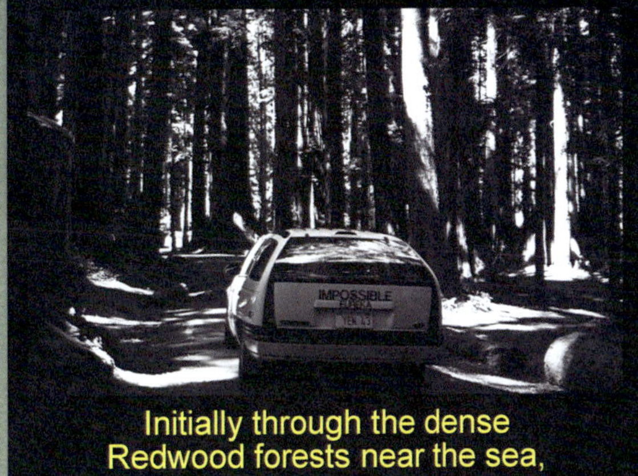

Initially through the dense
Redwood forests near the sea,

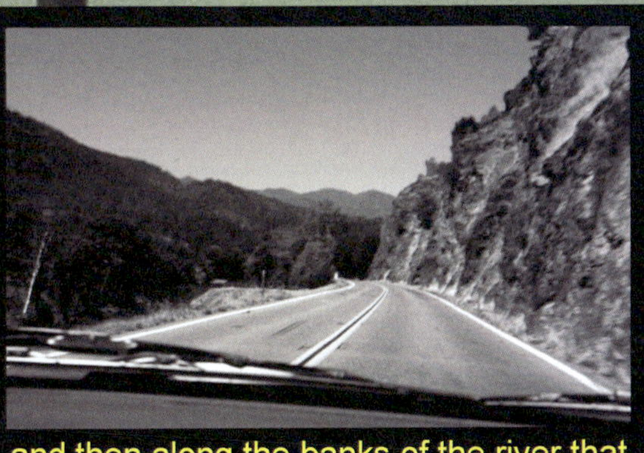

and then along the banks of the river that
formed a pass to the interior –

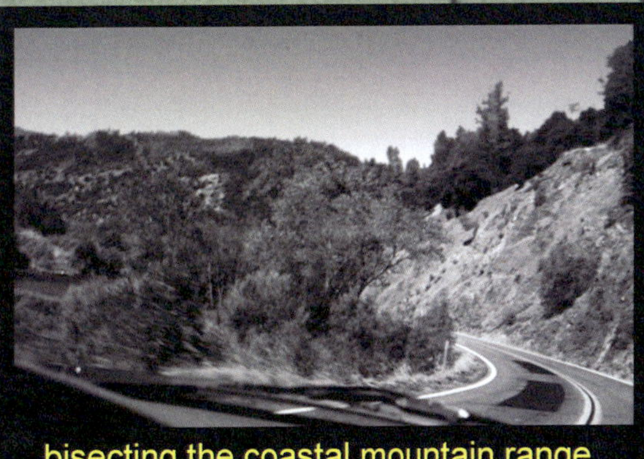

bisecting the coastal mountain range.
Ms. Falk passed the time drawing

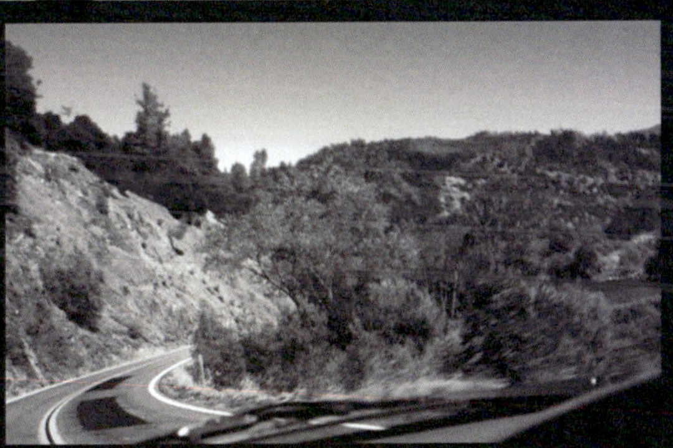

pencil caricatures of the group in
an artist's pad she always carried.

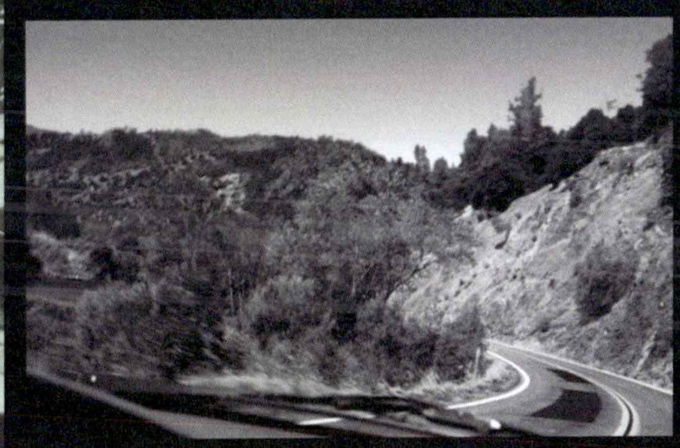

From her position in the back seat I
assumed they would have mainly been

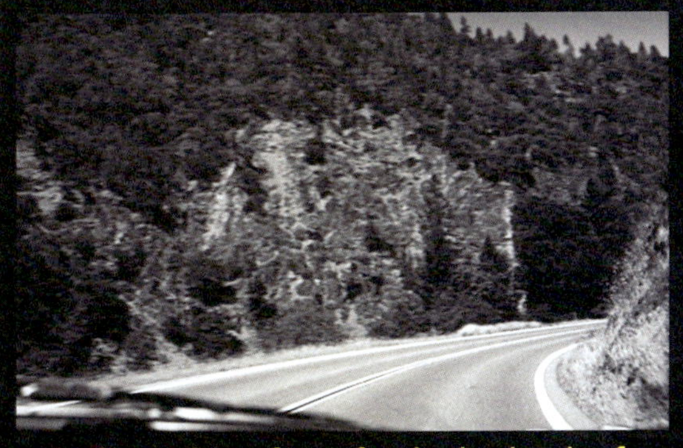

profiles with a few of only the back of a
head. My wife, with the great ability

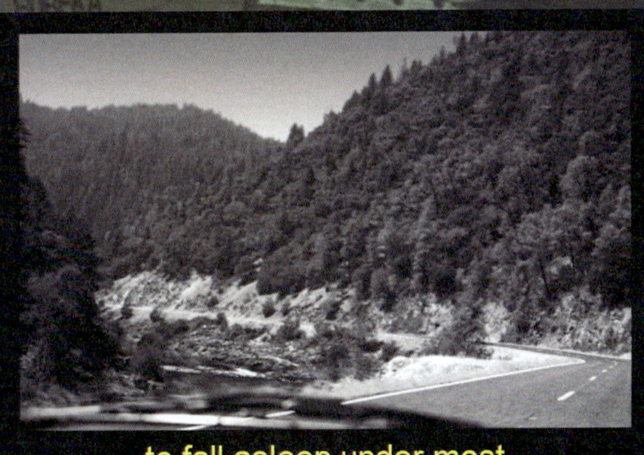

to fall asleep under most
any circumstance, did so.

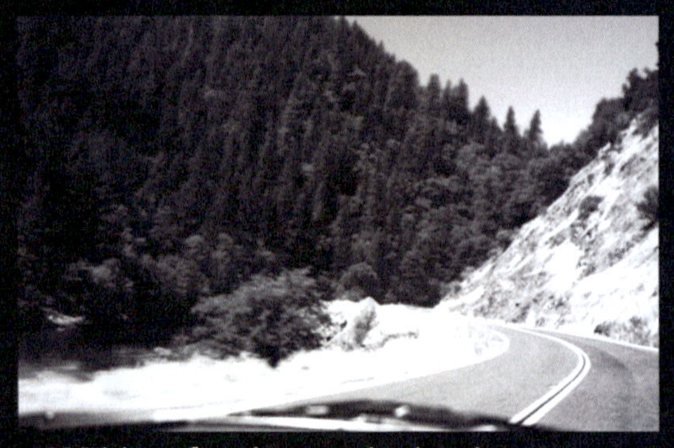

Within a few hours, the landscape we drove through changed dramatically.

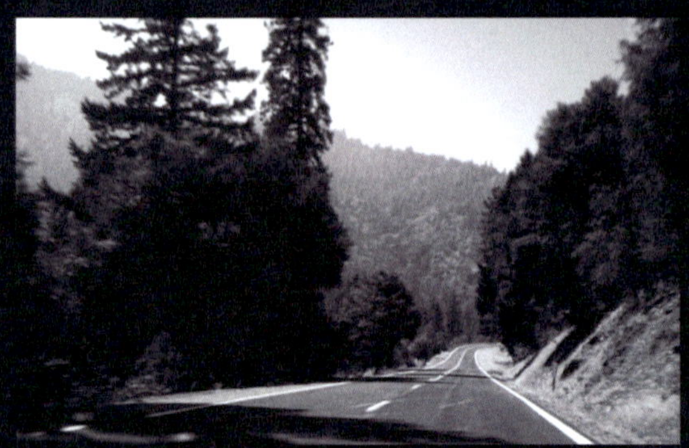

Brilliant sun on red earth – with muted dry brush and oak predominating.

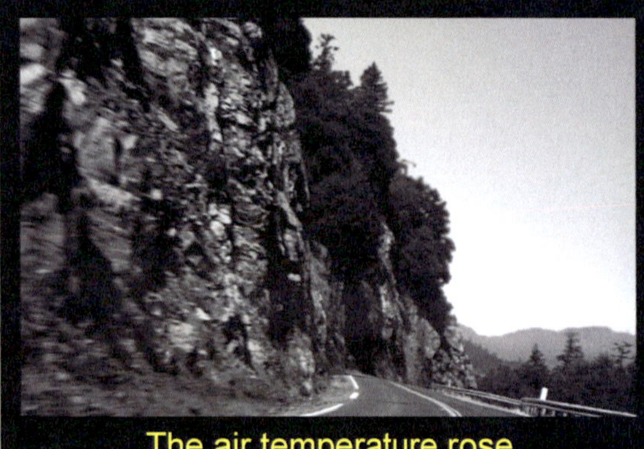

The air temperature rose to nearly double that of the coast.

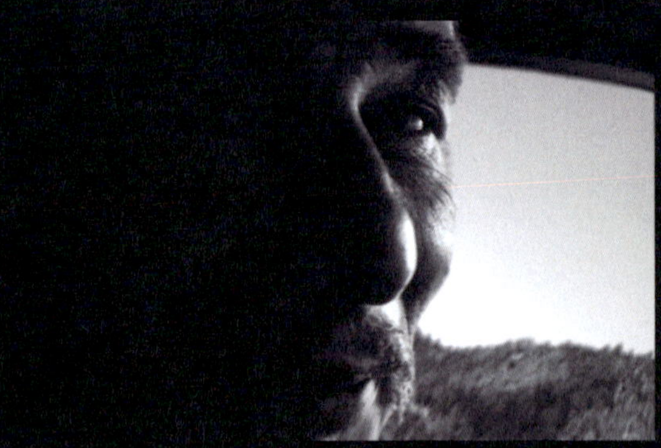

Herr Dockter drove quickly but smoothly

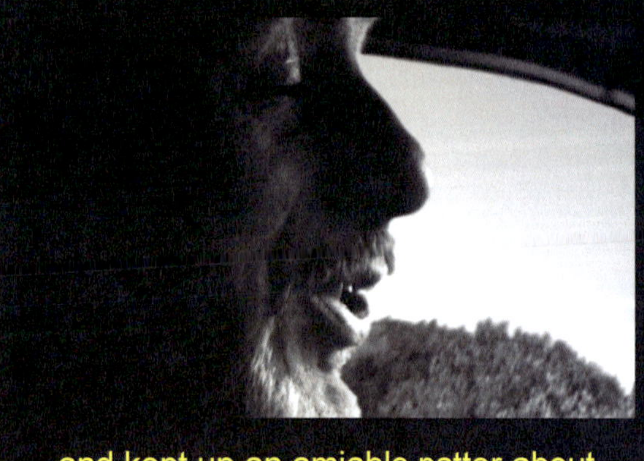

and kept up an amiable patter about

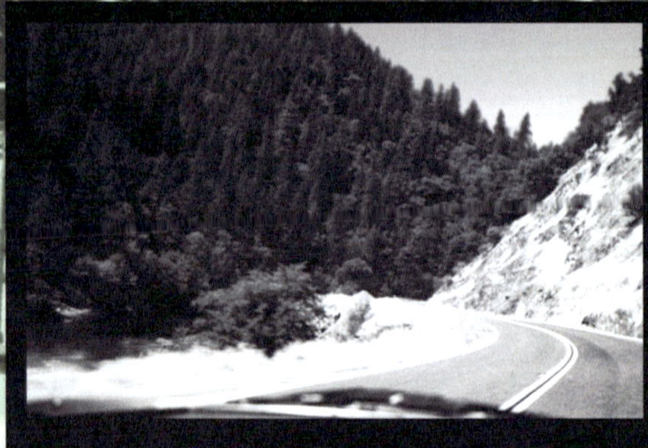

flora and fauna alongside the highway.

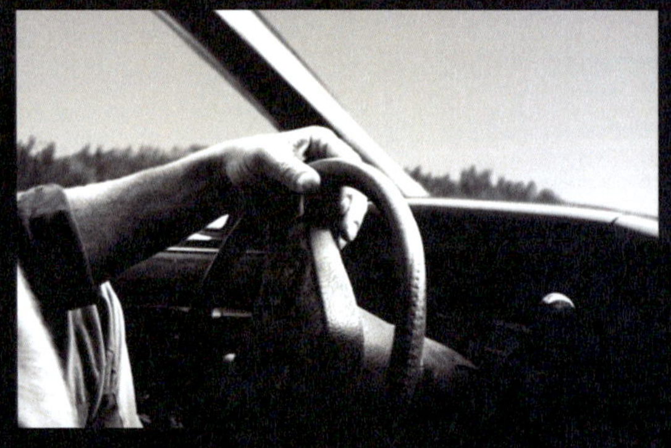

Inside, the high temperature abetted by

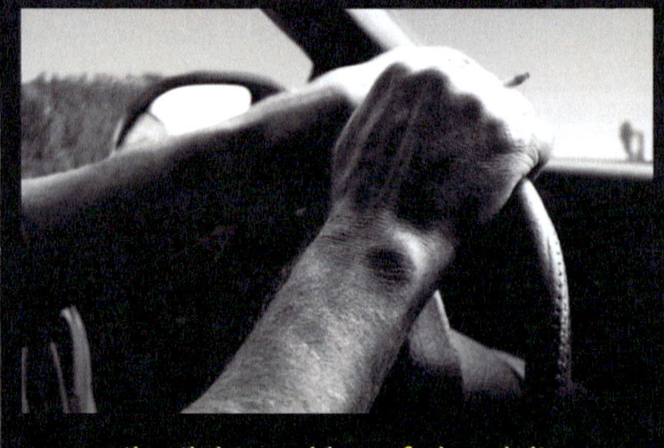

the tight packing of six adults

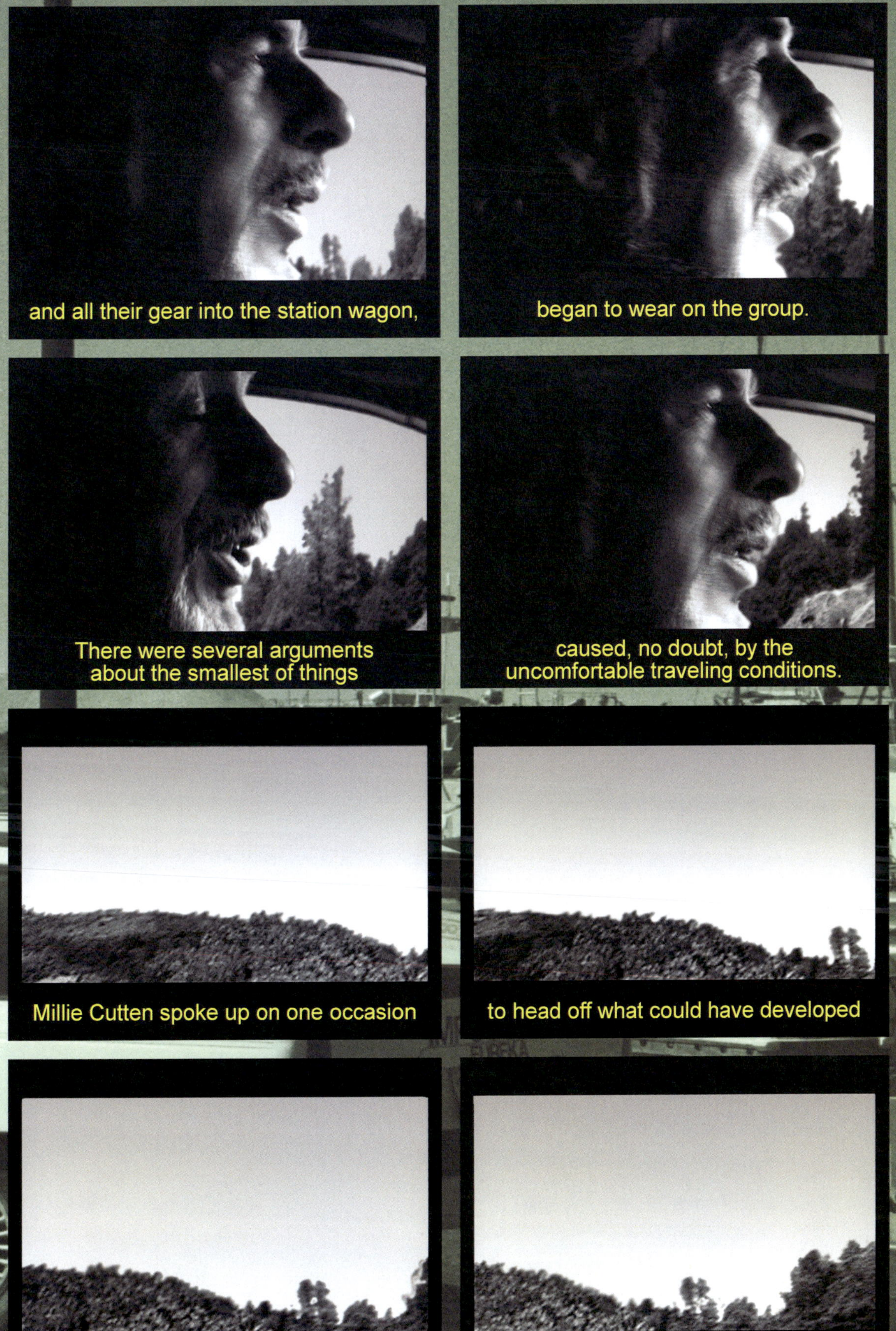

and all their gear into the station wagon,
began to wear on the group.
There were several arguments
about the smallest of things
caused, no doubt, by the
uncomfortable traveling conditions.
Millie Cutten spoke up on one occasion
to head off what could have developed
into a fist fight about body odor
between Mr. Pepperwood and myself.

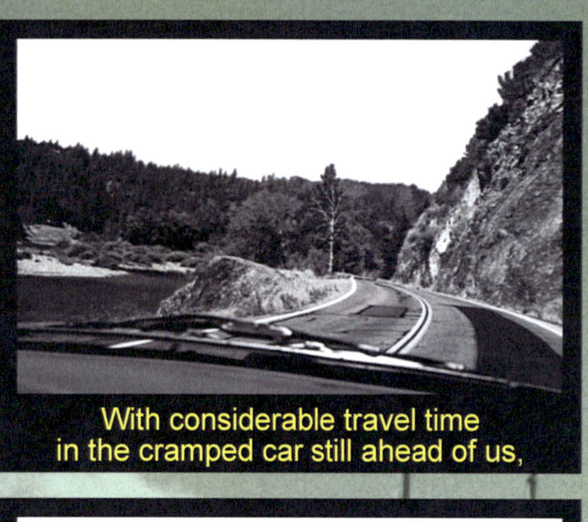

With considerable travel time
in the cramped car still ahead of us,

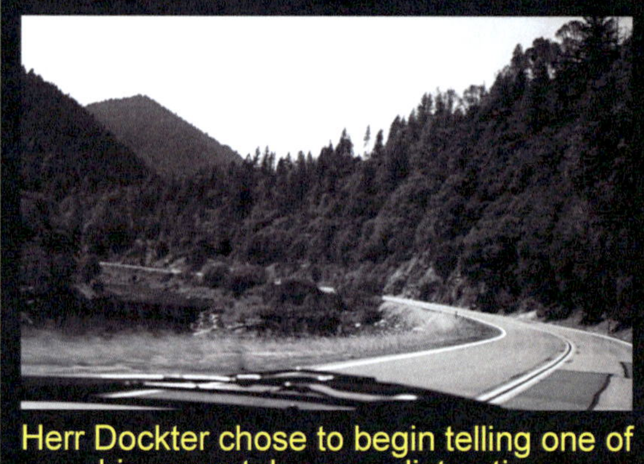

Herr Dockter chose to begin telling one of
his many tales as a distraction.

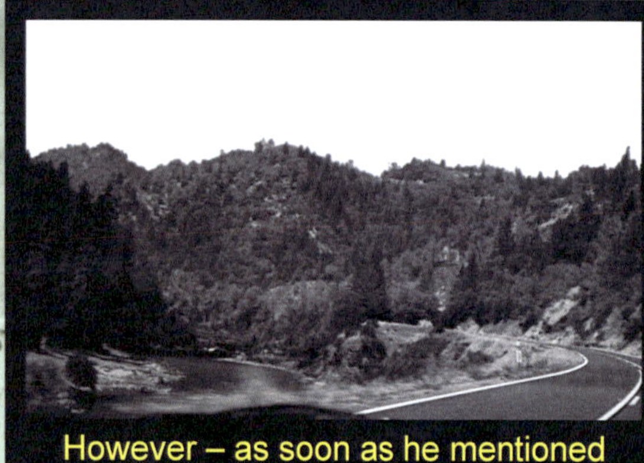

However – as soon as he mentioned
"Lemurians",

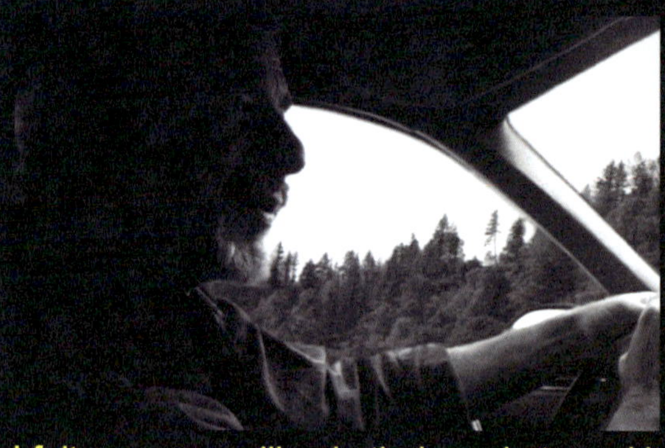

I felt my eyes rolling in their sockets and it
was all I could do to restrain a protest.

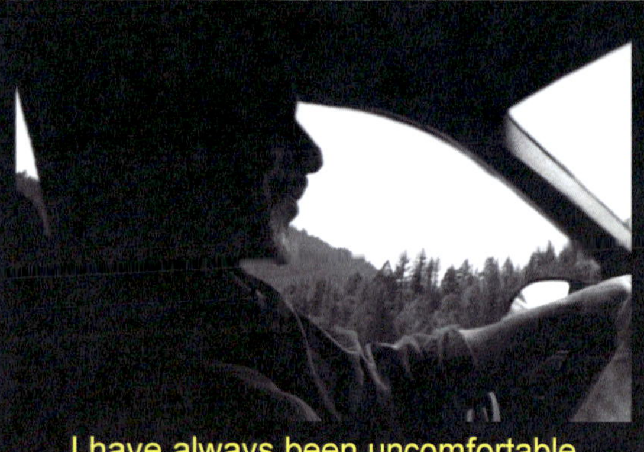

I have always been uncomfortable
with the need to include

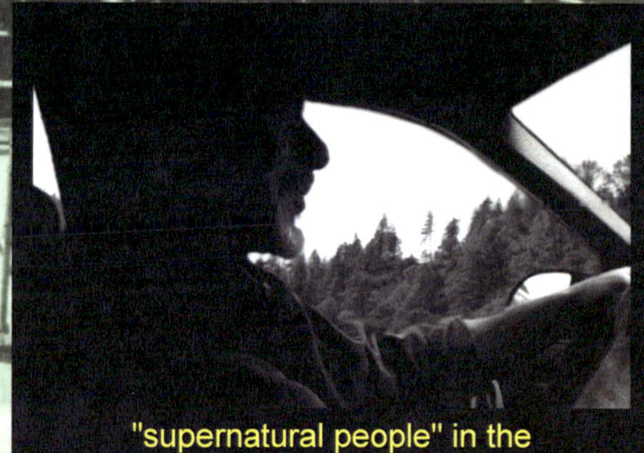

"supernatural people" in the
discussion of metaphysics.

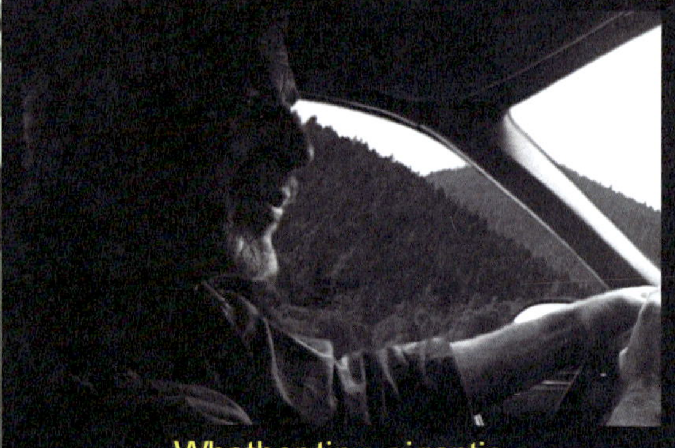

Whether tiny, gigantic,
covered with fur or green,

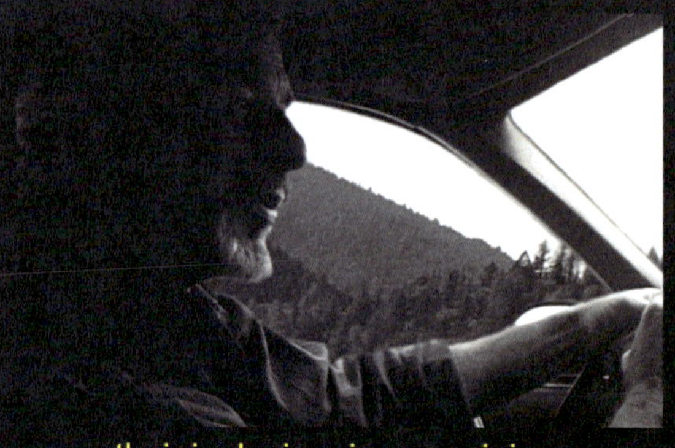

their inclusion, in my opinion,
is always to the detriment of

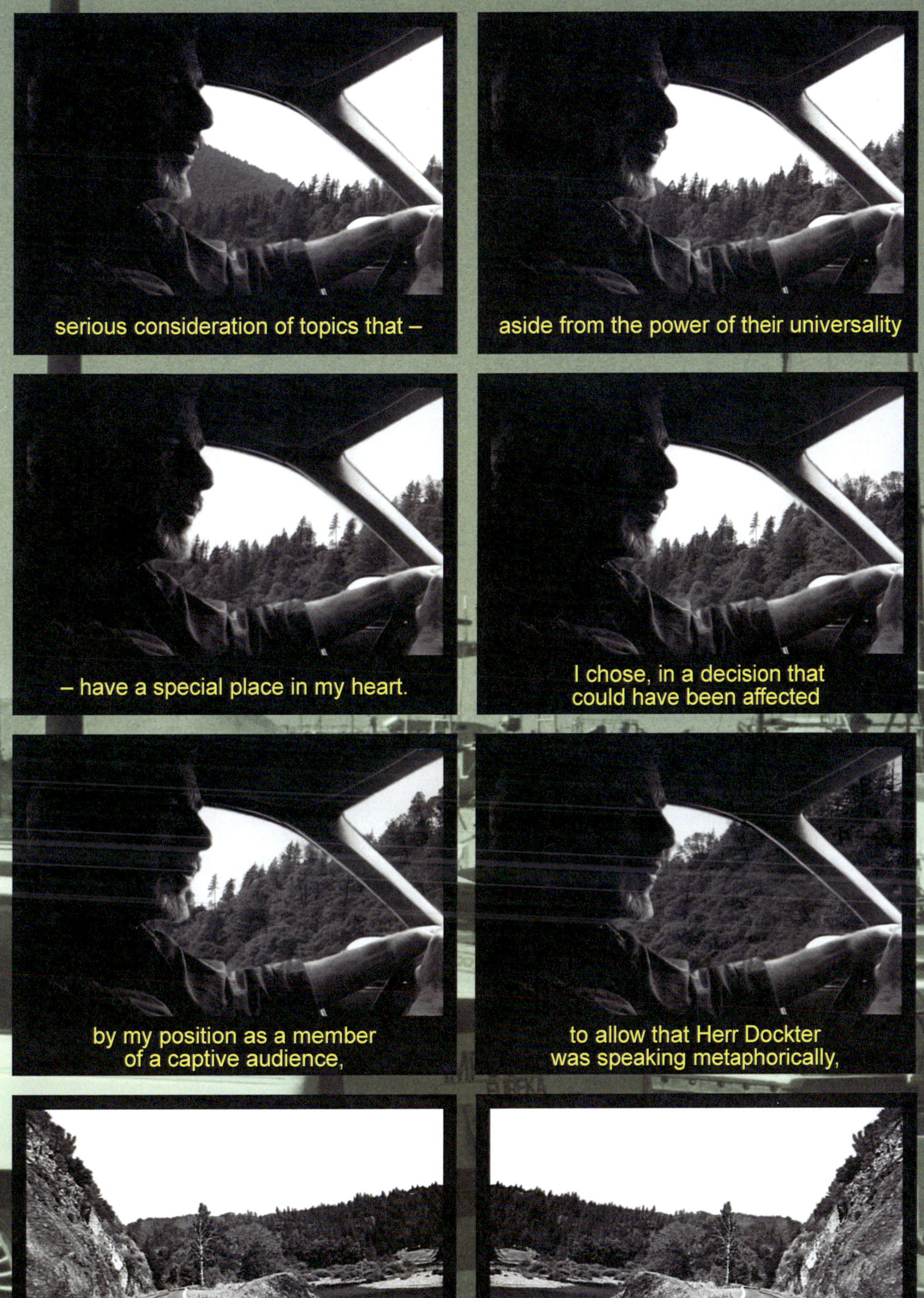
serious consideration of topics that —
aside from the power of their universality
— have a special place in my heart.
I chose, in a decision that
could have been affected
by my position as a member
of a captive audience,
to allow that Herr Dockter
was speaking metaphorically,
remained silent,
and listened as I gazed out the window.

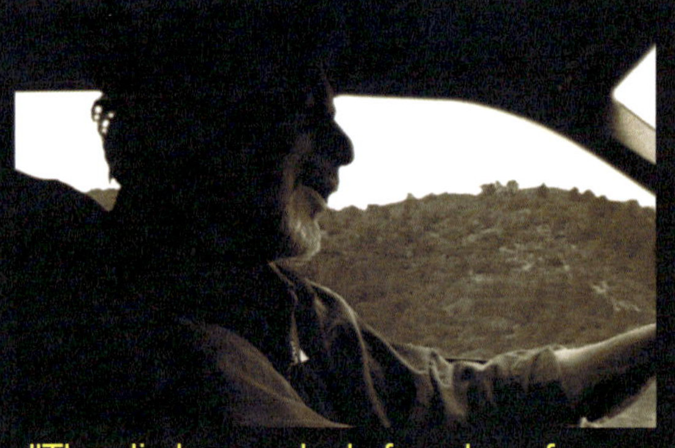
"The climber awoke before dawn from a fitful sleep and noticed immediately

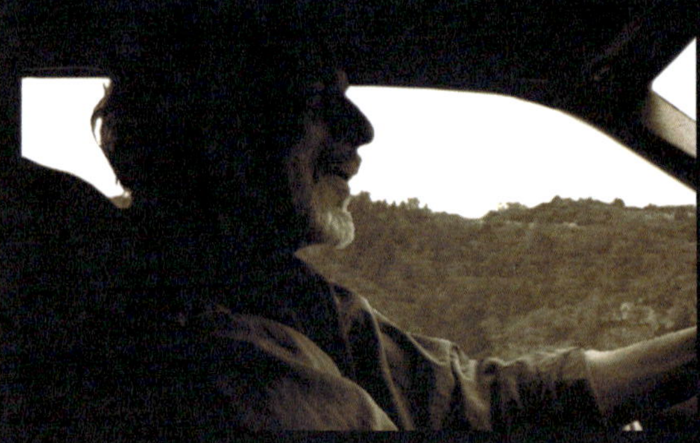
his partner's absence. The tent flap was partially unzipped allowing a fine dusting

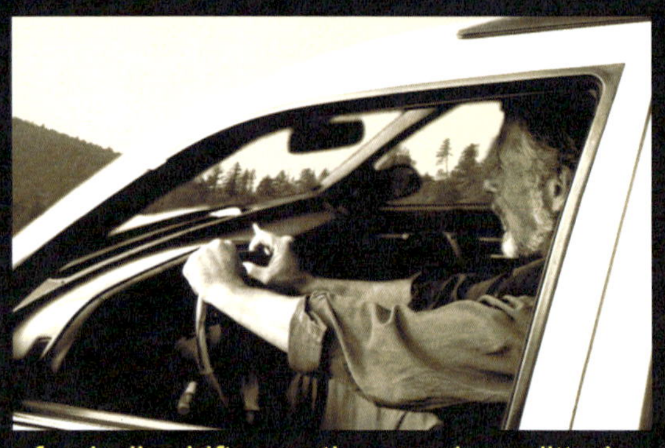
of spindle drift near the opening, glittering in the flashlight's beam.

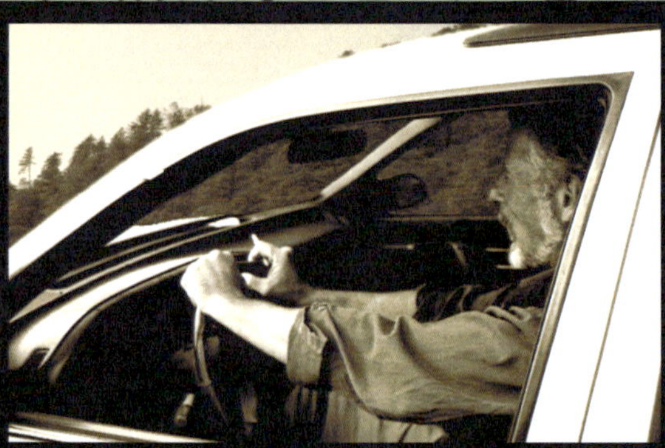
As he stuck his head out to locate his friend, he saw, not three meters distant,

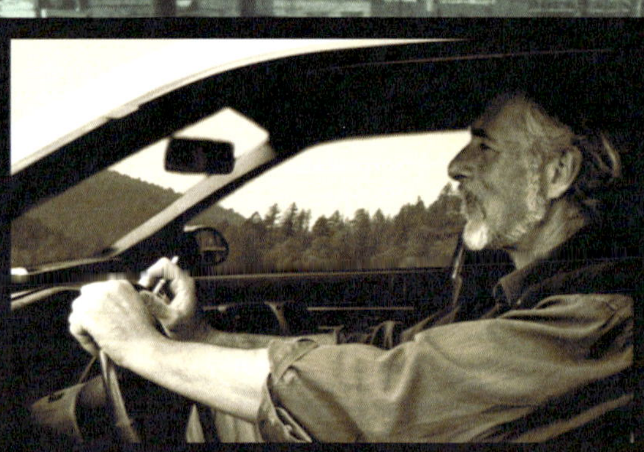
a very tall man with hair of Biblical length, oddly dressed in white robes.

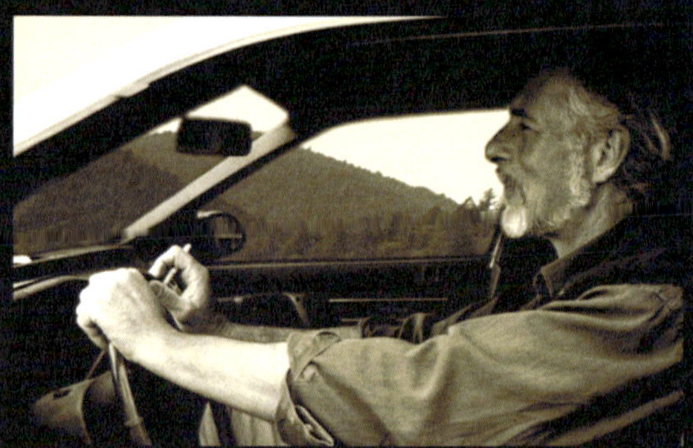
The climber recalled that the strange man welcomed him and bid him to follow.

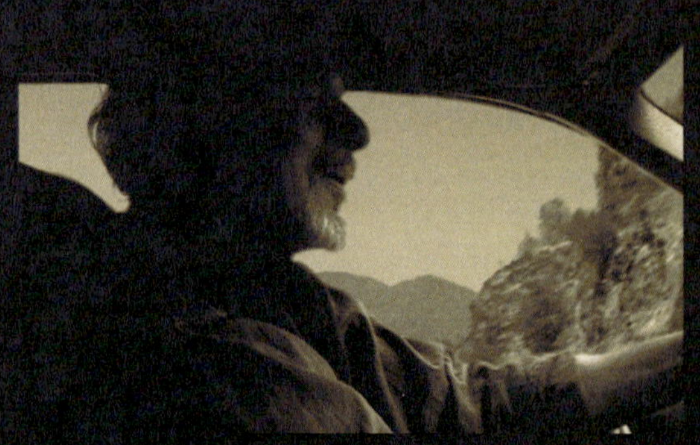
As they walked together across the snow in silence, the climber was quite

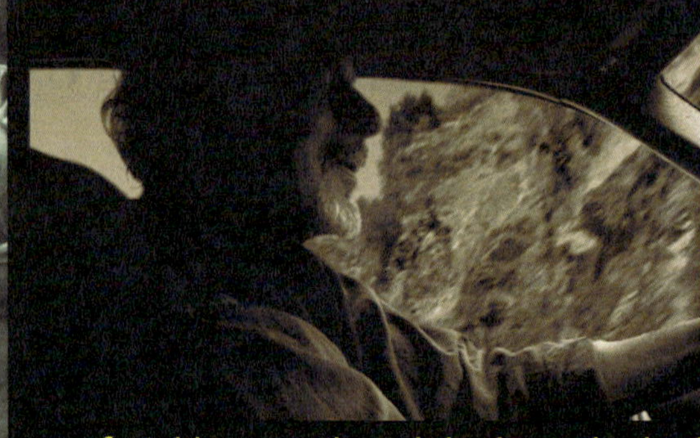
comfortable even though he knew he had not put on his parka and felt certain –

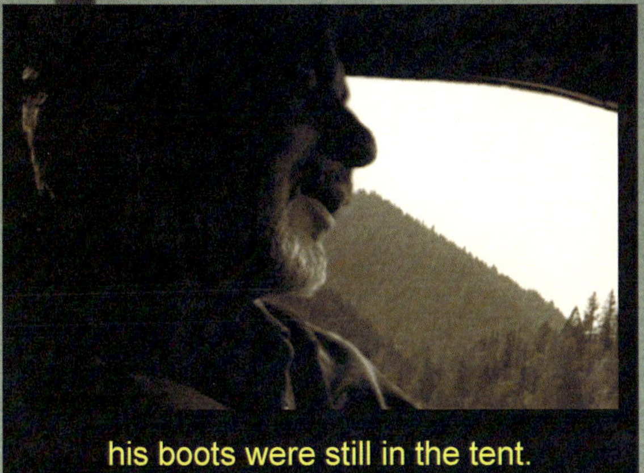

his boots were still in the tent.

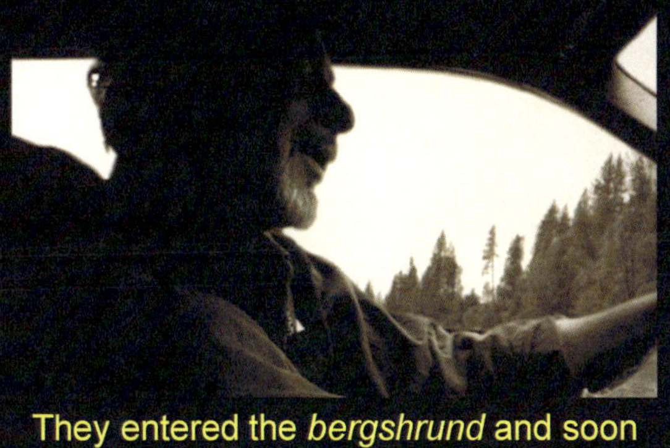

They entered the *bergshrund* and soon
turned down a sloping shaft which

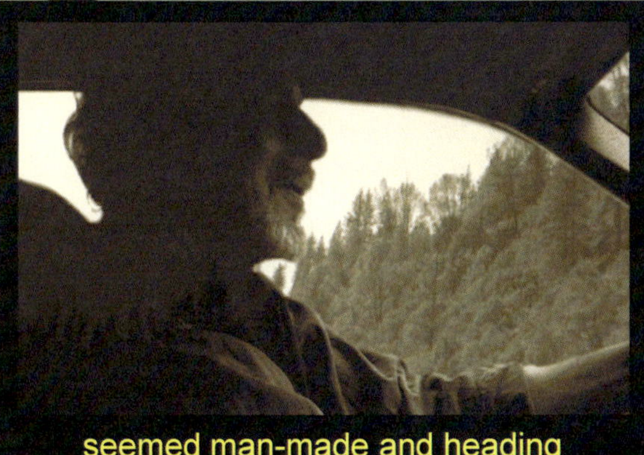

seemed man-made and heading
for the heart of Mount Shasta.

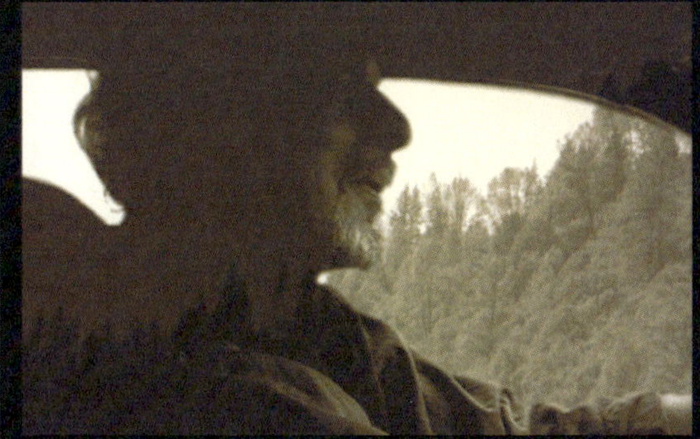

At once, the shaft opened into a large
chamber, lined in gold and lit from within.

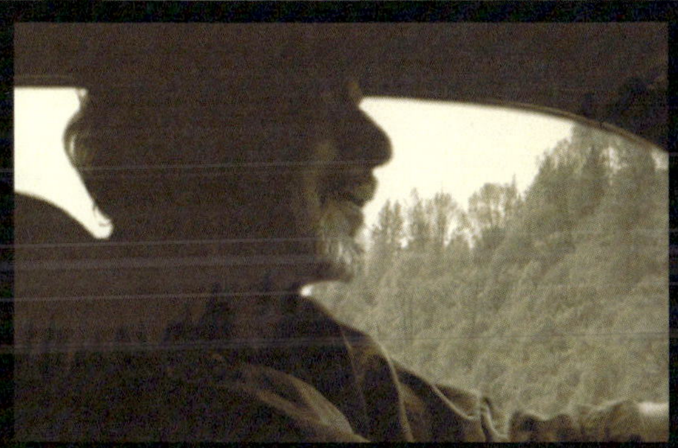

The strange man said he was a *Lemurian*
and that these were his living quarters.

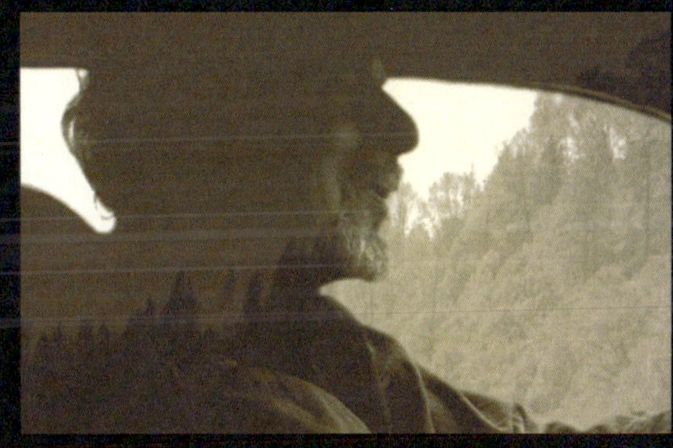

The climber was invited to rest on a slab
of solid gold. Later, they could meet

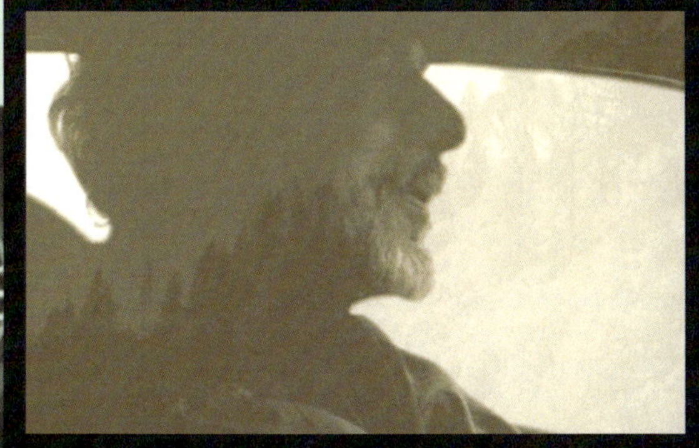

other *Lemurians and learn much
of this ancient civilization* –

But first, he was told, if he would just lay
his head upon this pillow of gold..."

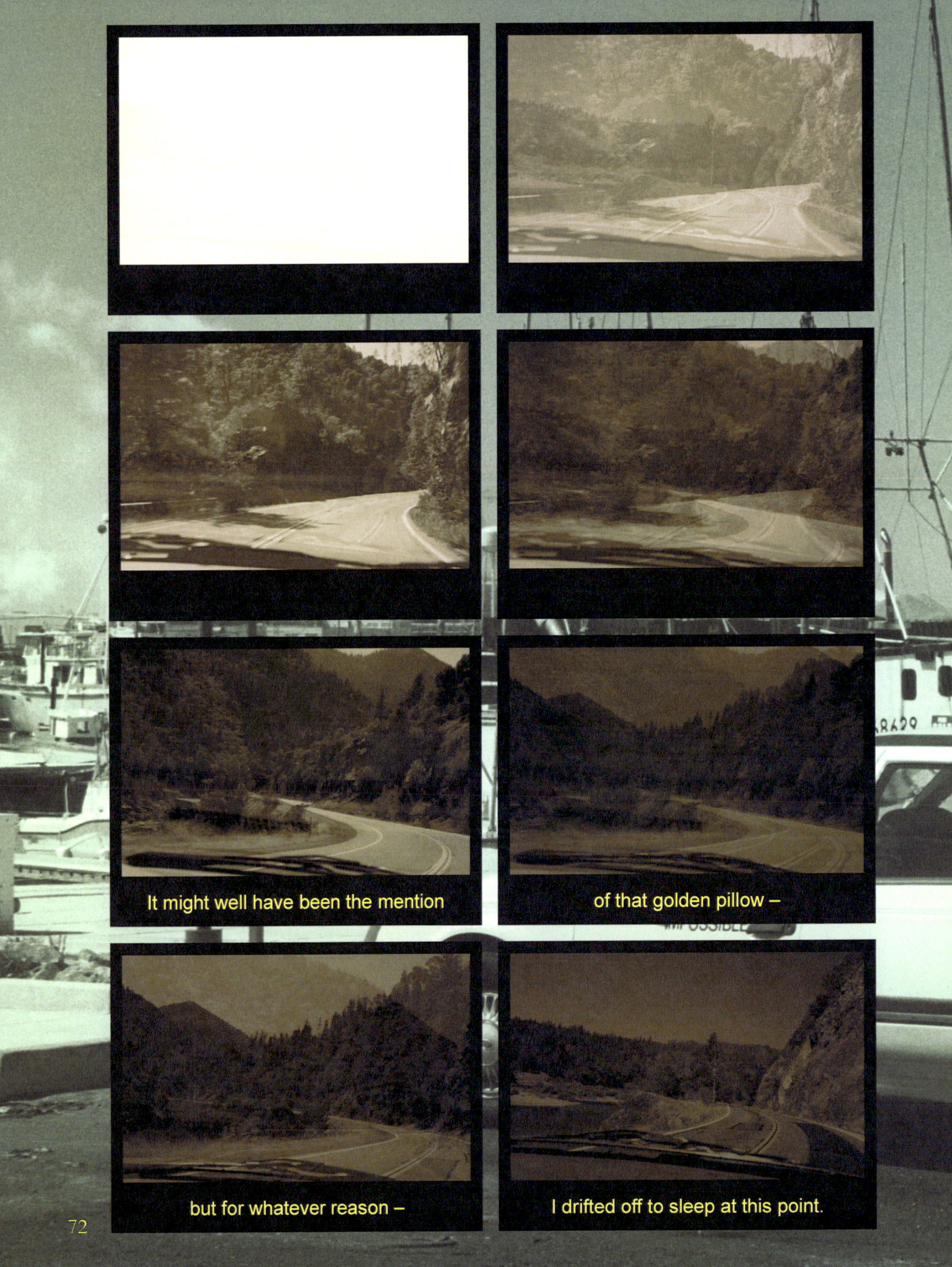

It might well have been the mention
of that golden pillow –
but for whatever reason –
I drifted off to sleep at this point.

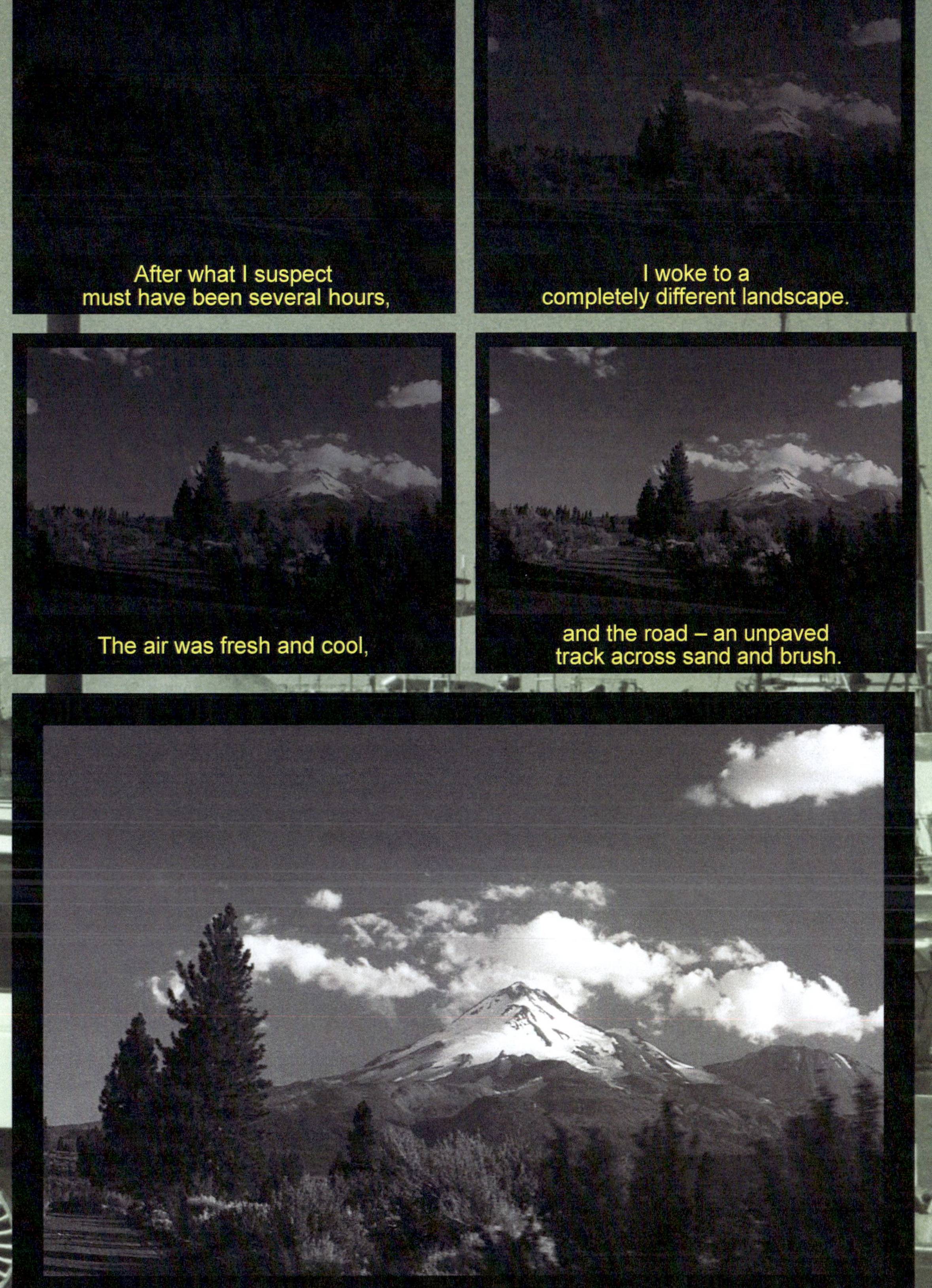

After what I suspect
must have been several hours,

I woke to a
completely different landscape.

The air was fresh and cool,

and the road – an unpaved
track across sand and brush.

In the sky, small white puffy clouds
above a horizon that held my first view of our mountain.

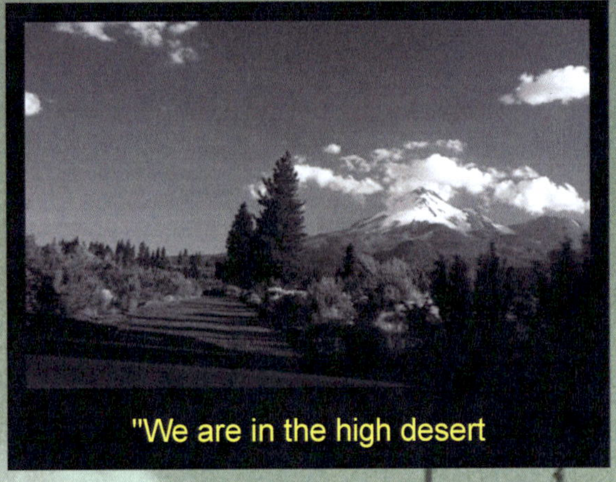
"We are in the high desert

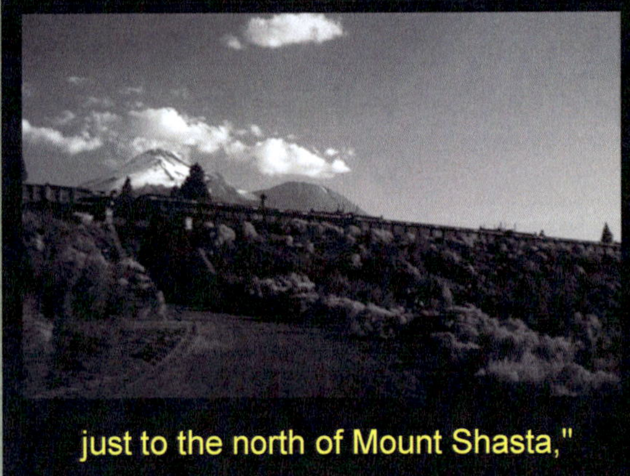
just to the north of Mount Shasta,"

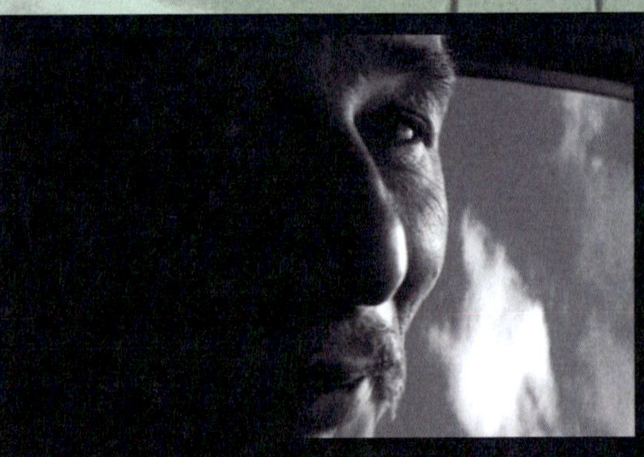
Herr Dockter said

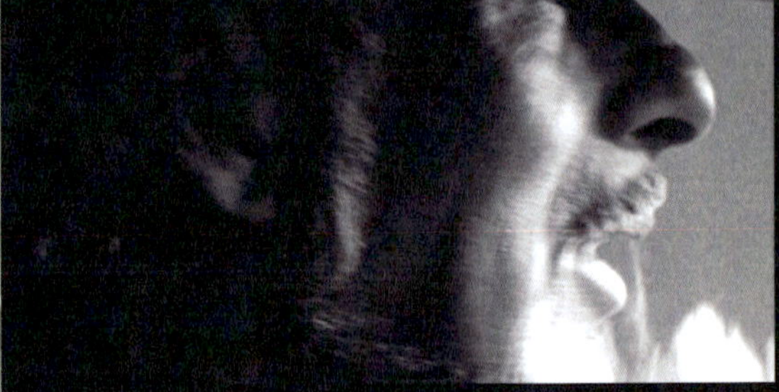
when he noticed I was awake.

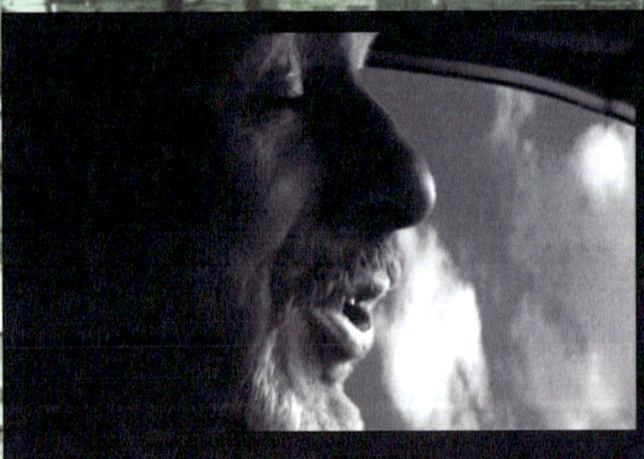
"Not too much further to the trail head.

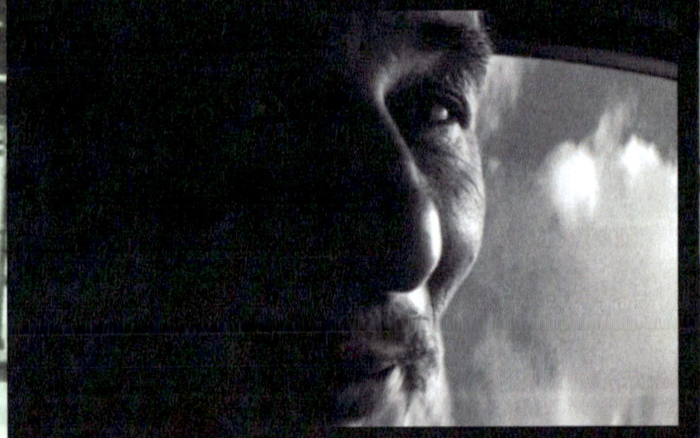
The air is much nicer now,
don't you agree?"

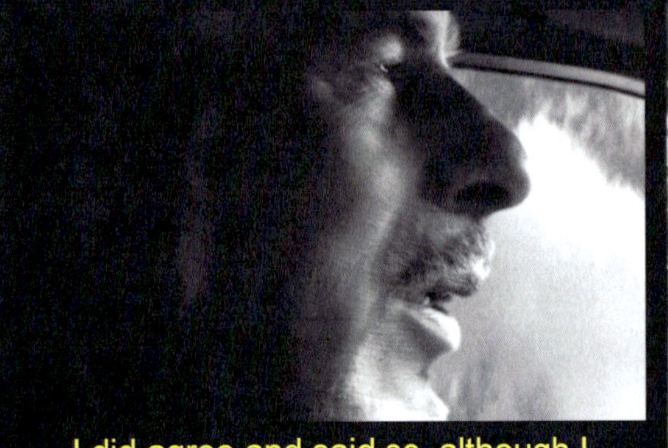
I did agree and said so, although I
added that the road was much worse.

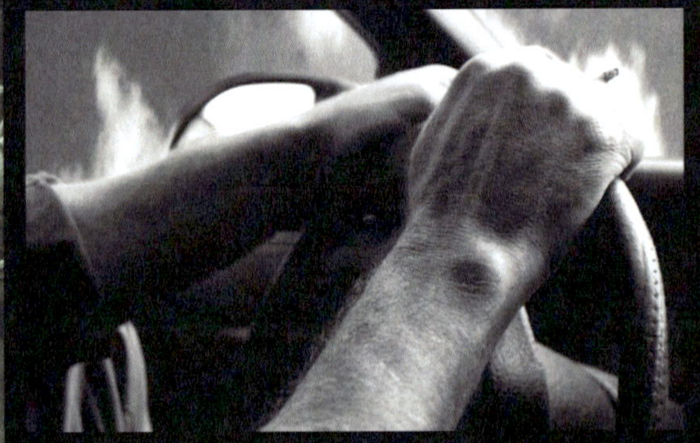
I was happy for the seatbelt and
hung on to whatever I could

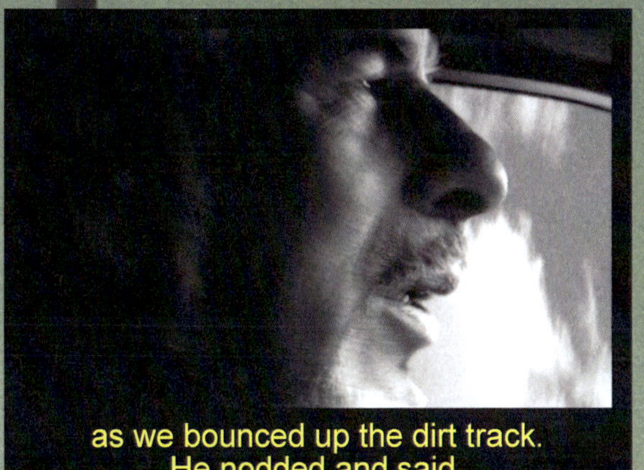
as we bounced up the dirt track.
He nodded and said,

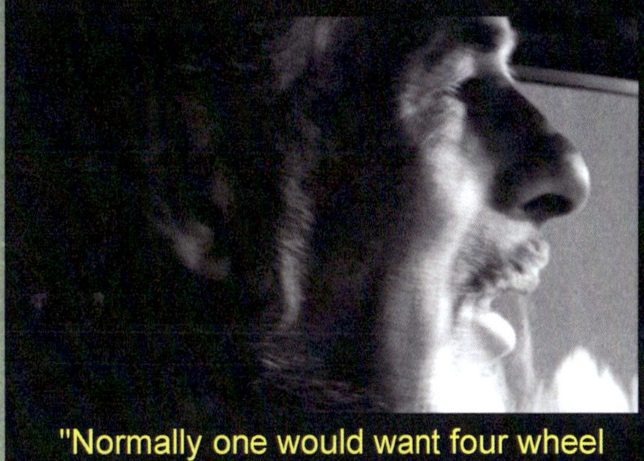
"Normally one would want four wheel
drive for this, but as long as we

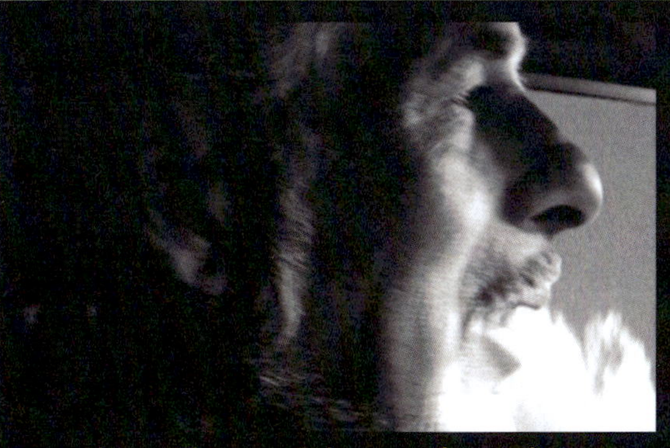
can keep the speed up and not damage
the oil pan by bottoming out, we'll be fine."

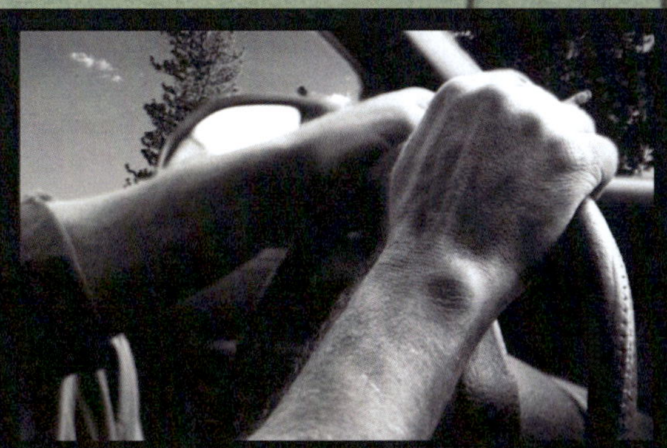
As we climbed higher up the slope, for the
first time during the drive I began to worry

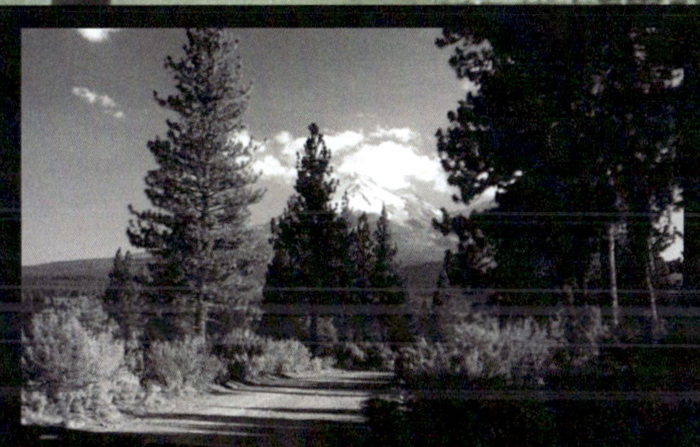
whether the old station wagon could make
it.   The road had deteriorated to not more

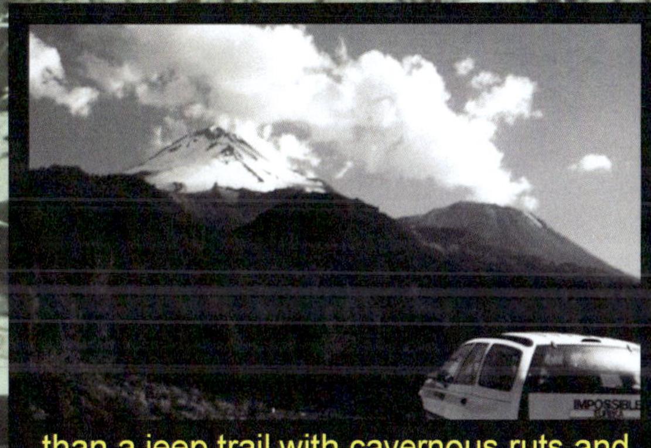
than a jeep trail with cavernous ruts and
huge boulders that had to negotiated.

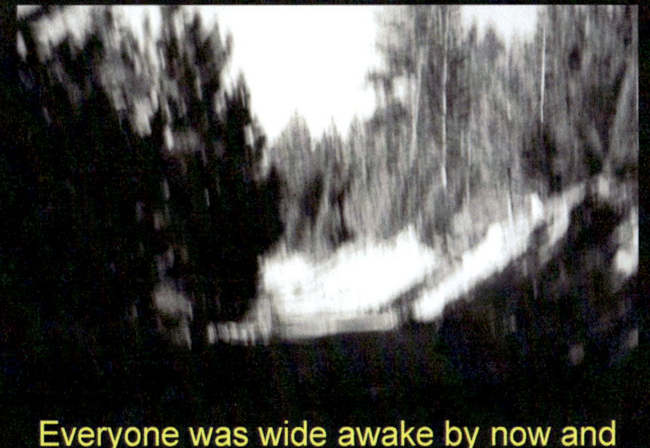
Everyone was wide awake by now and
looking about with that combination of

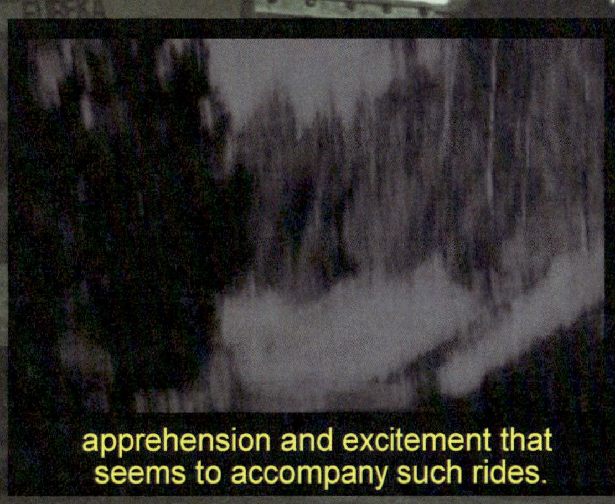
apprehension and excitement that
seems to accompany such rides.

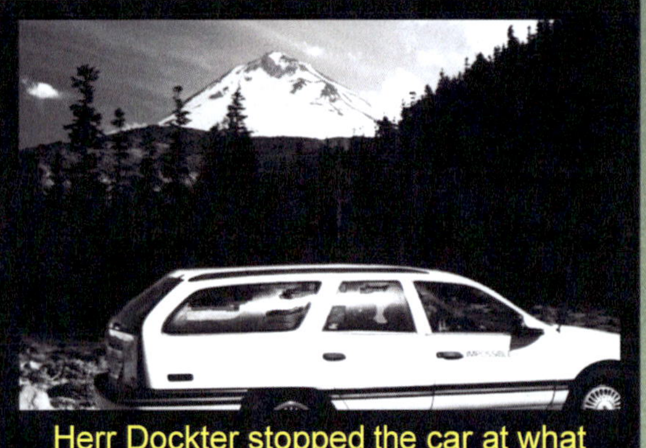

Herr Dockter stopped the car at what
seemed to be the end of the road –

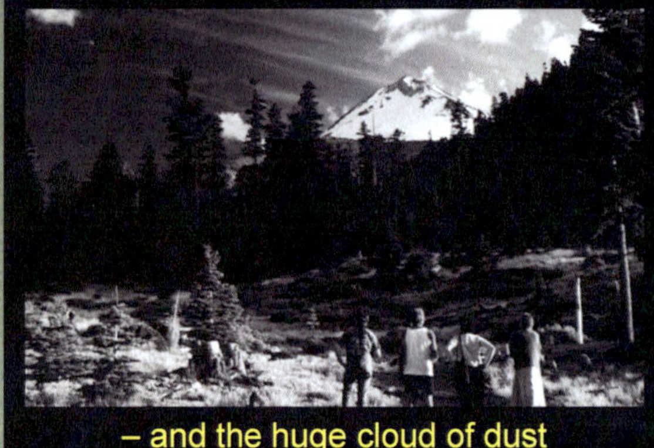

– and the huge cloud of dust
that had been following close behind,

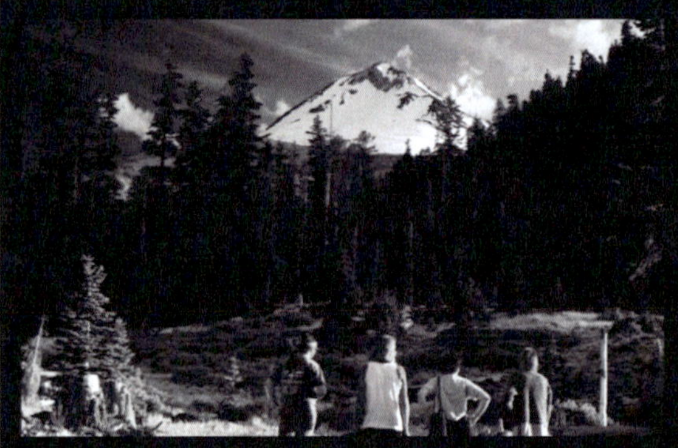

engulfed us and then settled. The air was
now clear and smelled sweetly of pine.

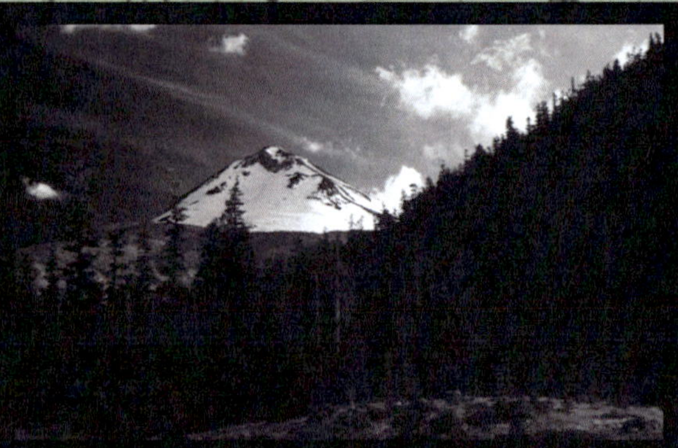

A smell that occurs only in the evening
after the forest has baked all day.

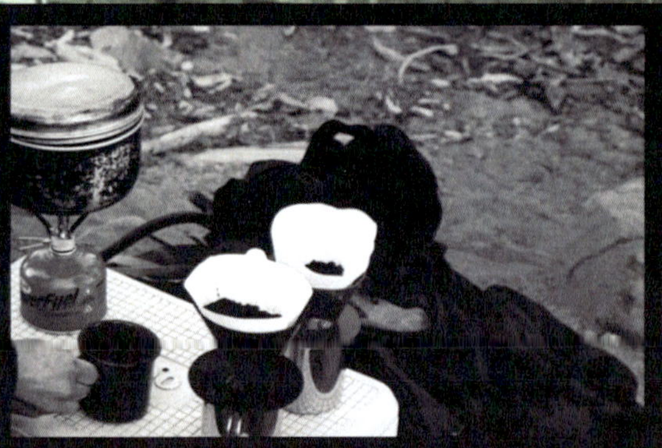

The group happily went about all the
chores necessary to make camp in

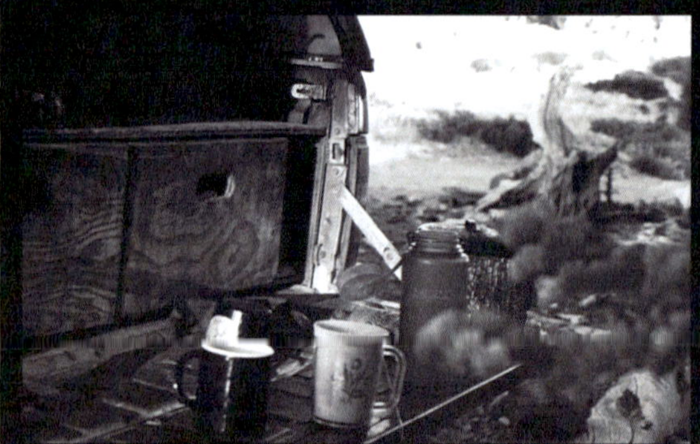

the hour of light remaining. Besides the
beauty of the location and the anticipation

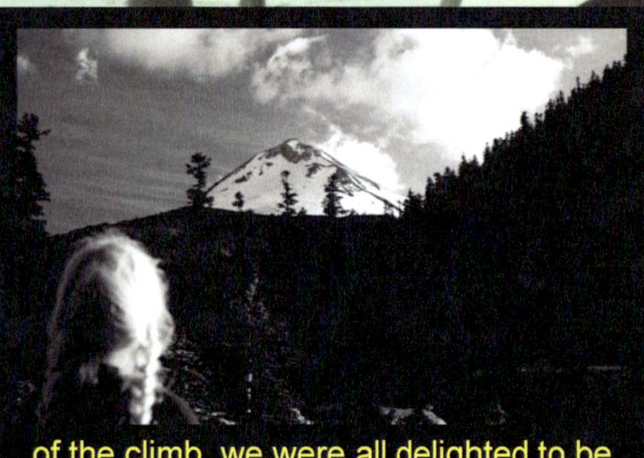

of the climb, we were all delighted to be
out of that car and standing upright.

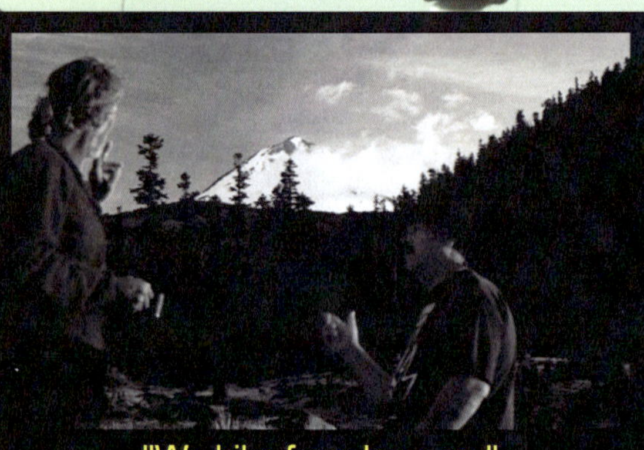

"We hike from here on,"
Herr Dockter explained to Pepperwood.

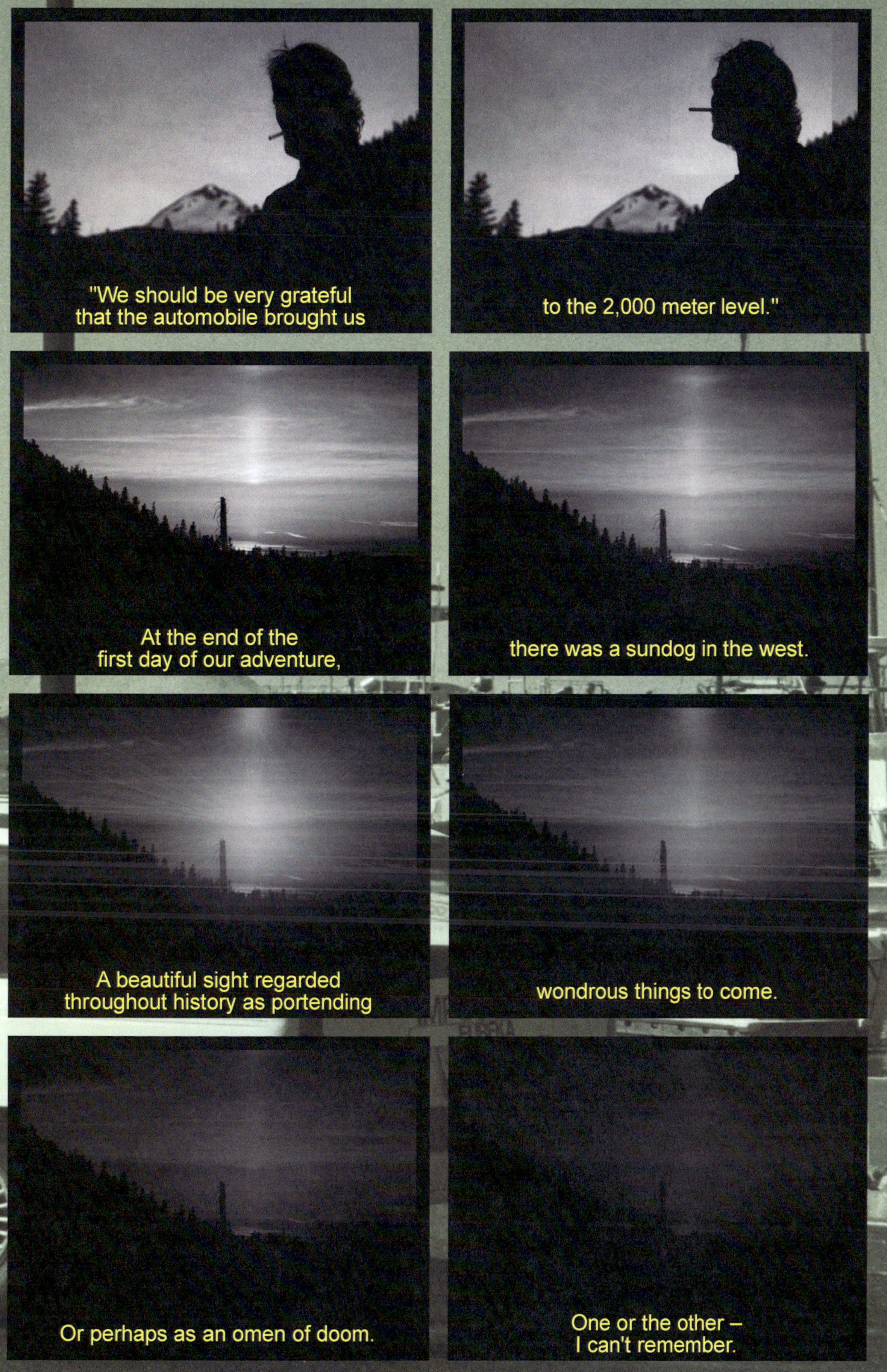

"We should be very grateful
that the automobile brought us
to the 2,000 meter level."
At the end of the
first day of our adventure,
there was a sundog in the west.
A beautiful sight regarded
throughout history as portending
wondrous things to come.
Or perhaps as an omen of doom.
One or the other –
I can't remember.

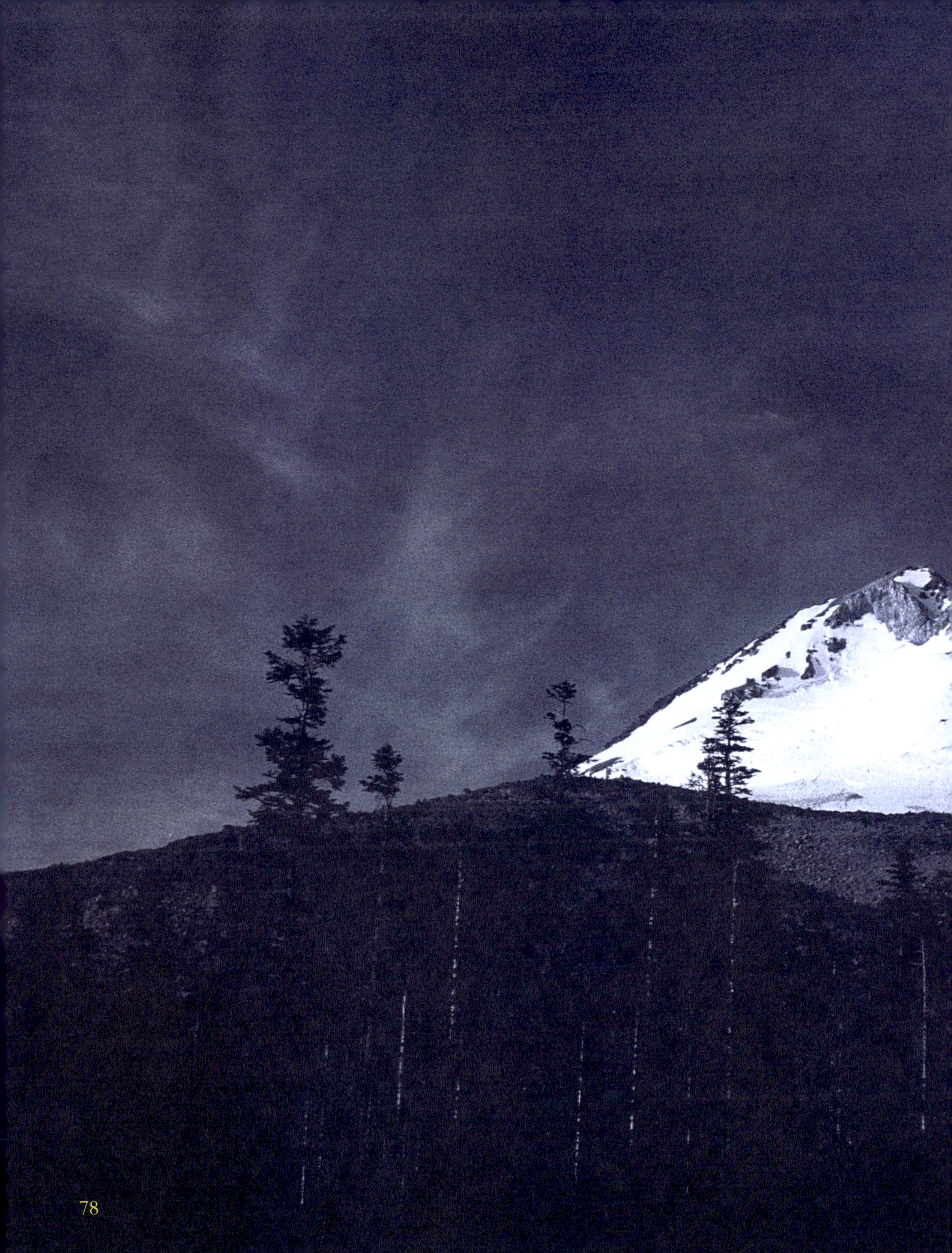

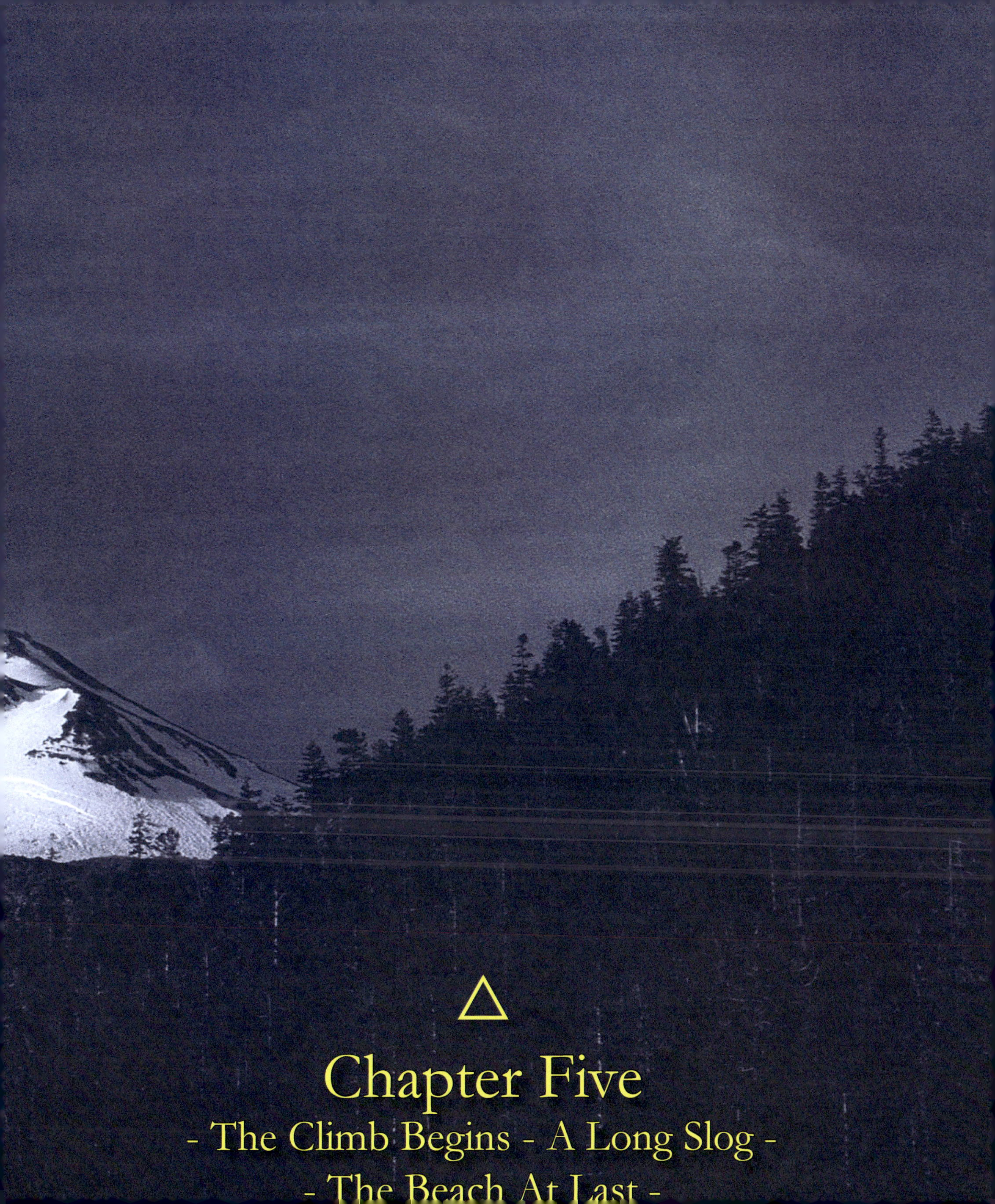
△

Chapter Five
- The Climb Begins - A Long Slog -
- The Beach At Last -

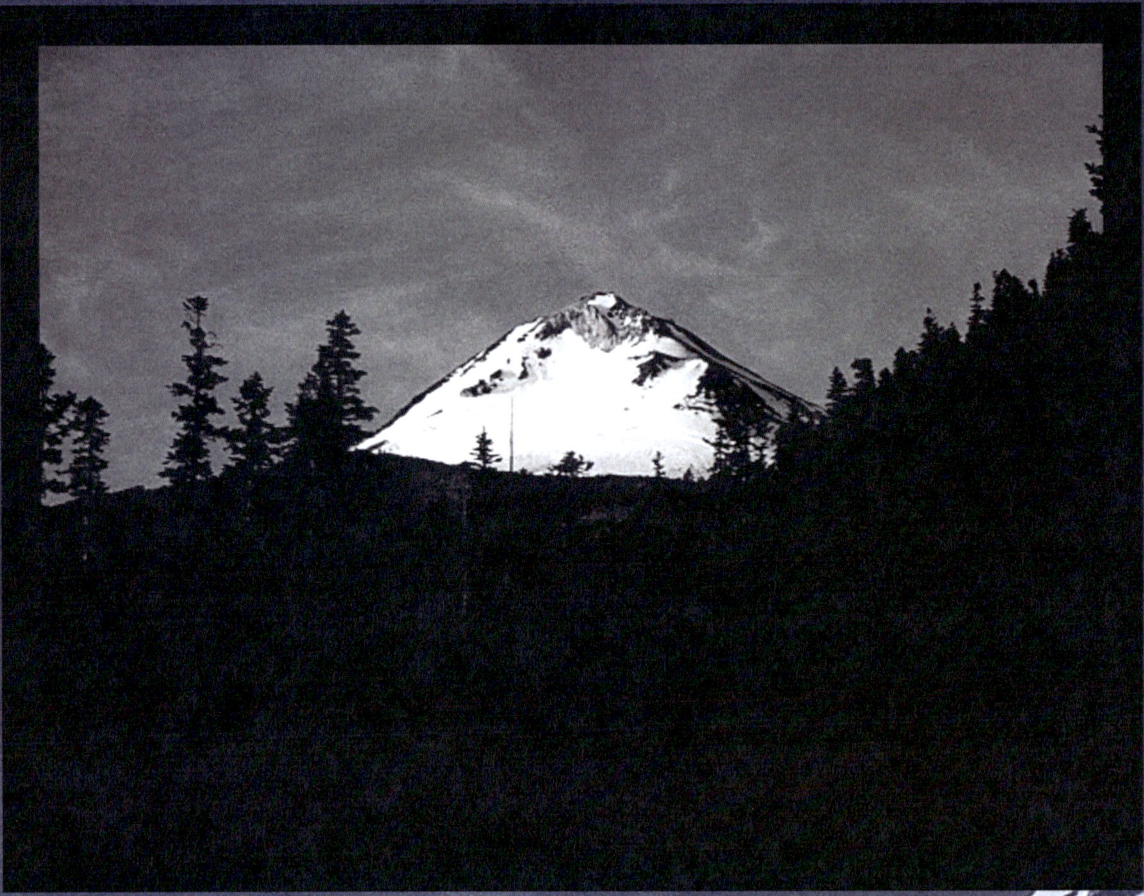

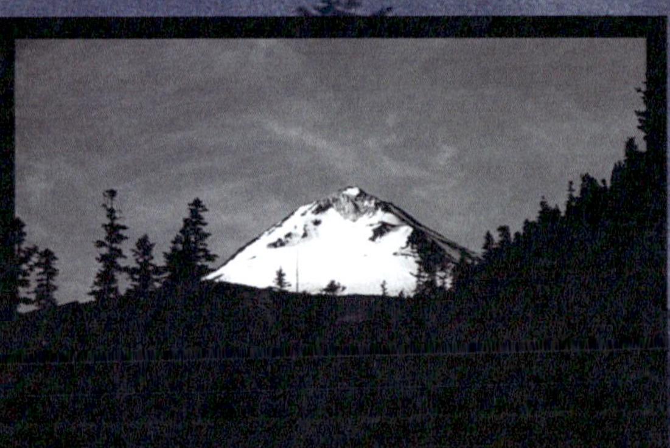

After Herr Dockter's assurances
that the climb to establish

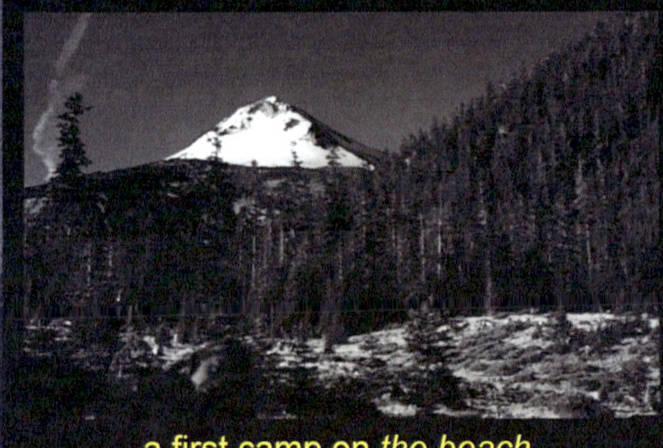

a first camp on *the beach,*
would neither be long nor strenuous,

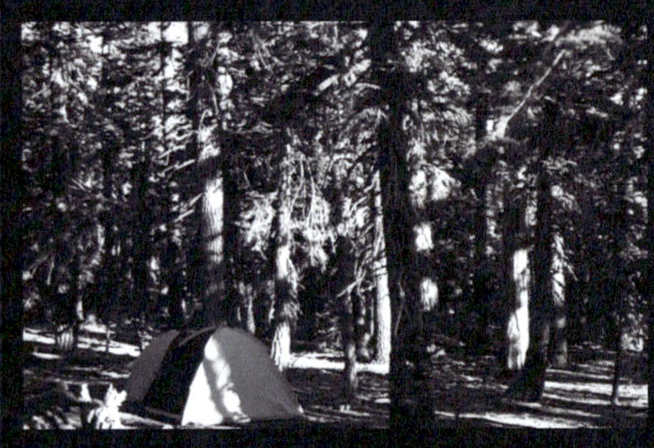

we chose to sleep in,

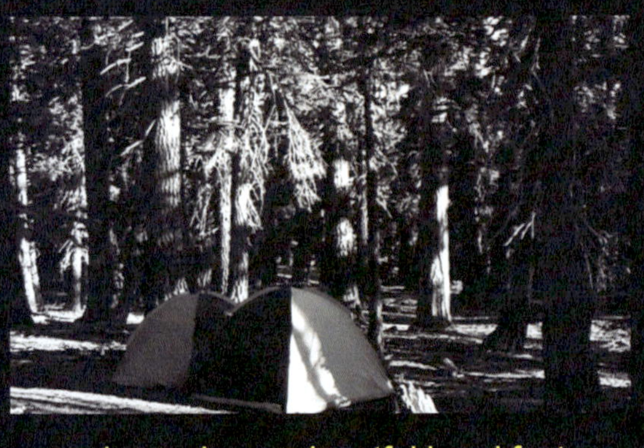

enjoy a slow and restful breakfast,

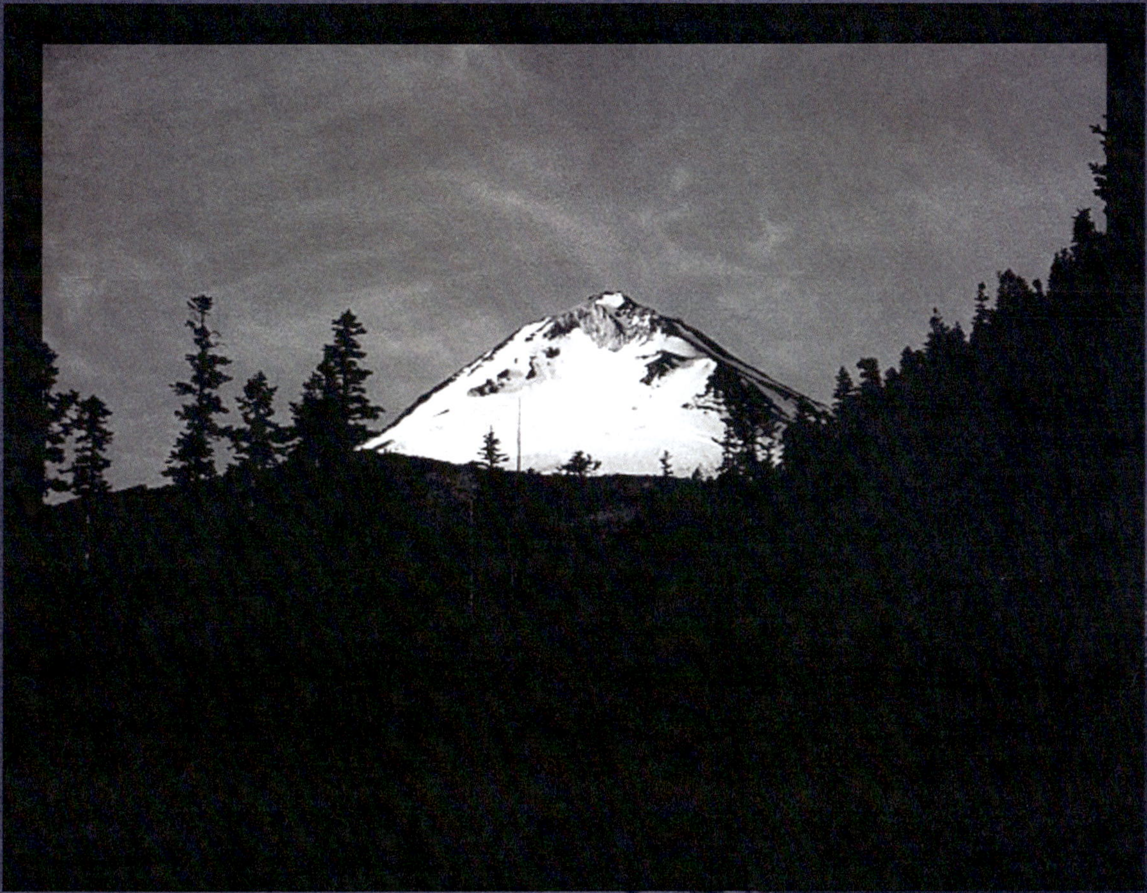

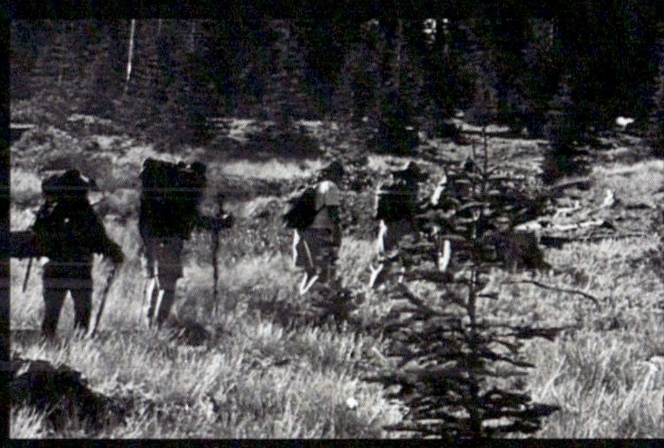
and begin our climb through the forest

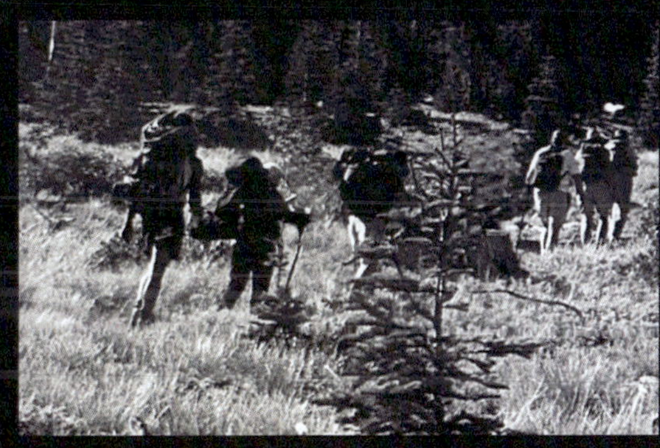
at midmorning.

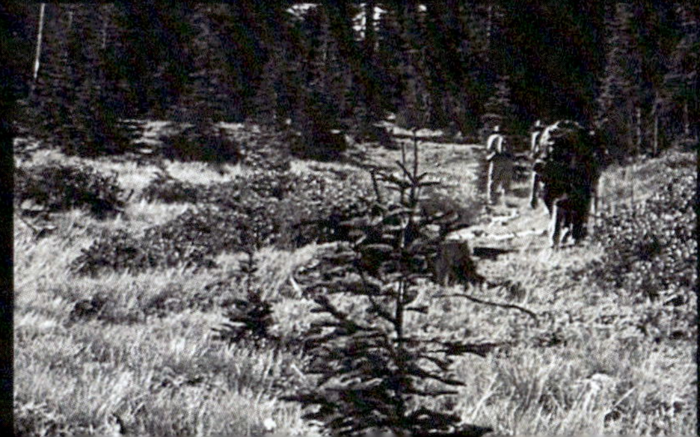

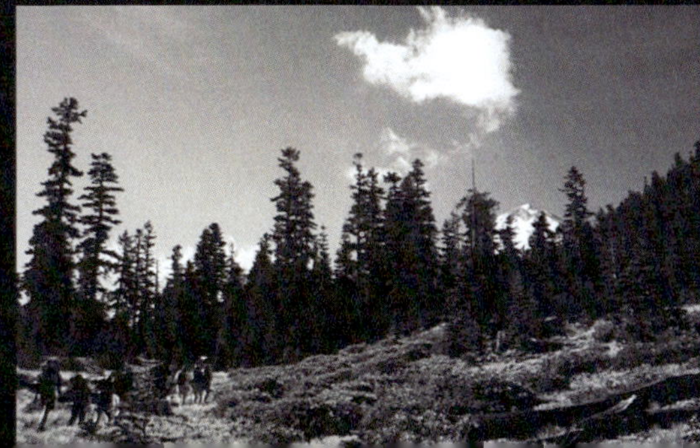

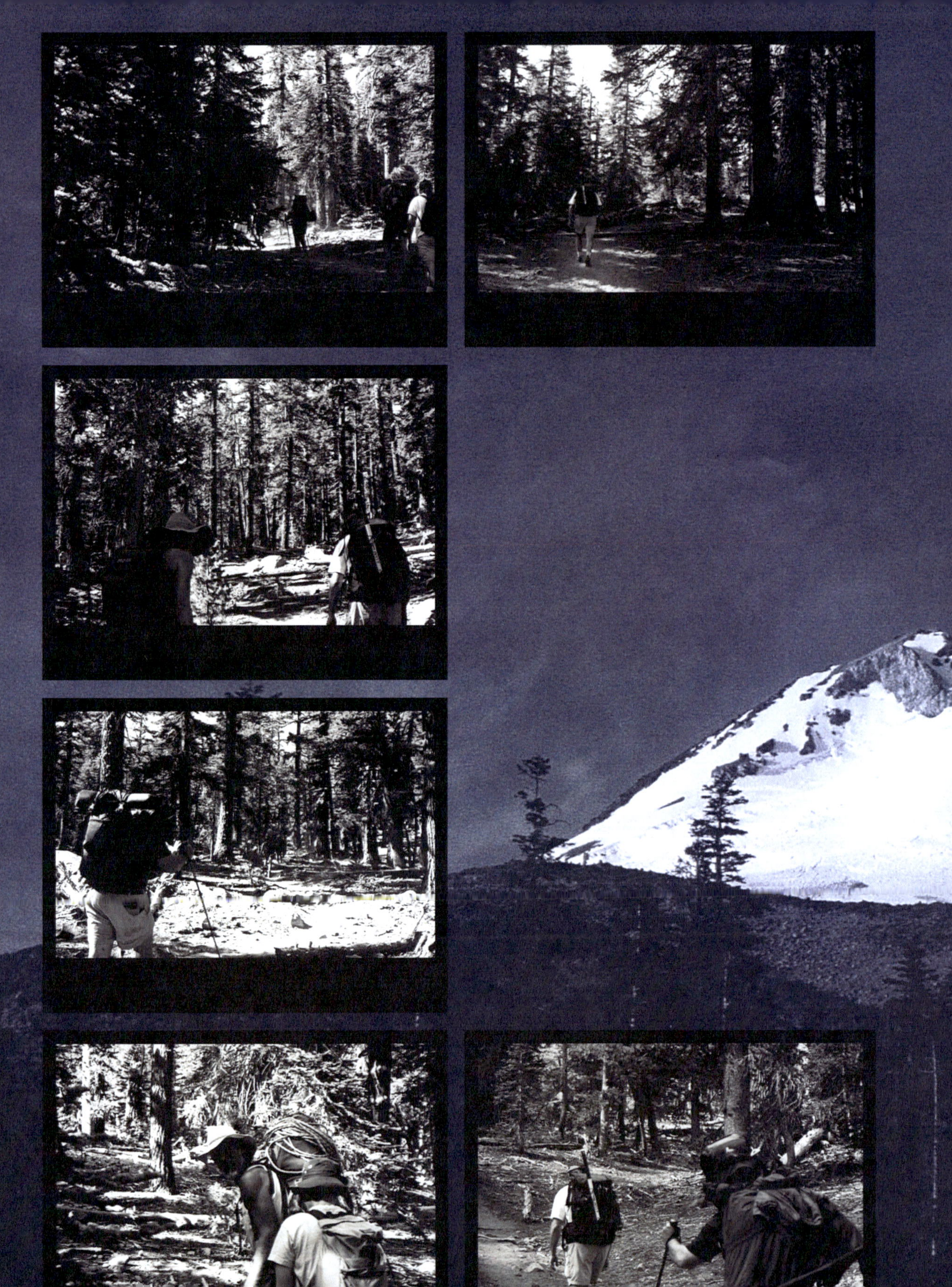

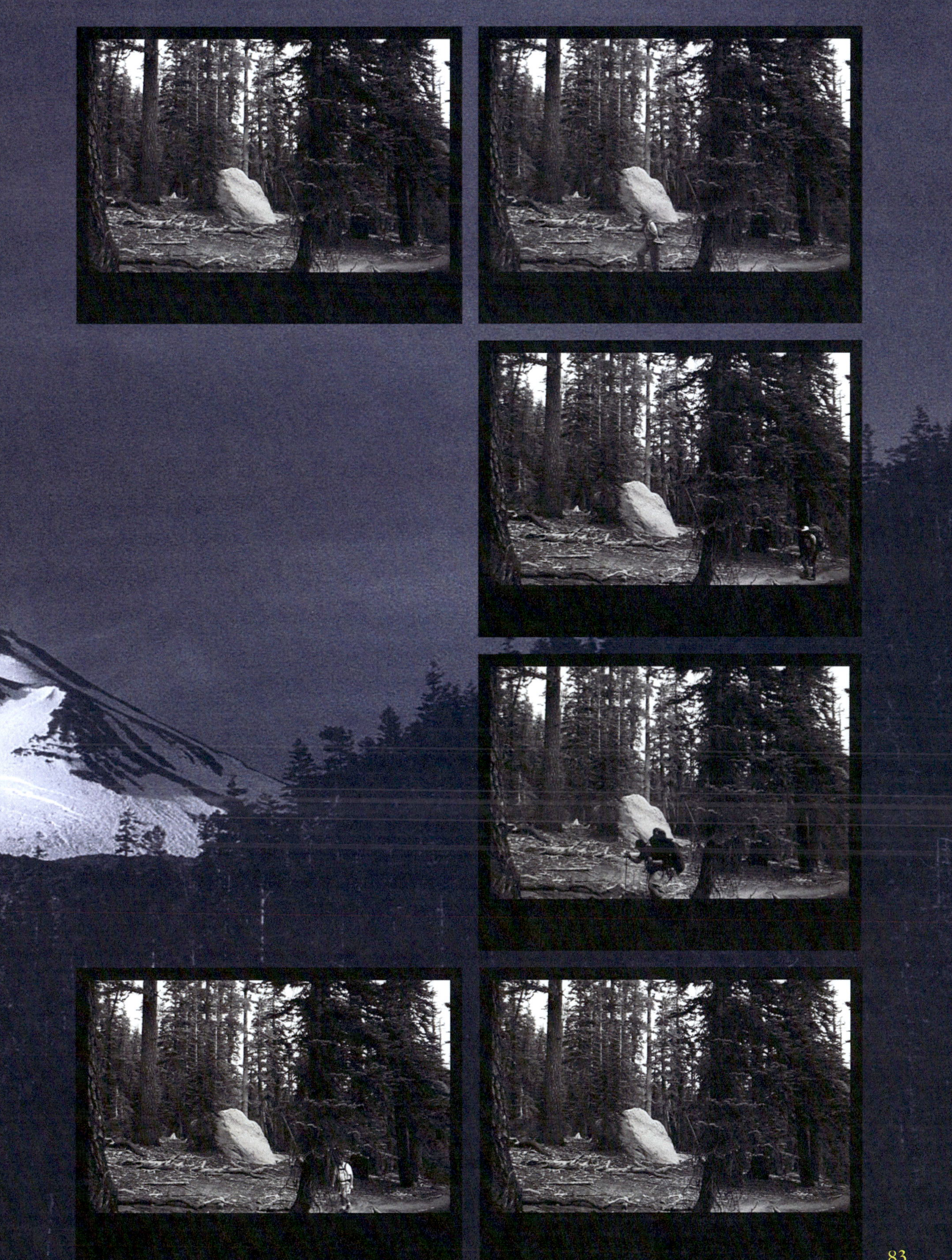

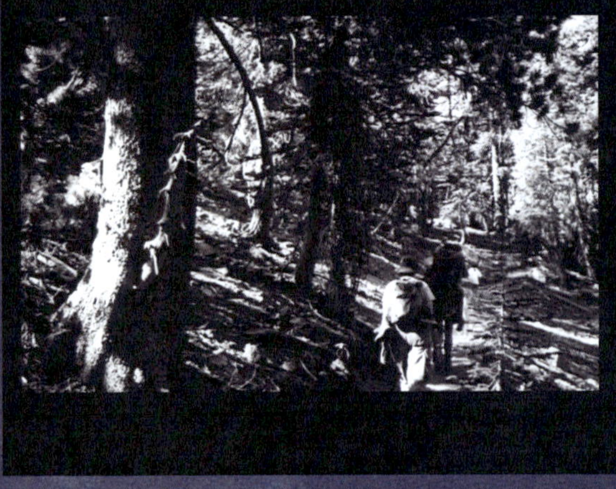

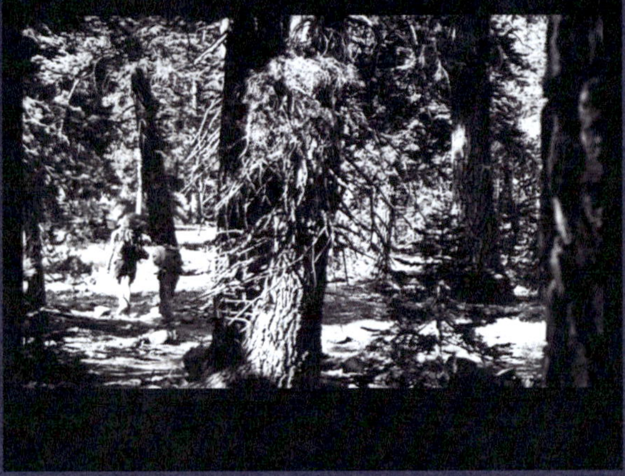

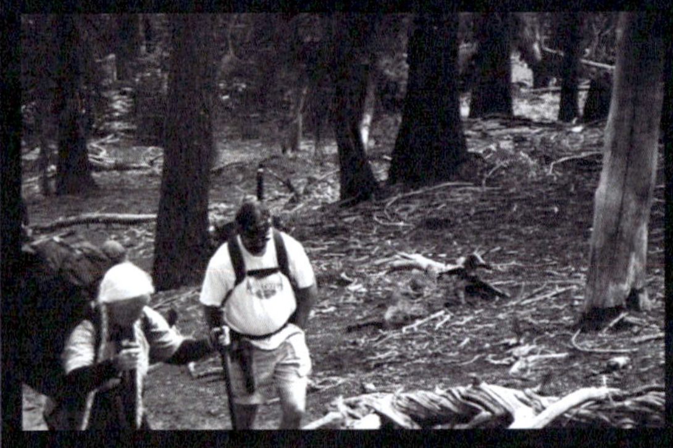

When exhaustion was complete

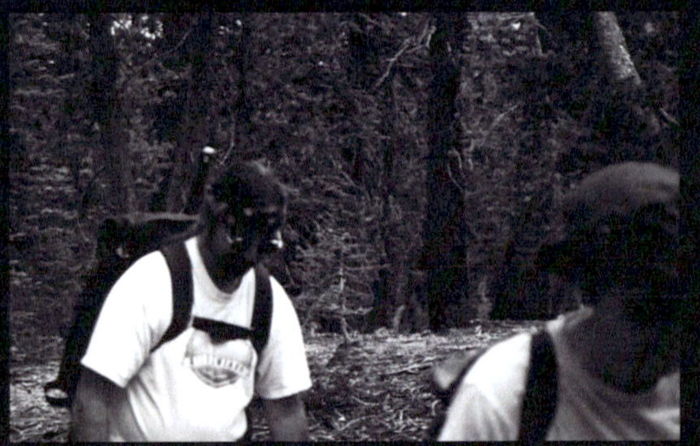

and we so desperately needed a rest,

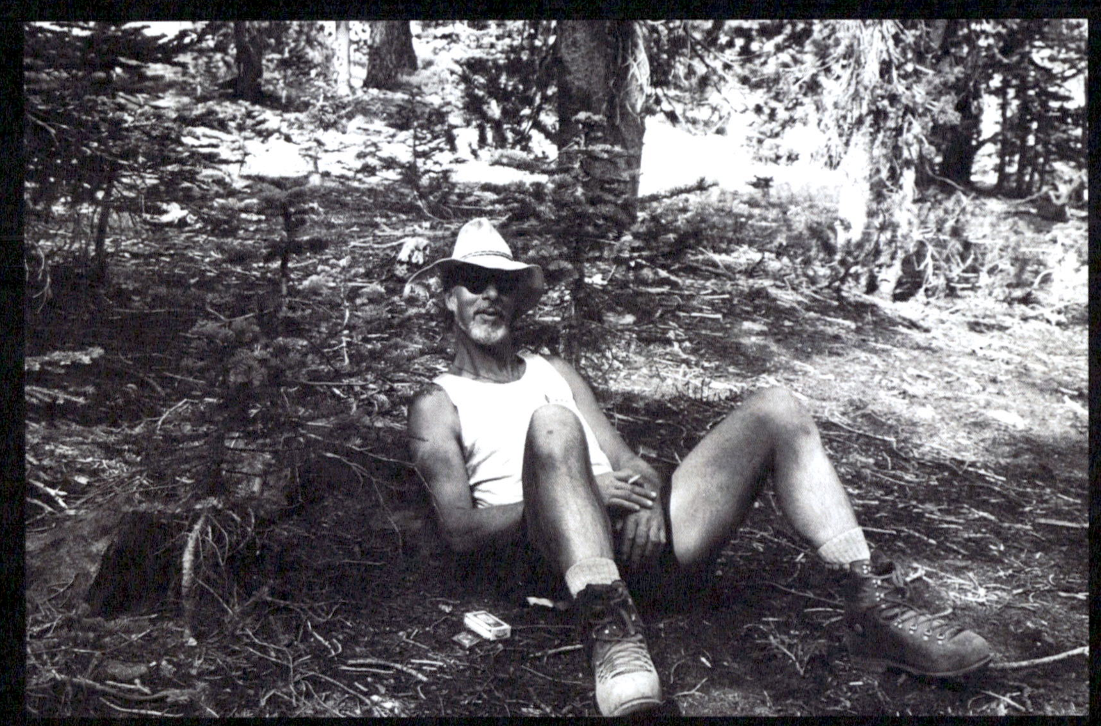

Herr Dockter was already there waiting for us – relaxing and smoking a cigarette.

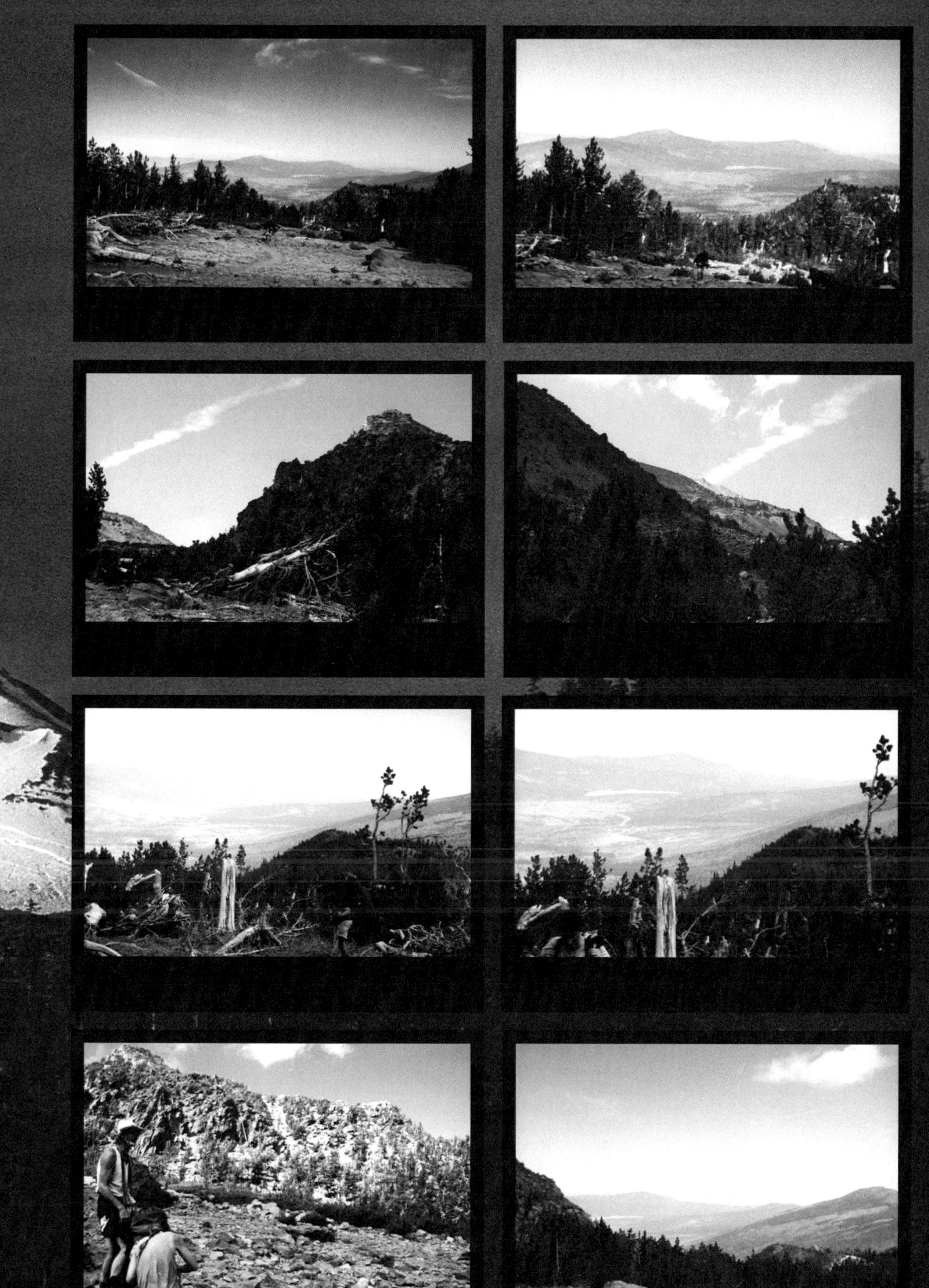

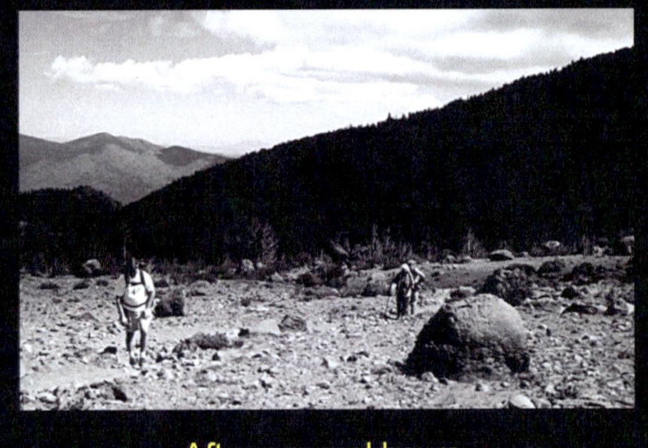

After several hours,

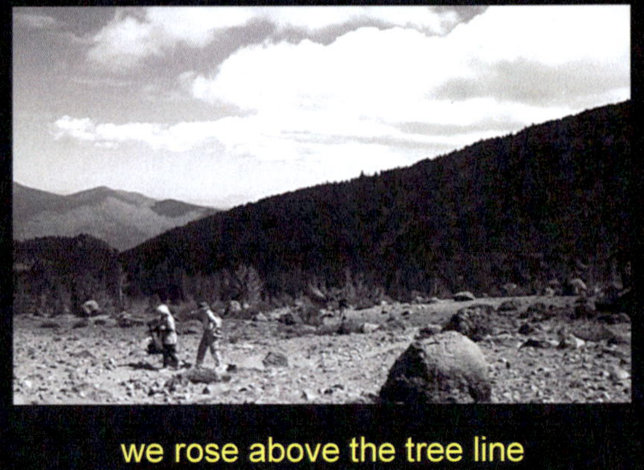

we rose above the tree line

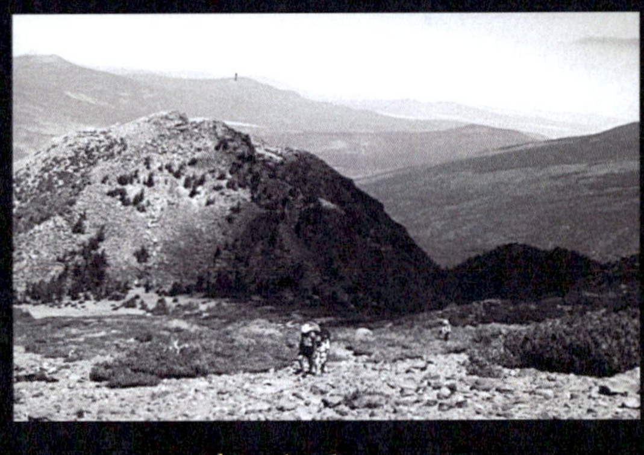

and got a true sense

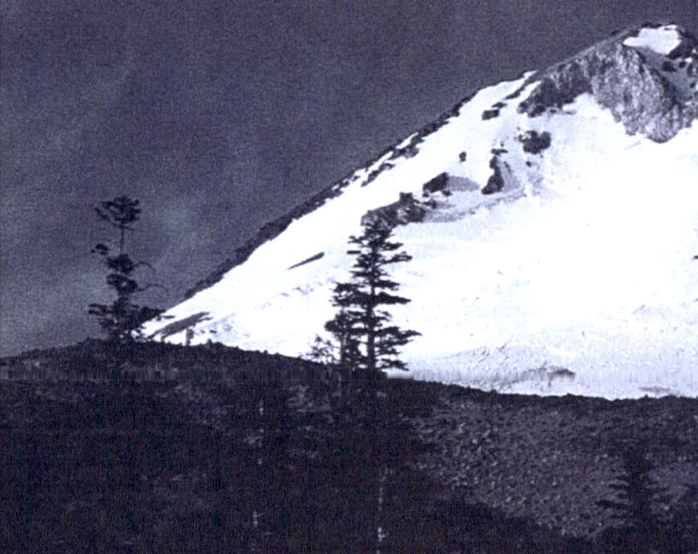

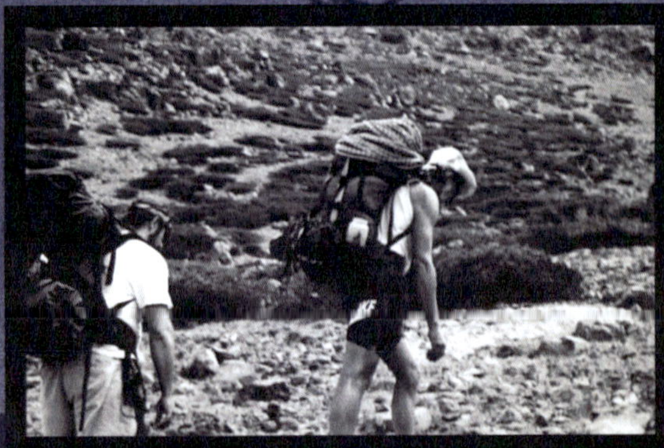

of our mountain.

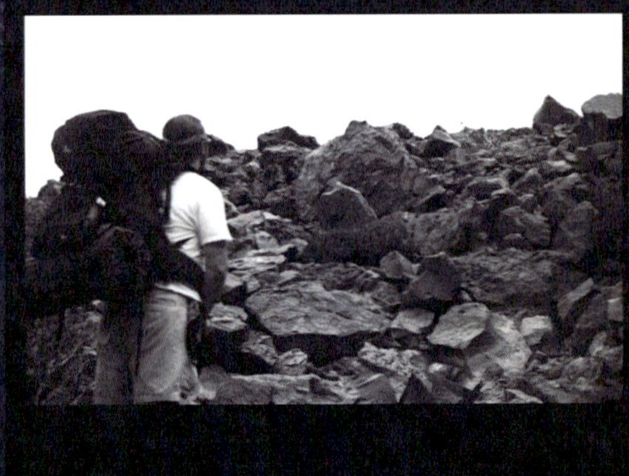

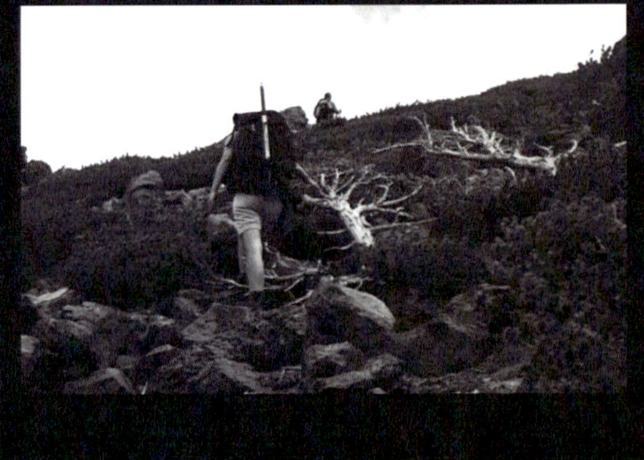

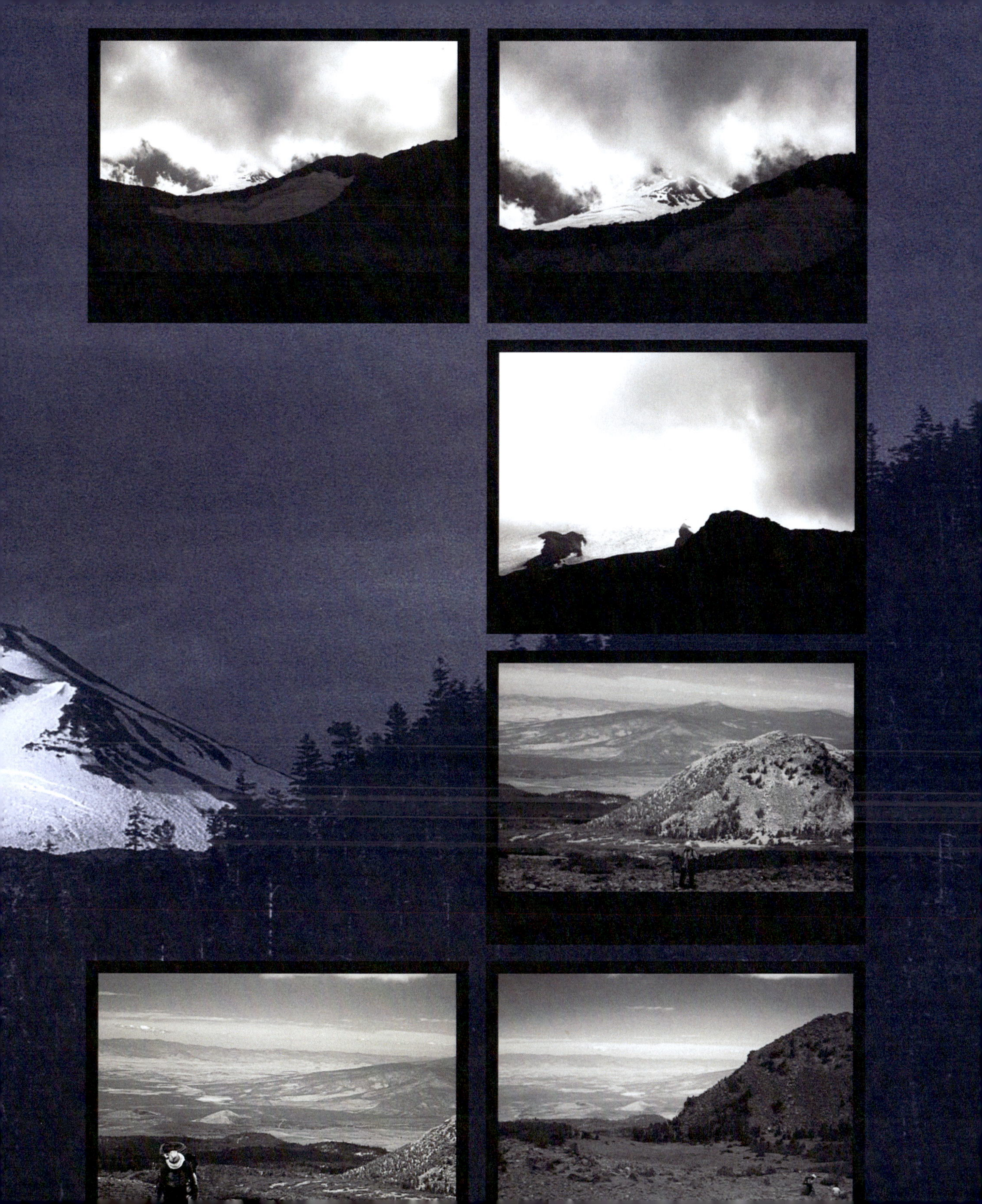

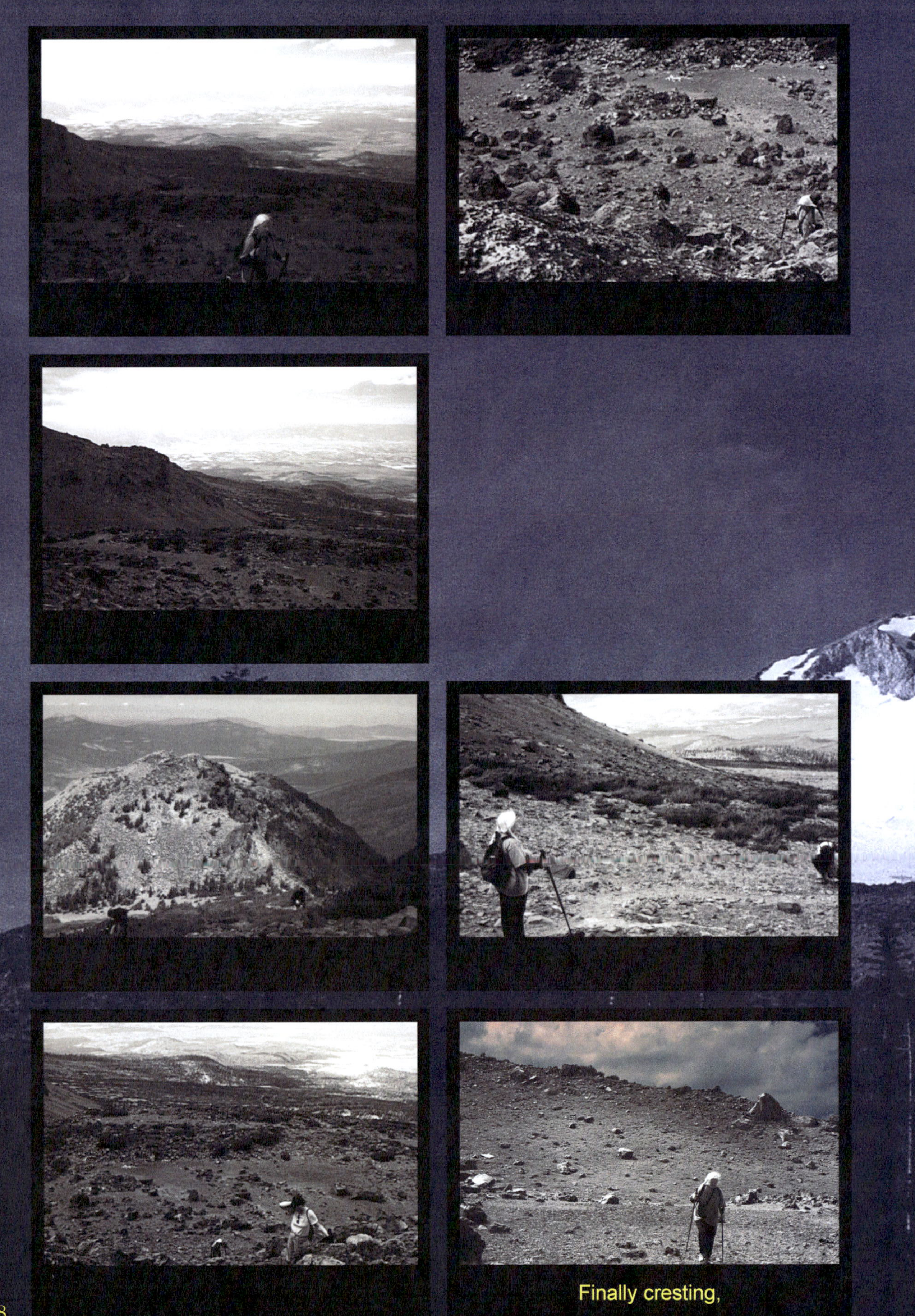
Finally cresting,

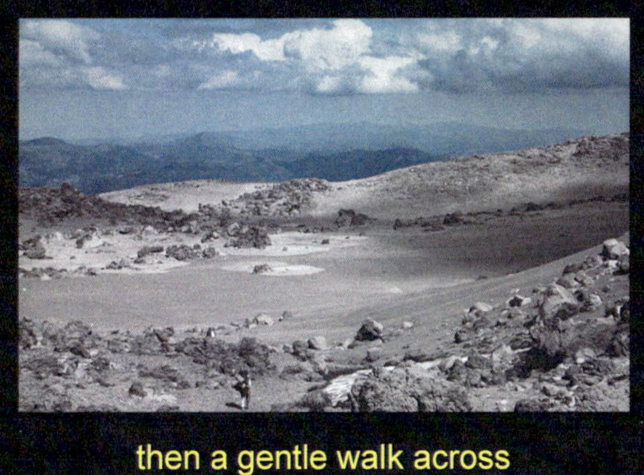

then a gentle walk across

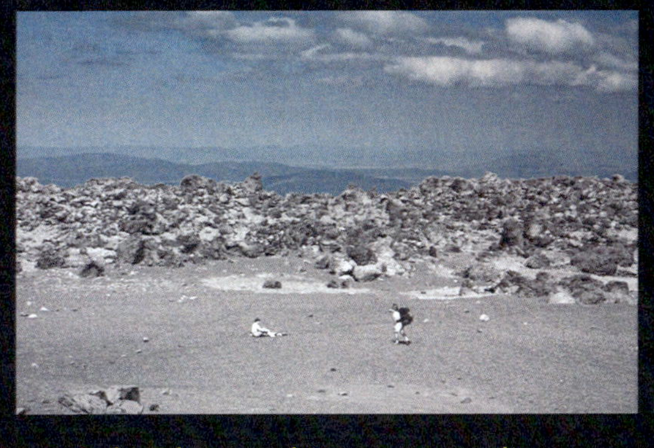

level ground to our campsite.

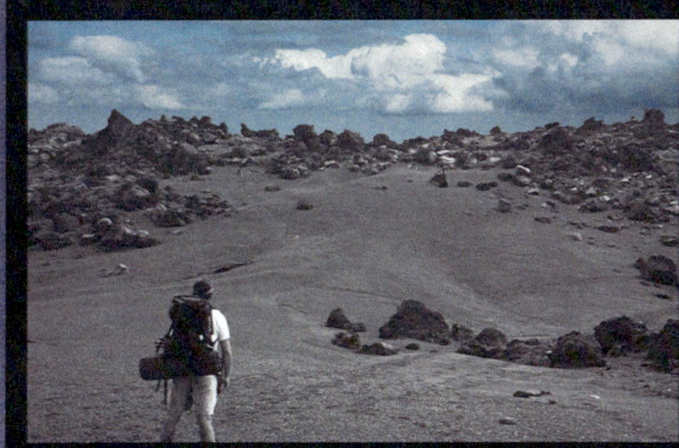

Shedding my pack,

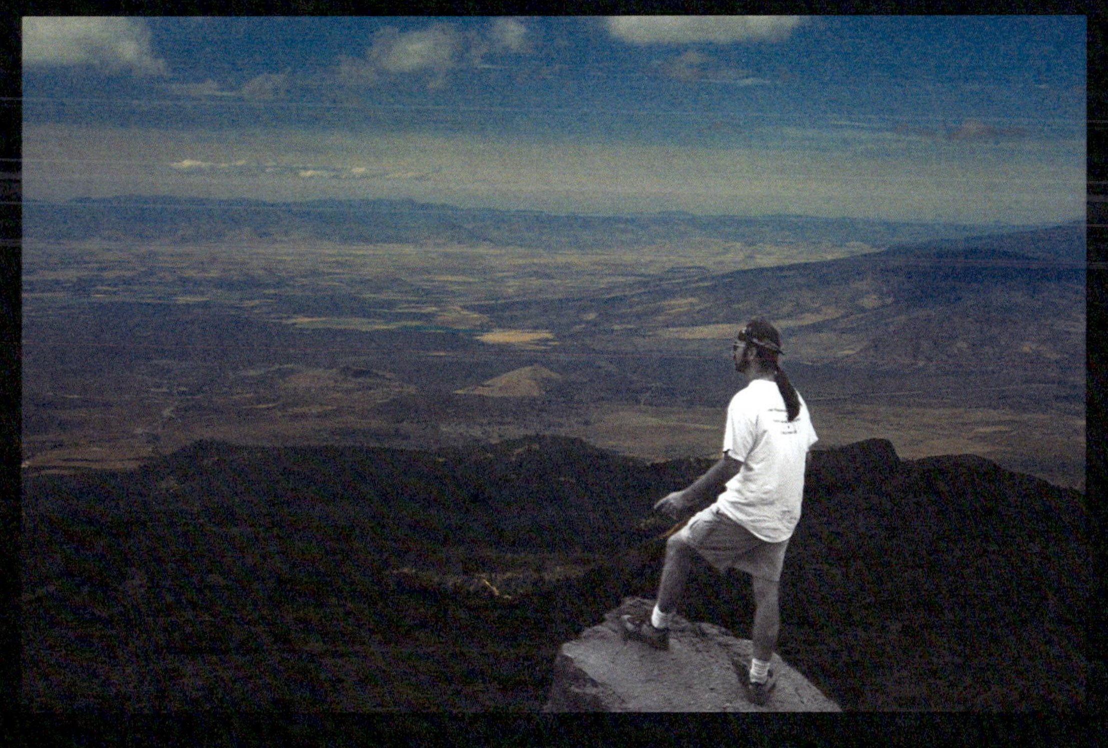

I scrambled to the top of the volcanic boulders that formed a natural wall around the beach. The view back down over our route to the valley seemed strangely familiar.

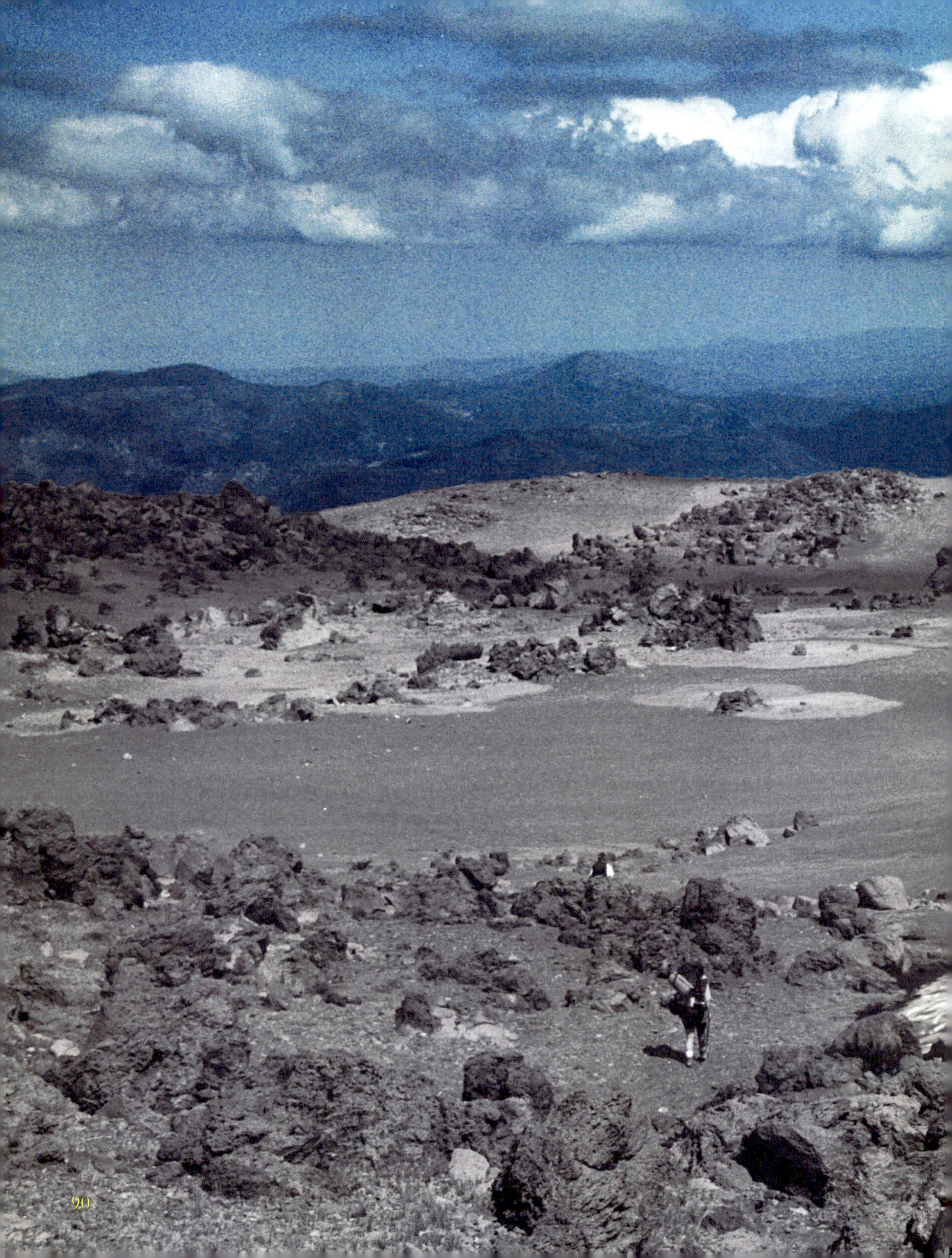

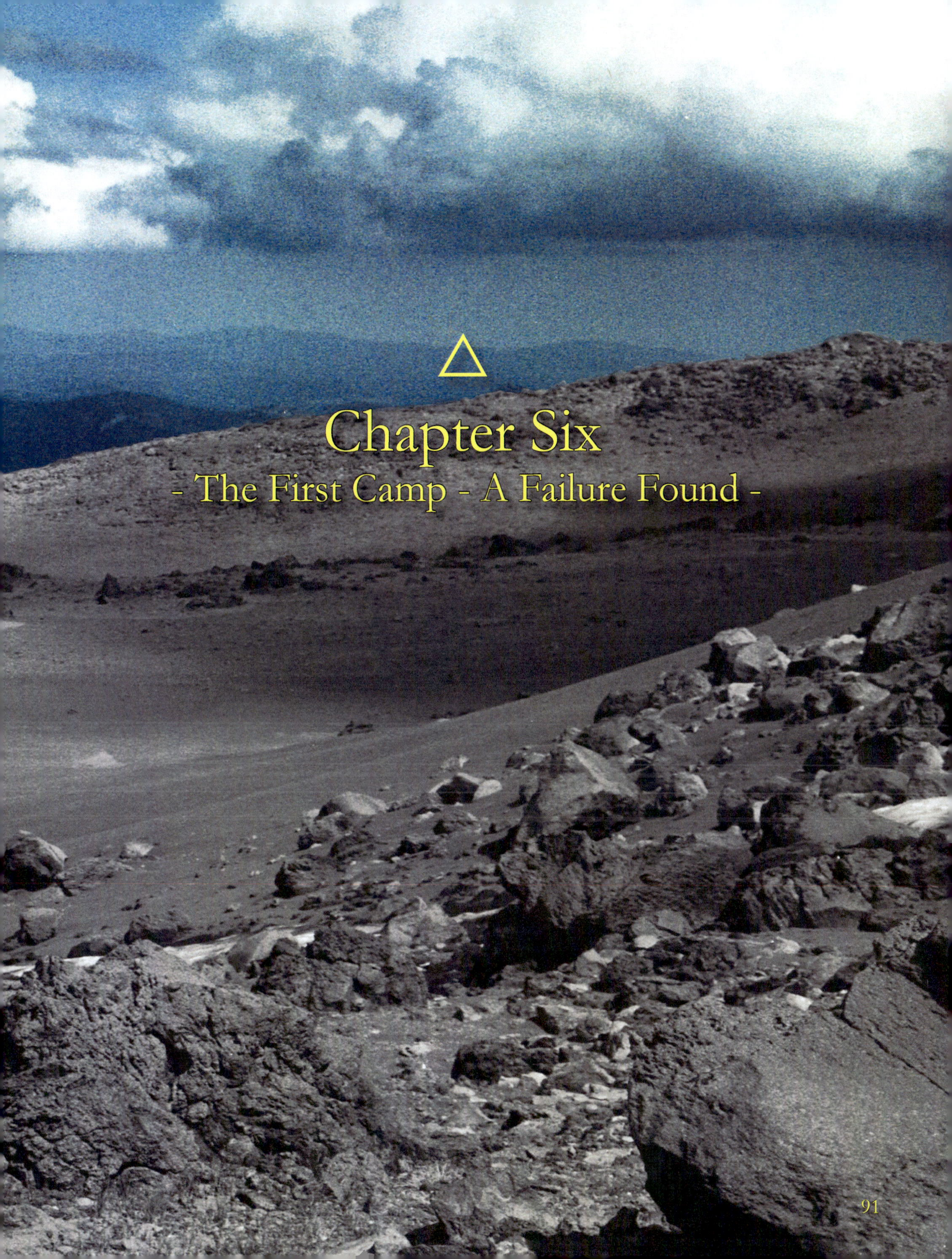
△

Chapter Six
- The First Camp - A Failure Found -

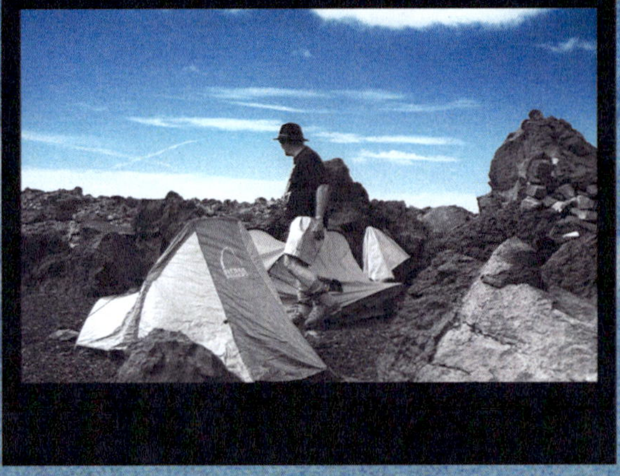

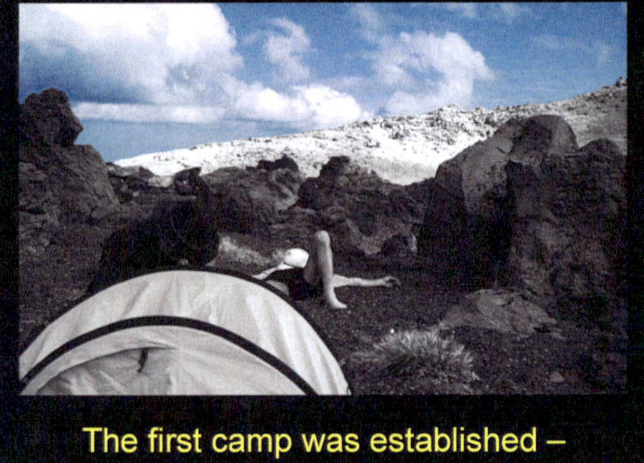

The first camp was established –

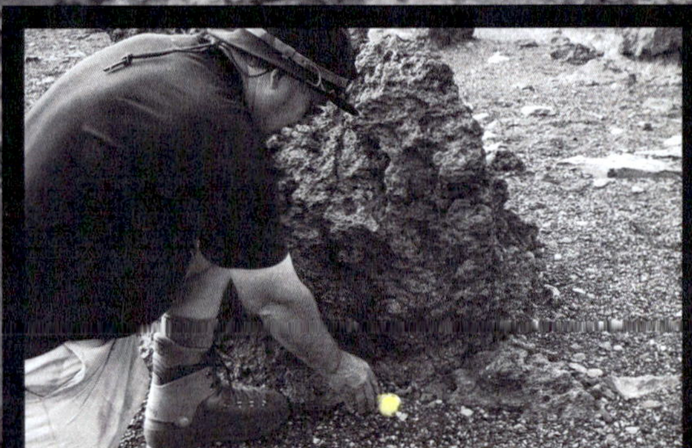

and there was a bit

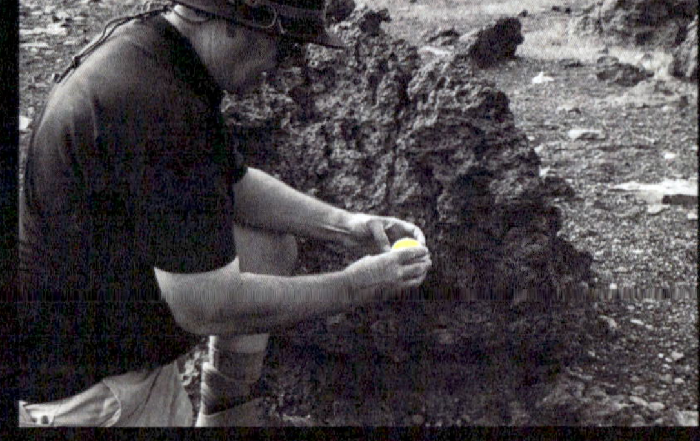

of free time for relaxation.

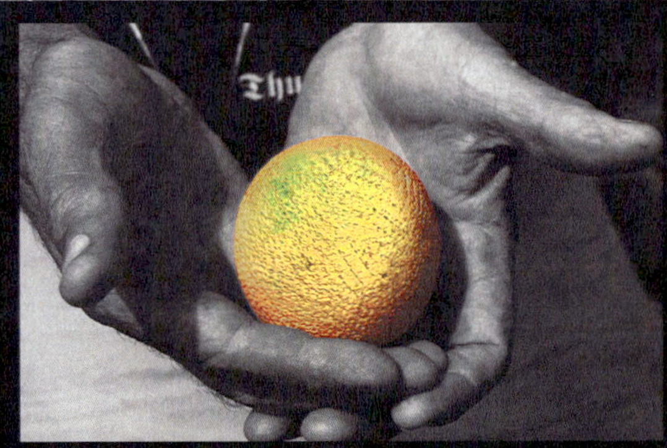

In his wanderings about the beach,
Lawrence Pepperwood discovered

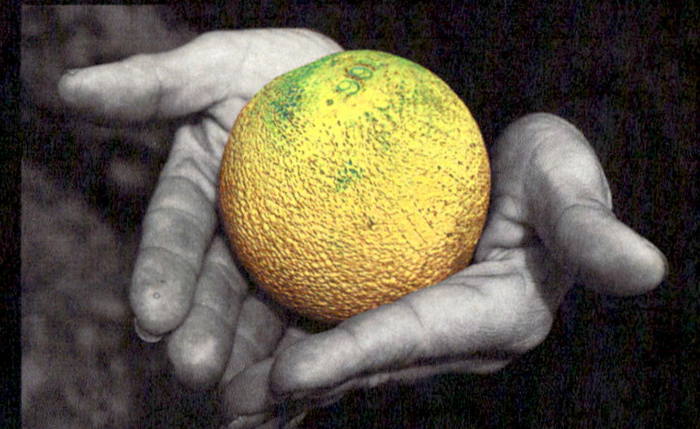

one of the hollow, ceramic spheres
we had been hoping to find.

The *failure* was passed among the group,

but no decision was reached
as to whether we ought keep it or not.

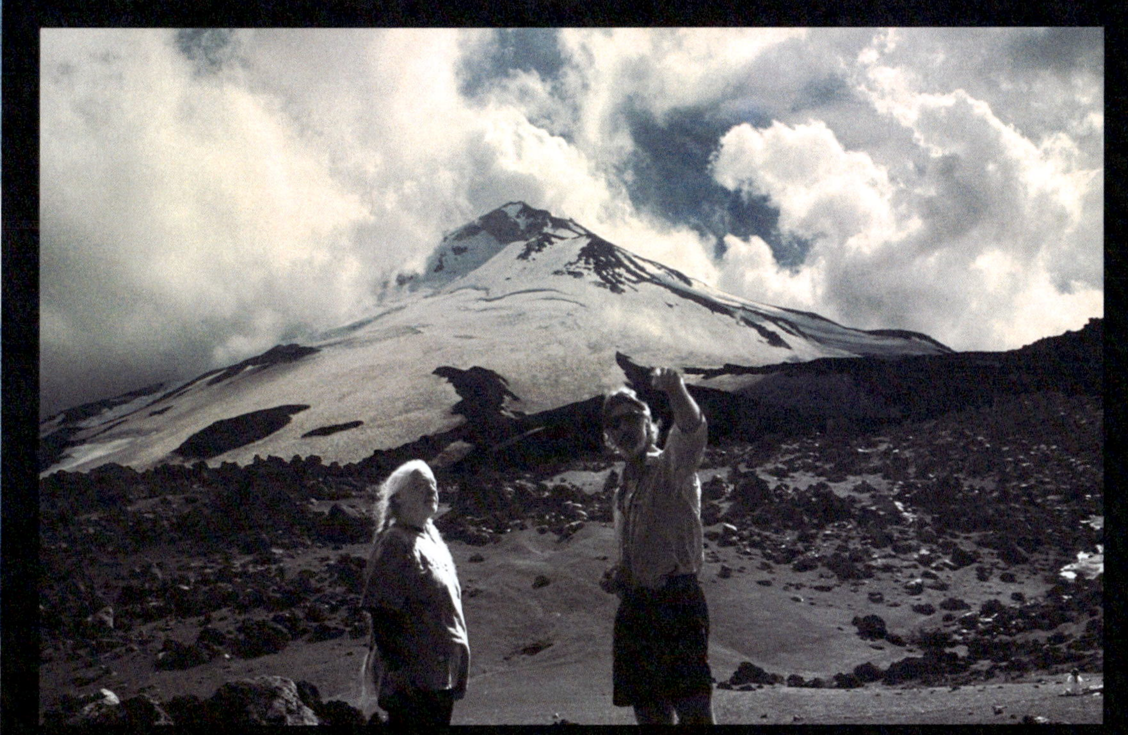

Herr Dockter explained "mountain-effect" clouds to Millie Cutten

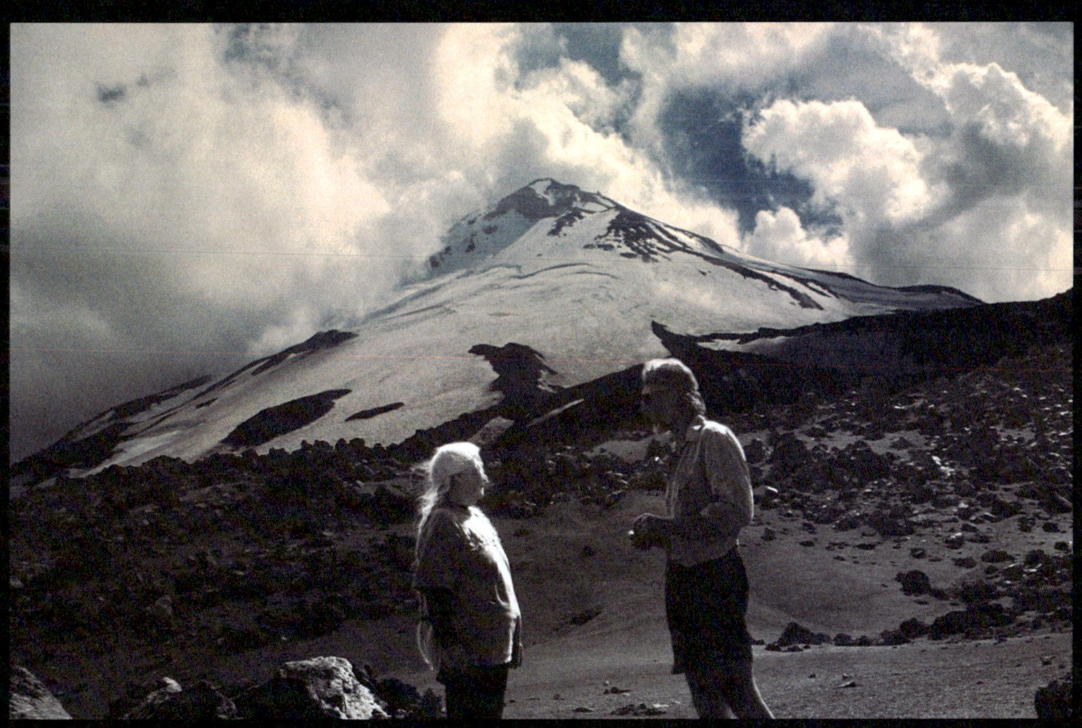

and what conditions would be propitious for the formation of lenticular clouds.

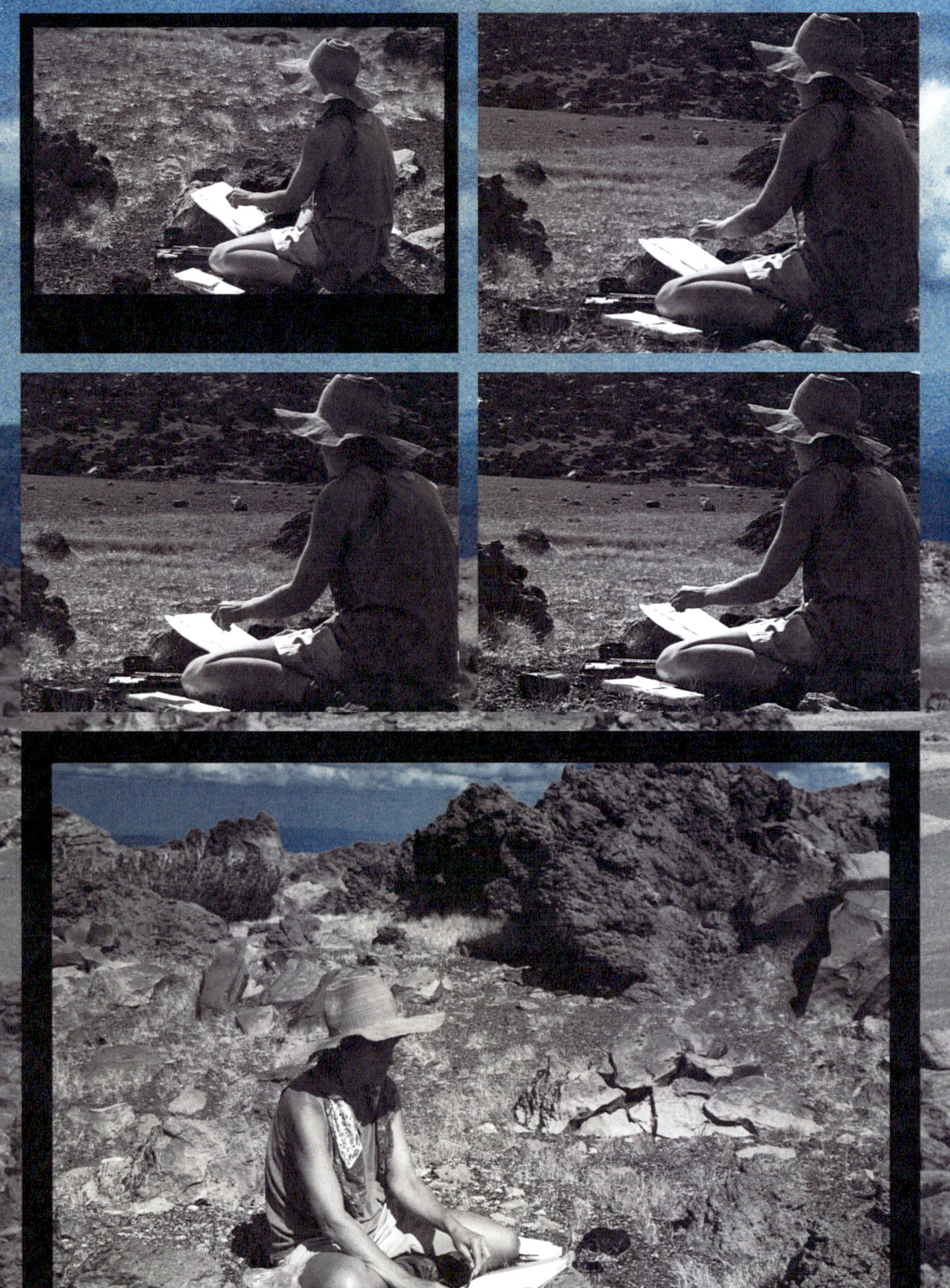

Judith Falk, our group's painter, spent an hour doing preliminary sketches

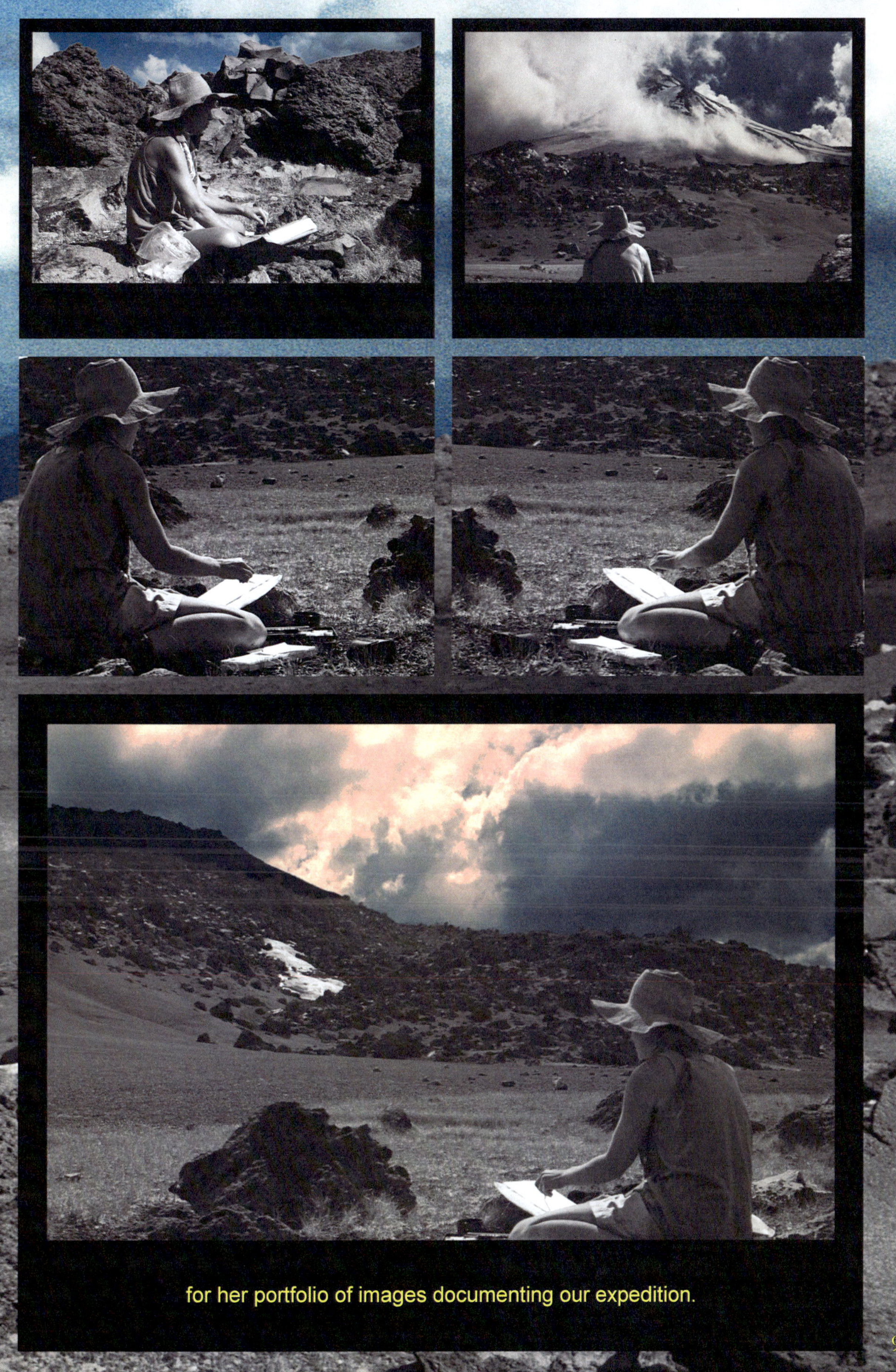

for her portfolio of images documenting our expedition.

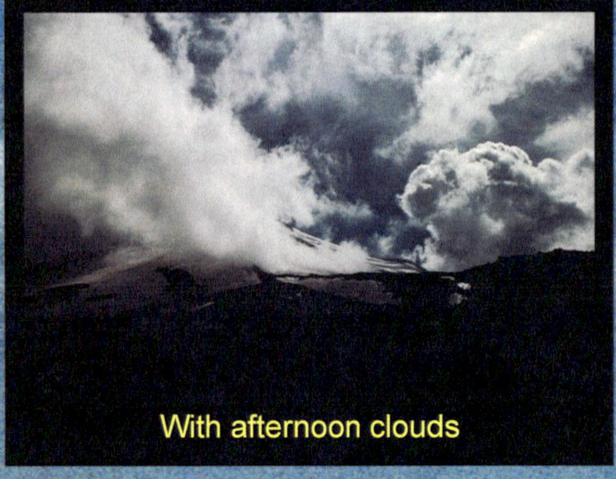

With afternoon clouds

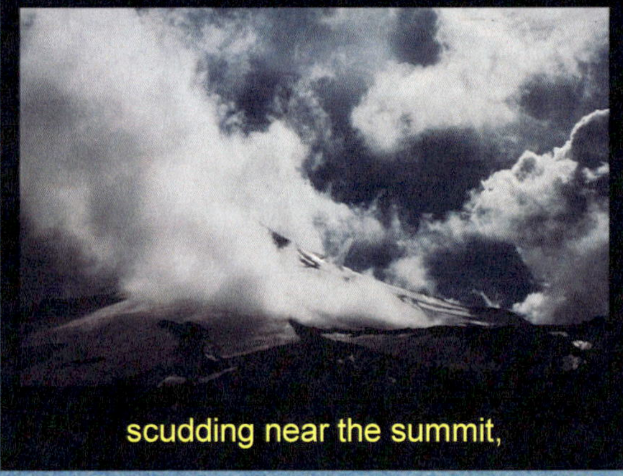

scudding near the summit,

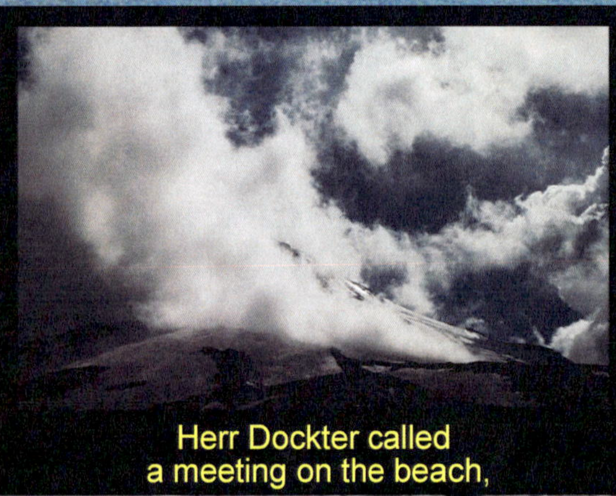

Herr Dockter called
a meeting on the beach,

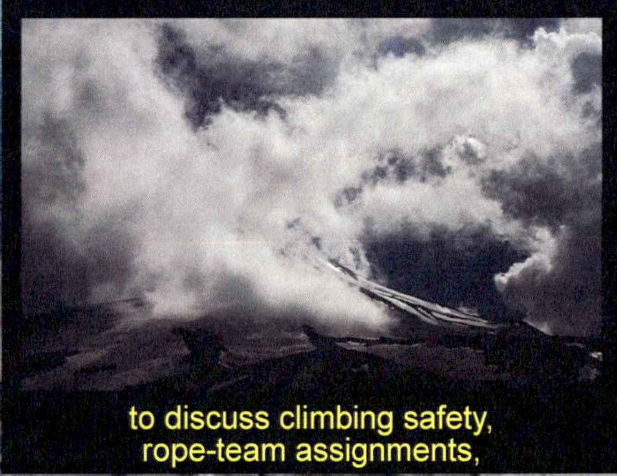

to discuss climbing safety,
rope-team assignments,

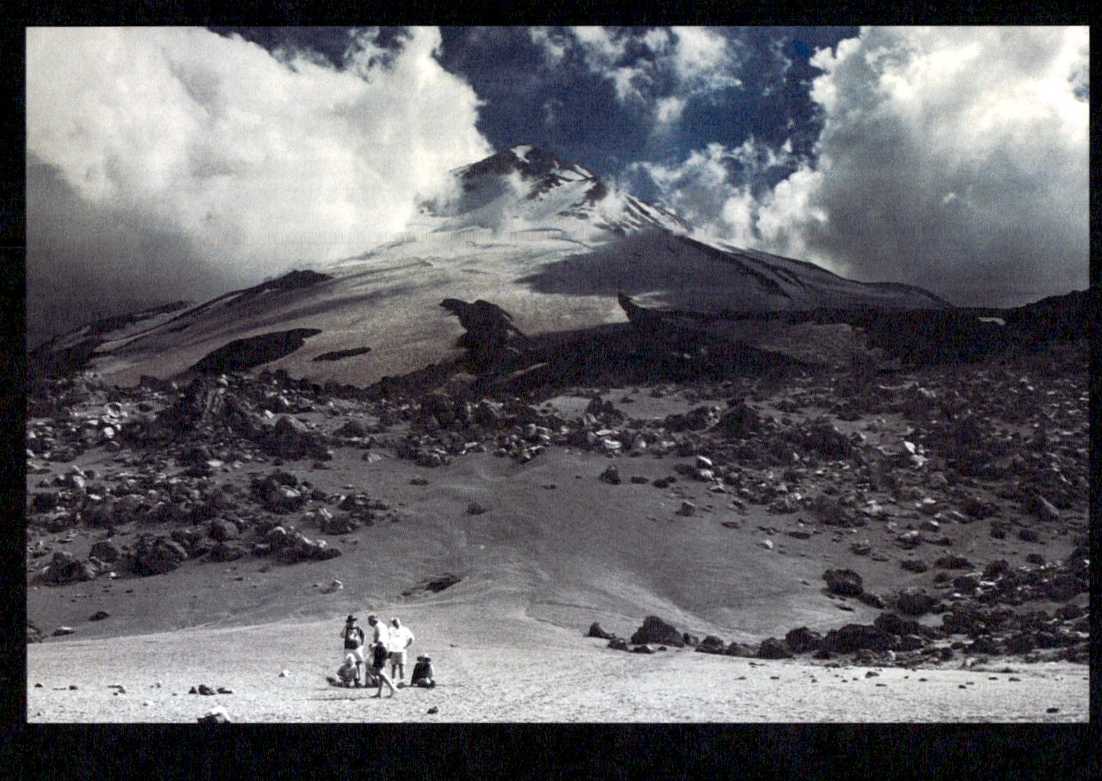

ice-axe arrest technique, our route, and above all – our attitude.

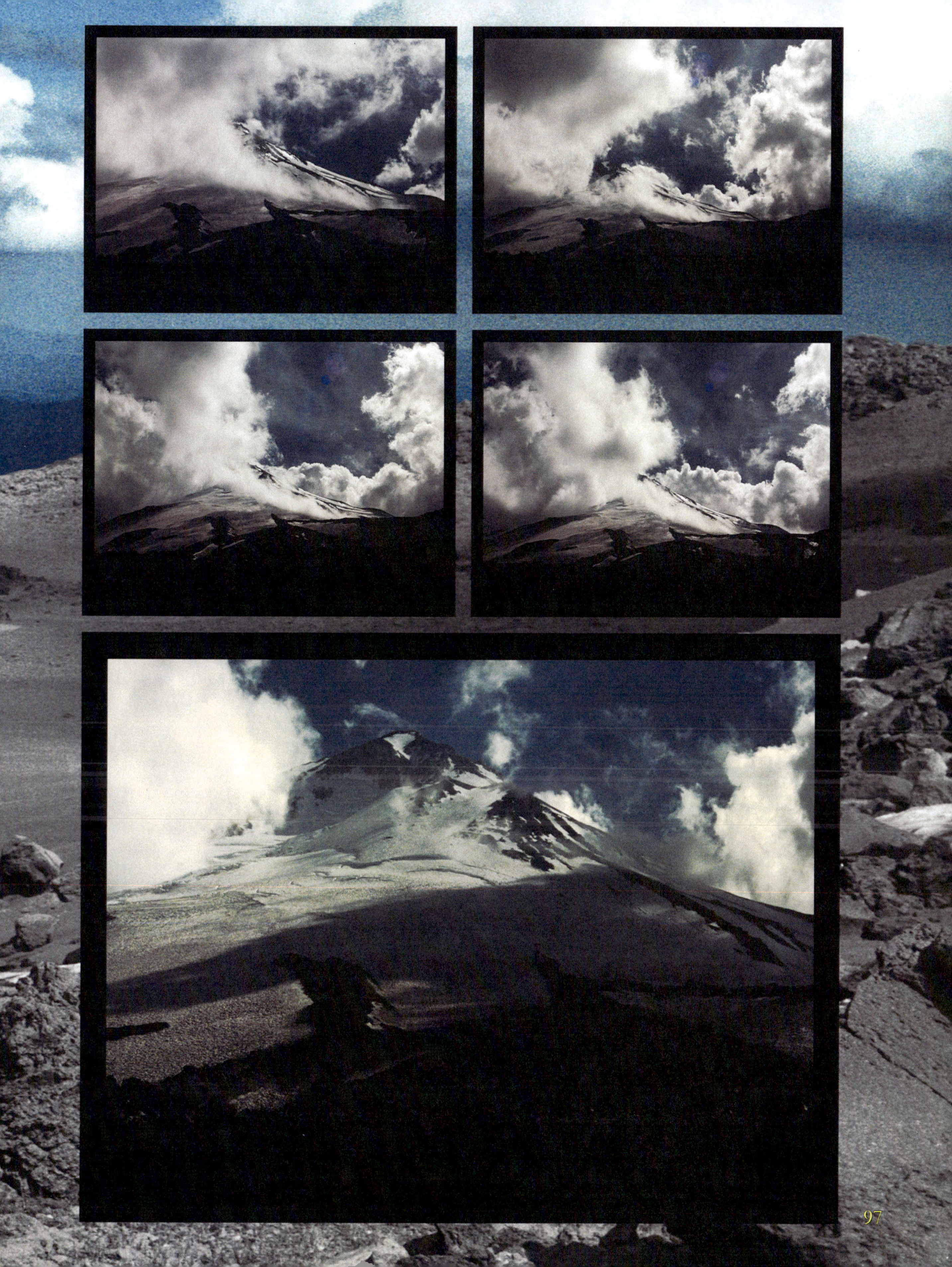

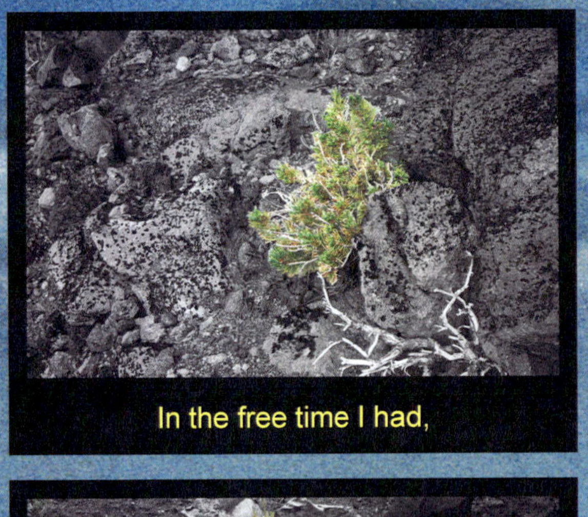

In the free time I had,

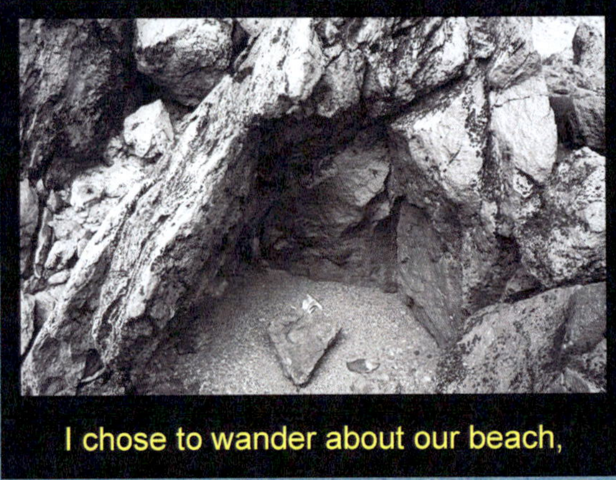

I chose to wander about our beach,

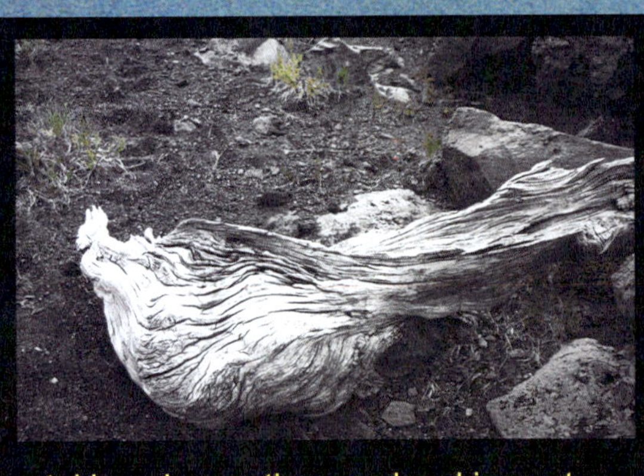

taking observations and making notes

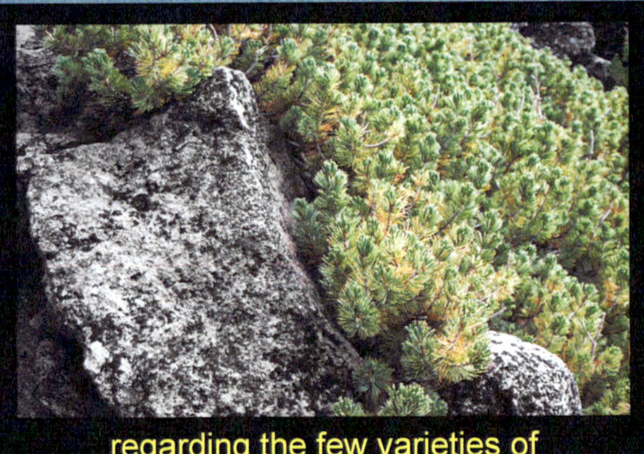

regarding the few varieties of
plant life – made so exotic by their rarity –

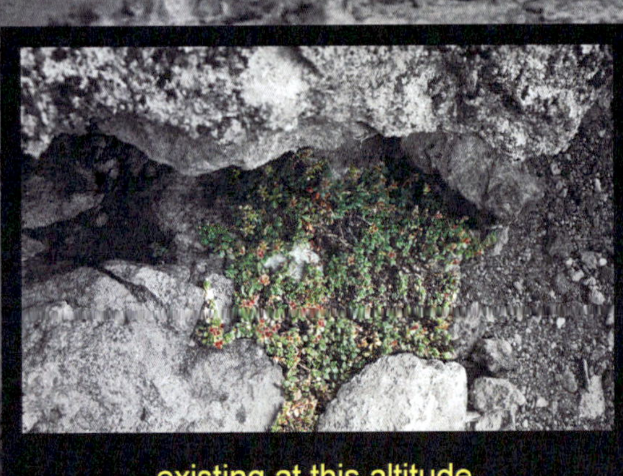

existing at this altitude.

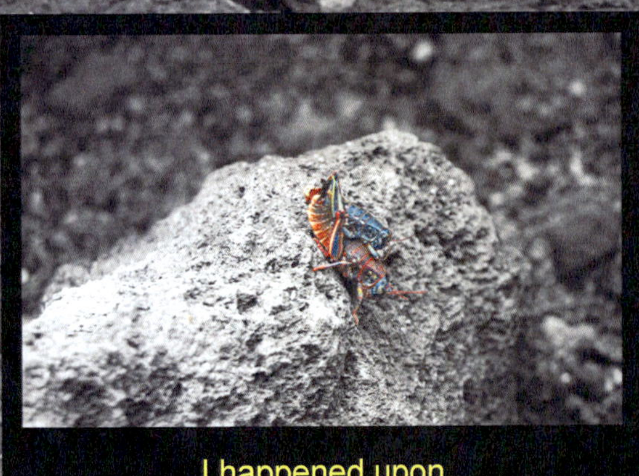

I happened upon

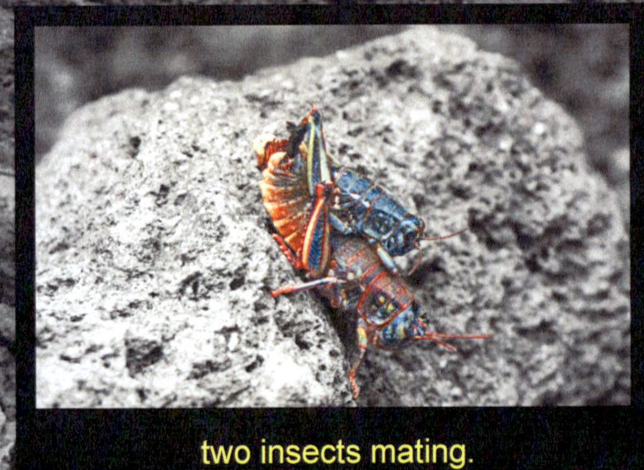

two insects mating.

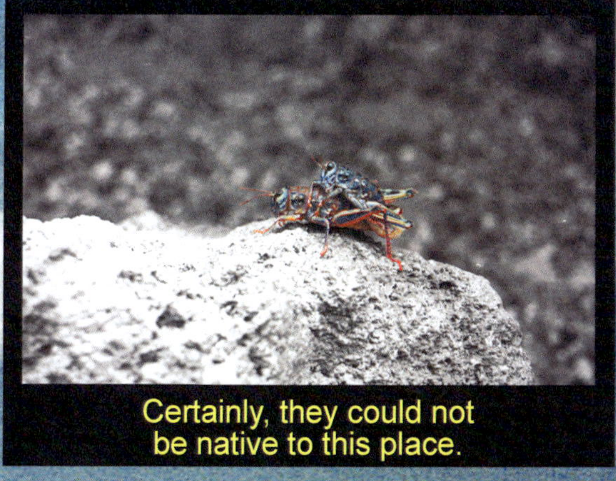

Certainly, they could not
be native to this place.

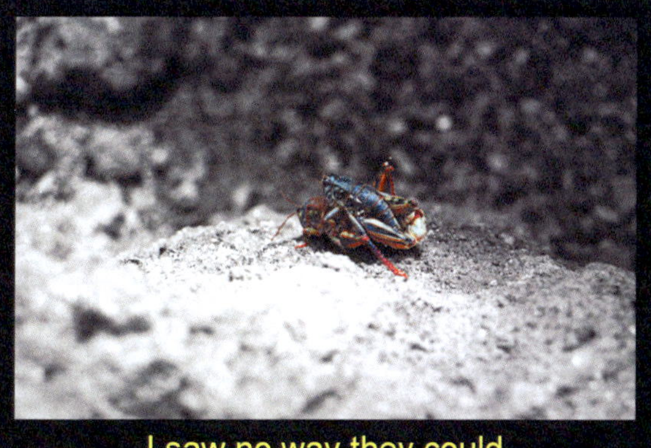

I saw no way they could
survive for long in a world that,

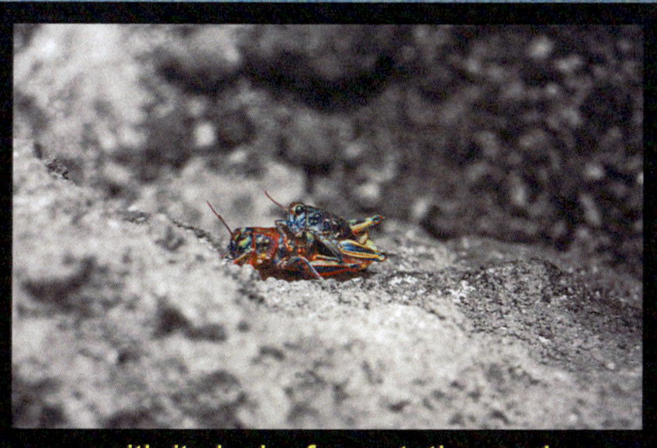

with its lack of vegetation and
freezing overnight temperatures,

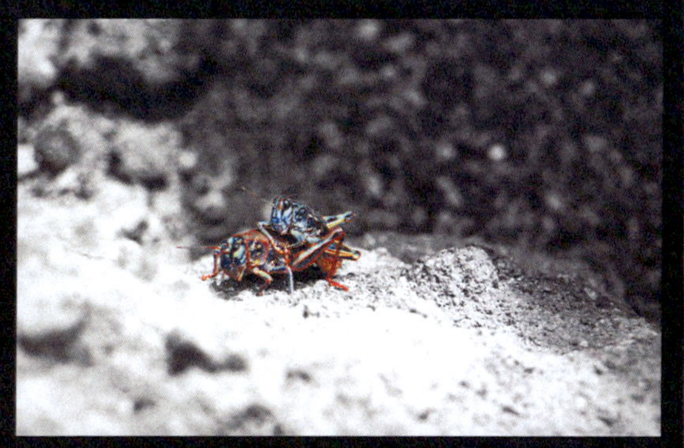

seemed so hostile.

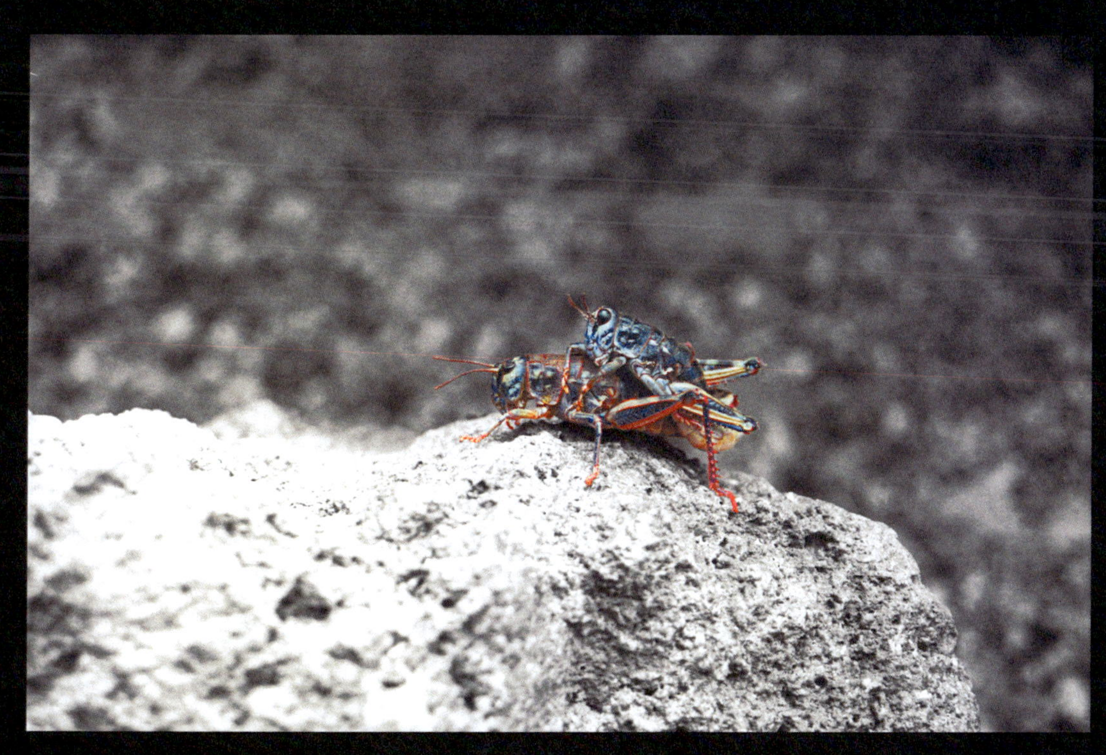

Yet they continued with this, the most important act
of their short lives, oblivious to the fact of its doomed outcome.
Perhaps they had been blown aloft together, already united, by some errant wi...

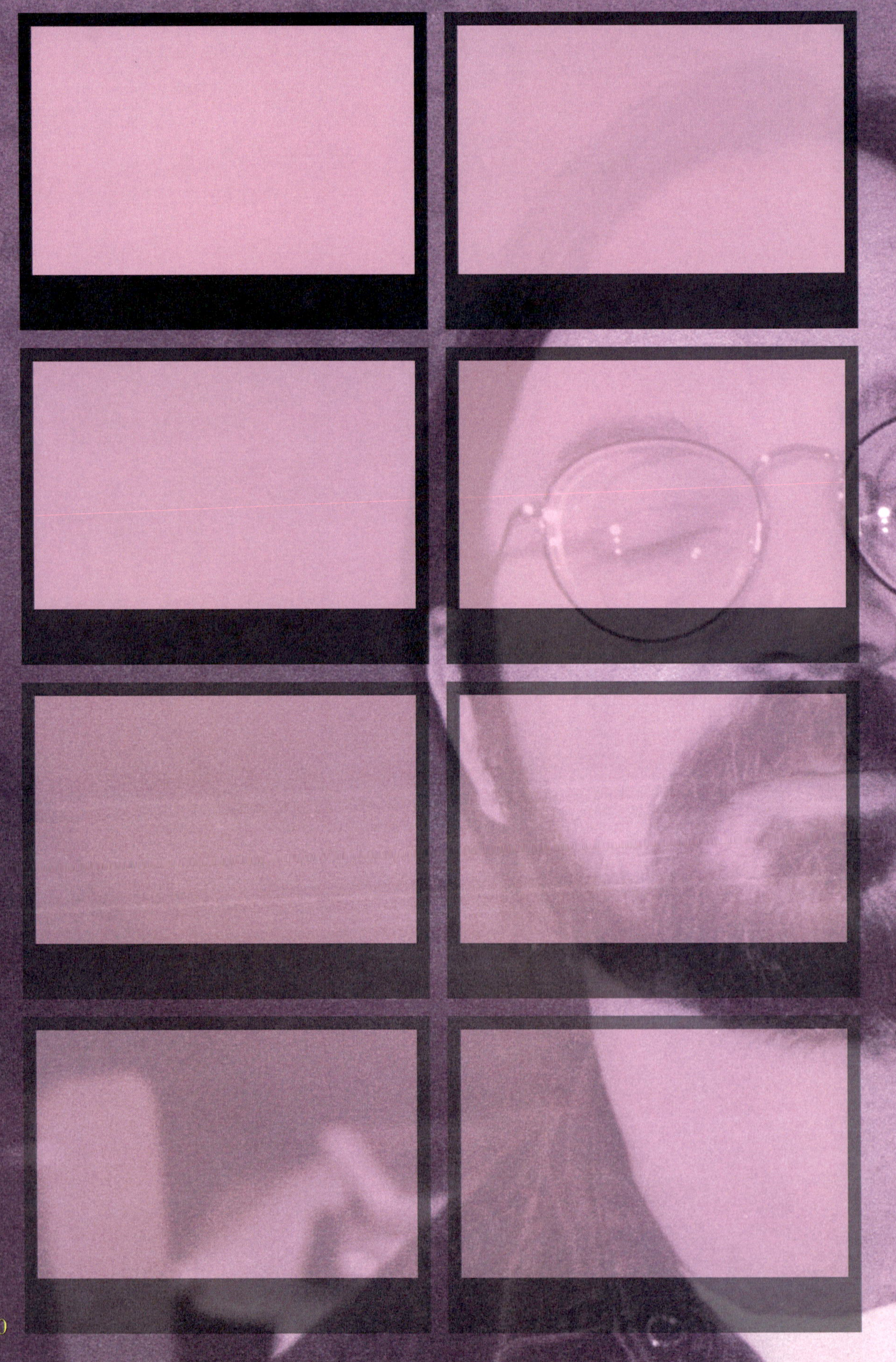

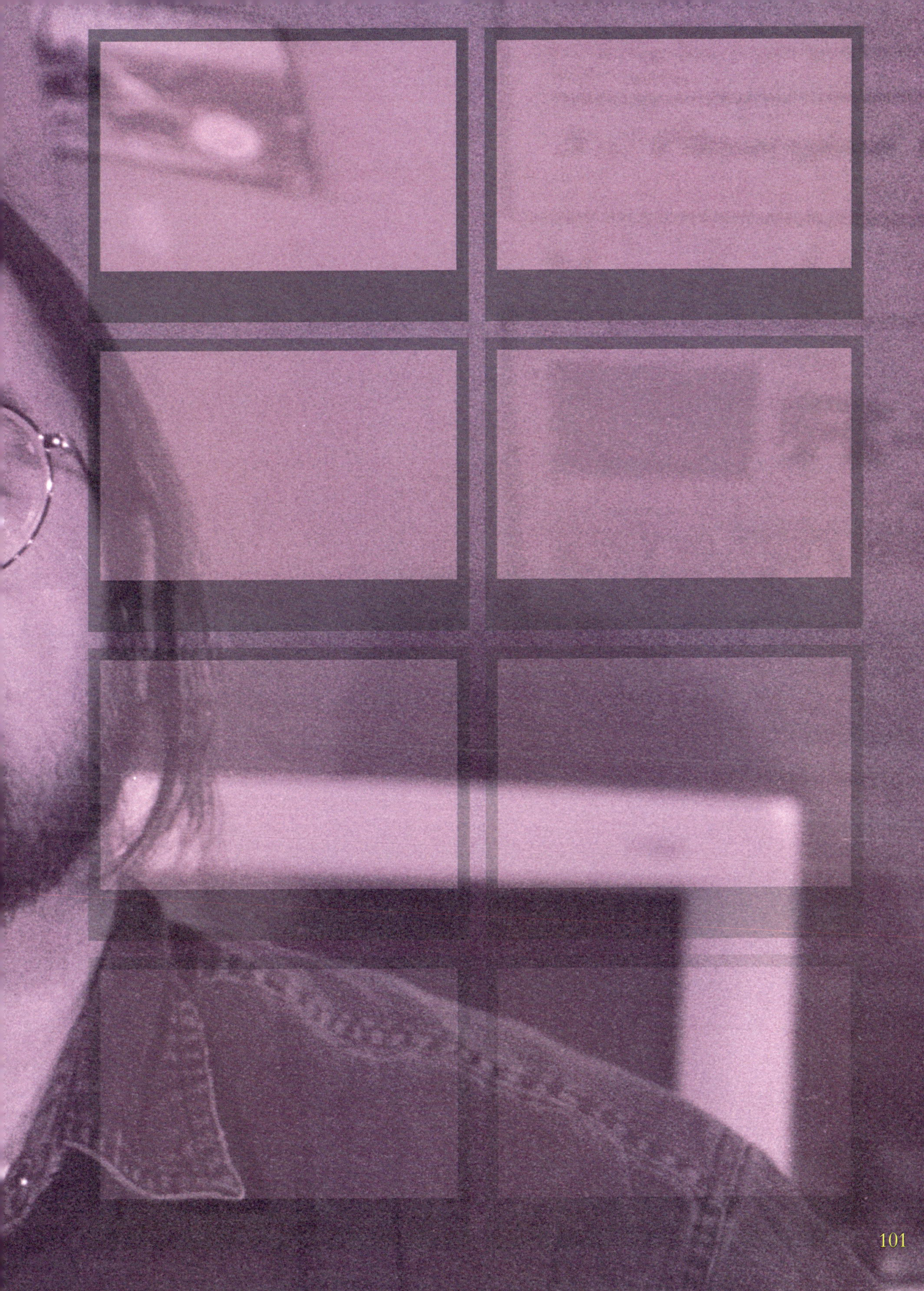

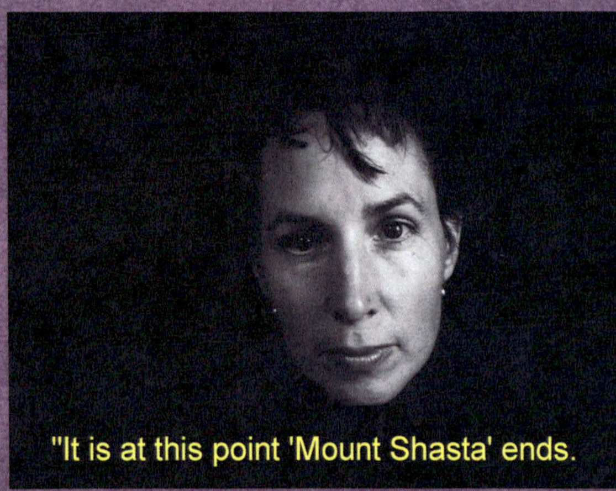
"It is at this point 'Mount Shasta' ends.

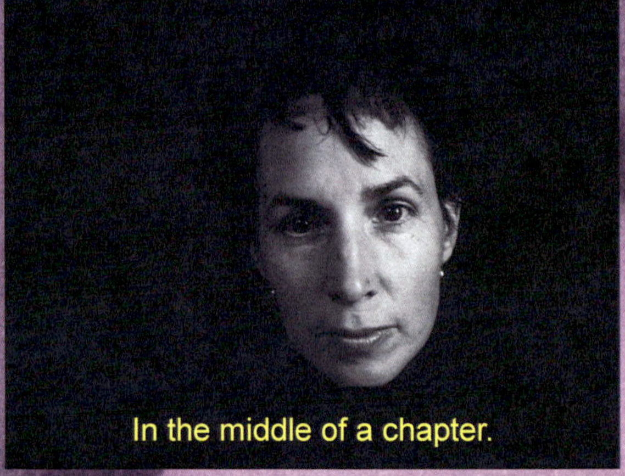
In the middle of a chapter.

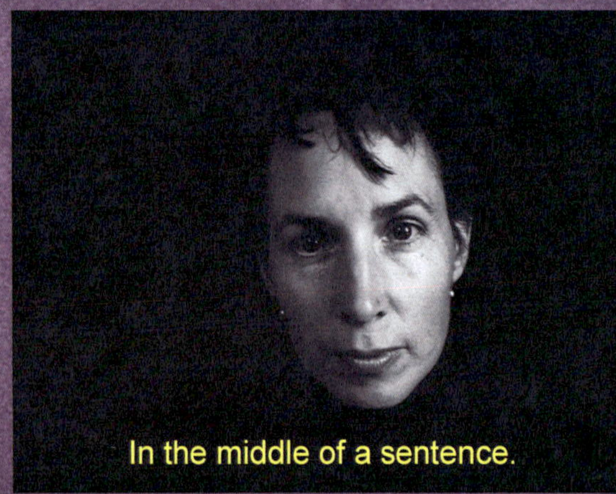
In the middle of a sentence.

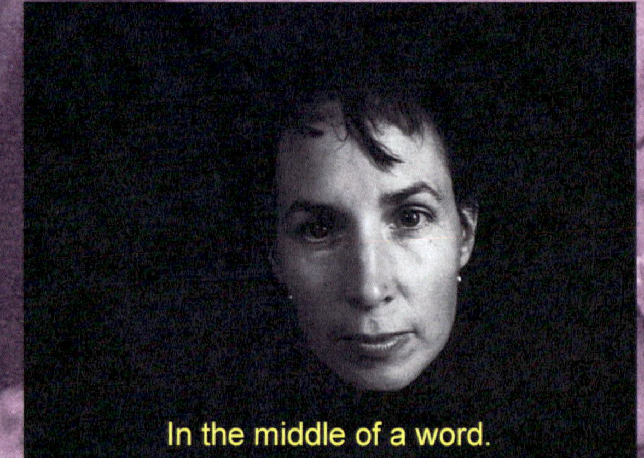
In the middle of a word.

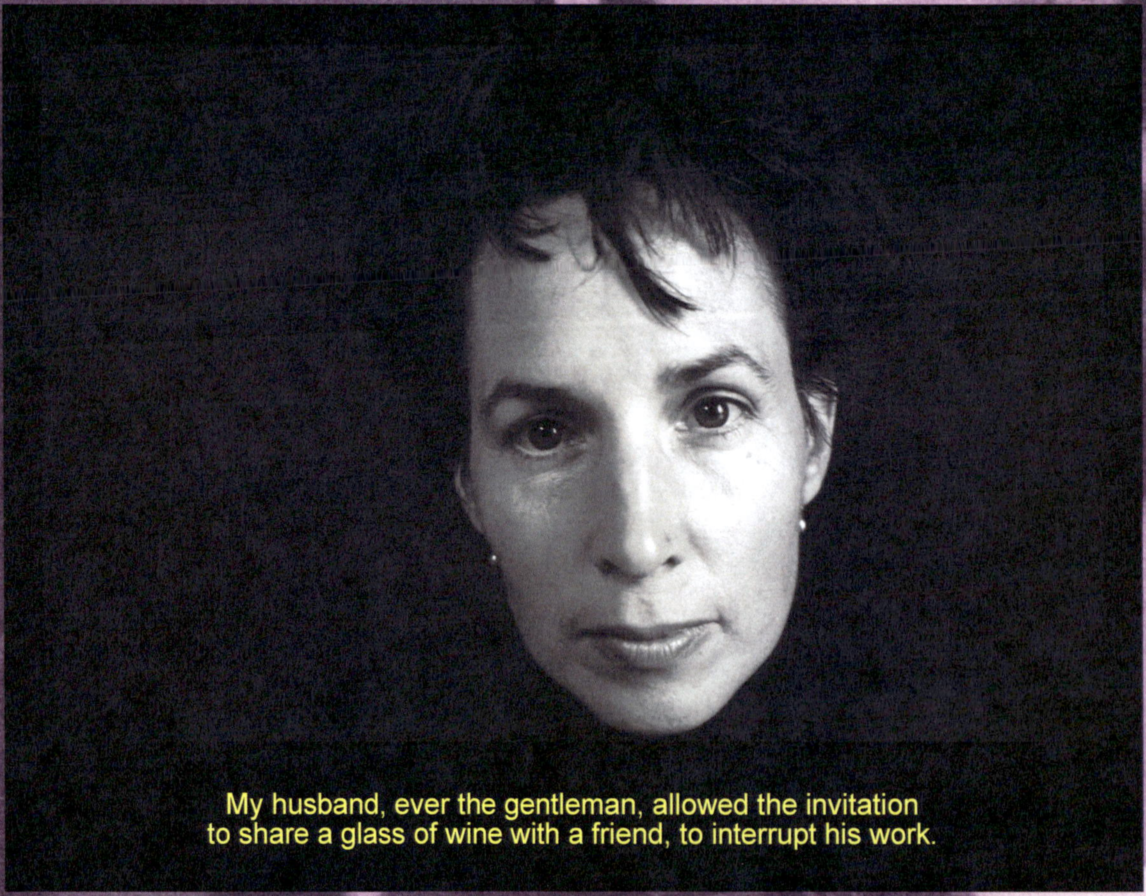

My husband, ever the gentleman, allowed the invitation
to share a glass of wine with a friend, to interrupt his work.

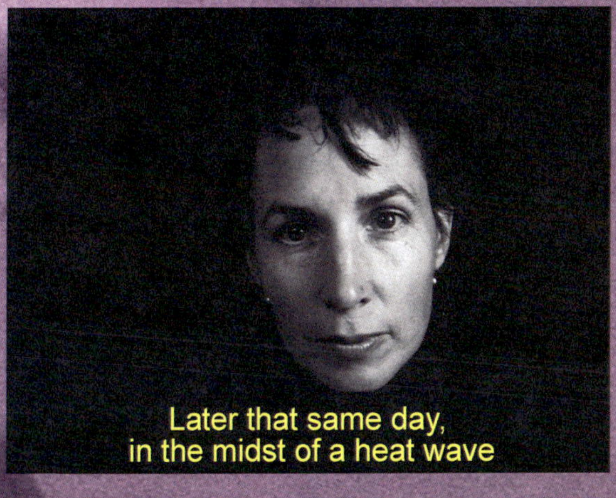

Later that same day,
in the midst of a heat wave

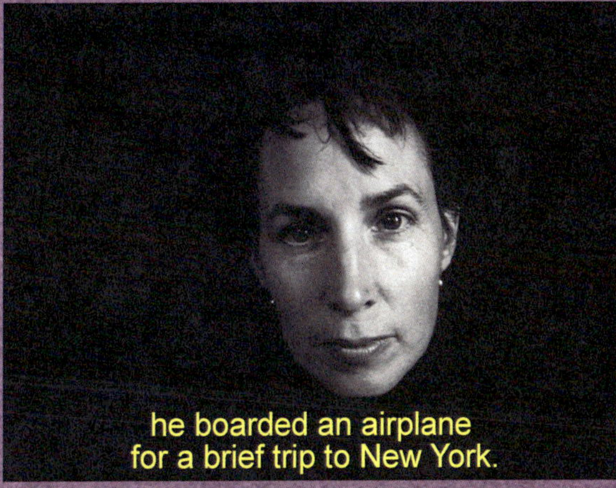

he boarded an airplane
for a brief trip to New York.

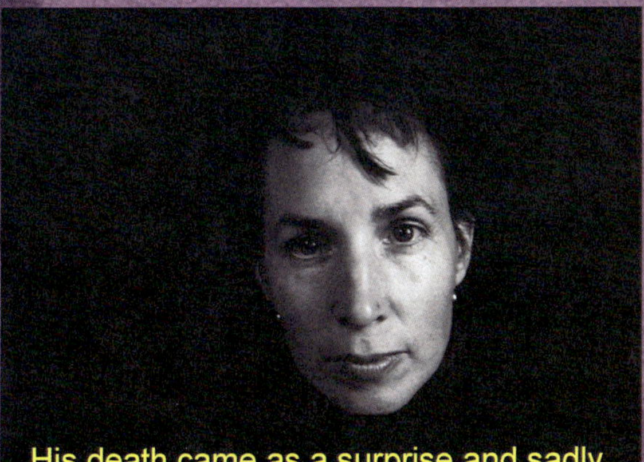

His death came as a surprise and sadly,

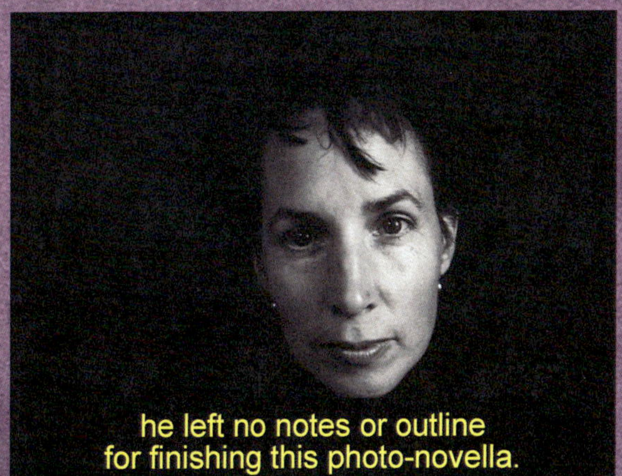

he left no notes or outline
for finishing this photo-novella.

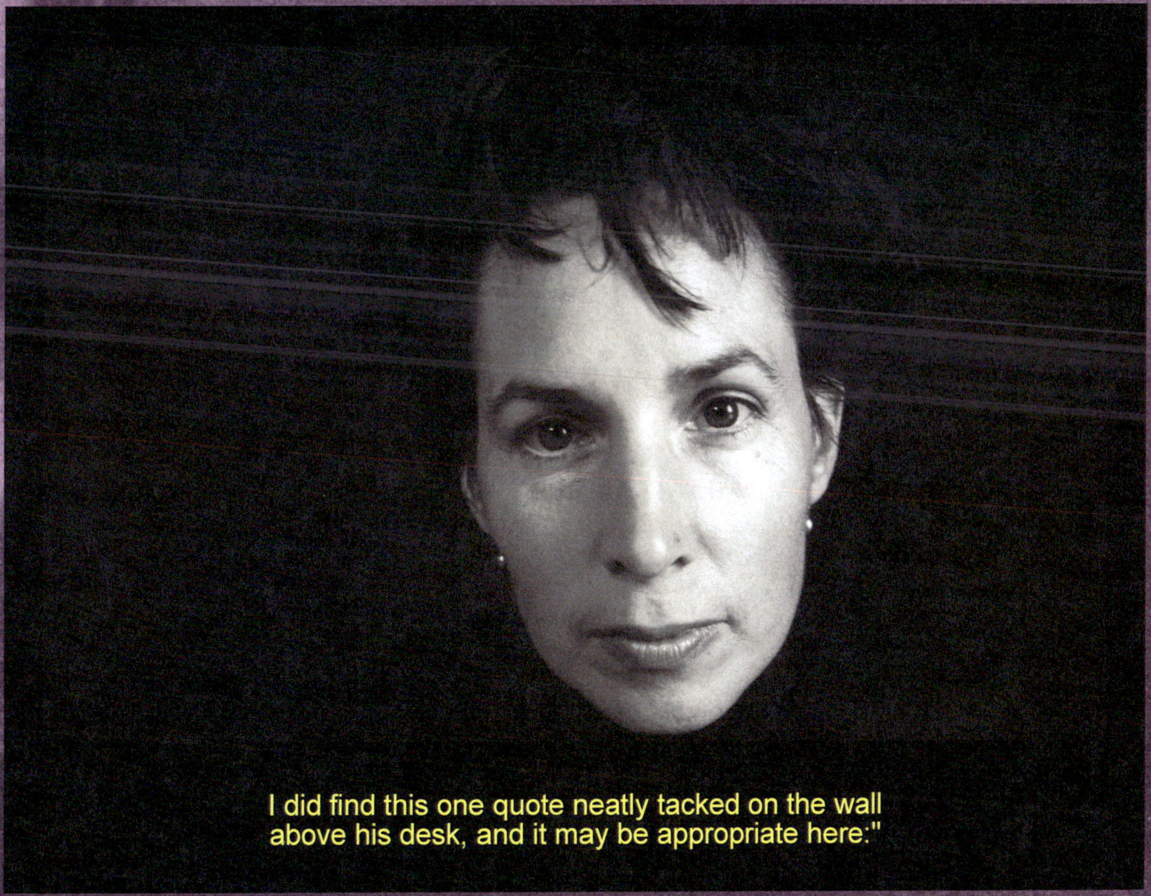

I did find this one quote neatly tacked on the wall
above his desk, and it may be appropriate here:"

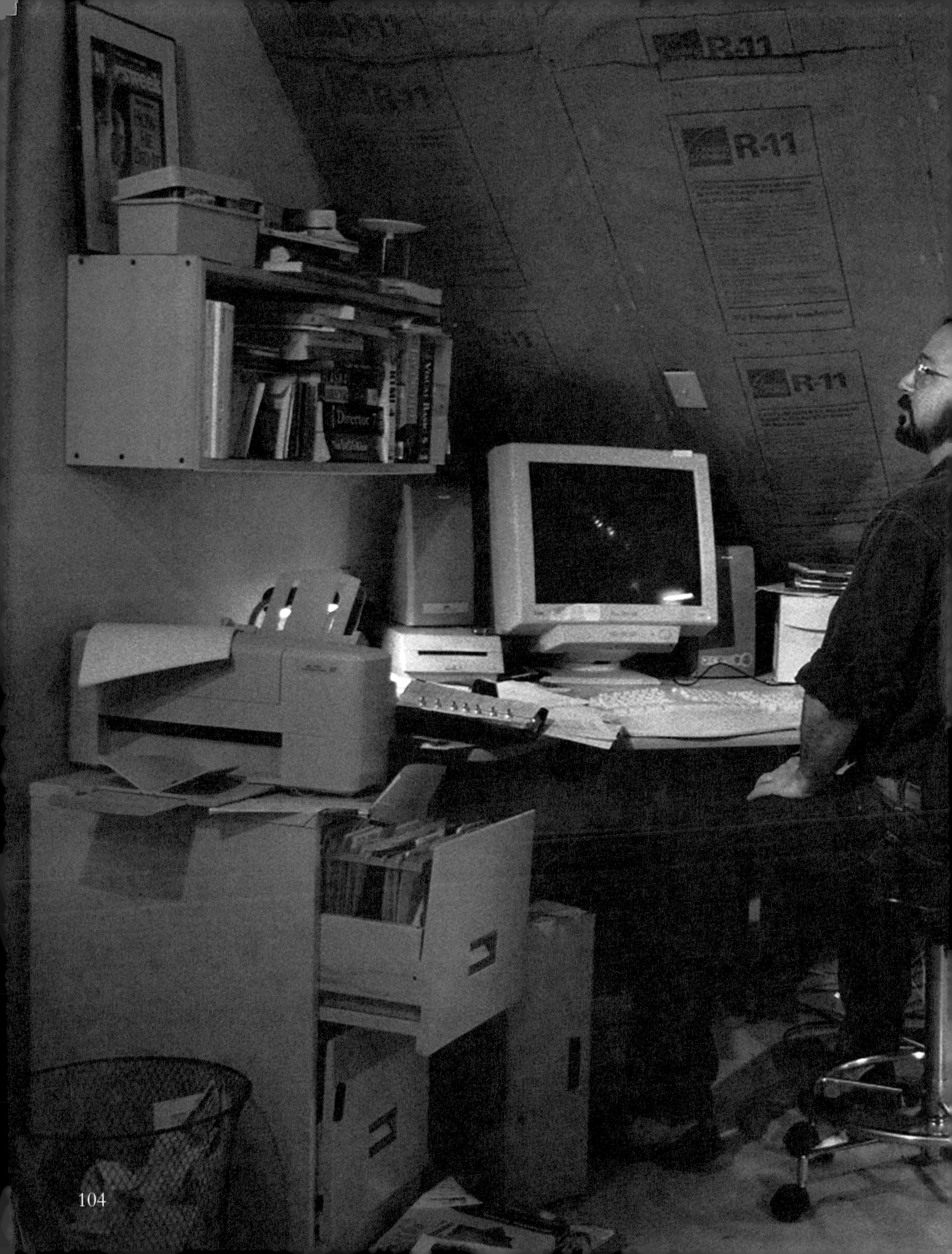
R-11
R-11
R-11

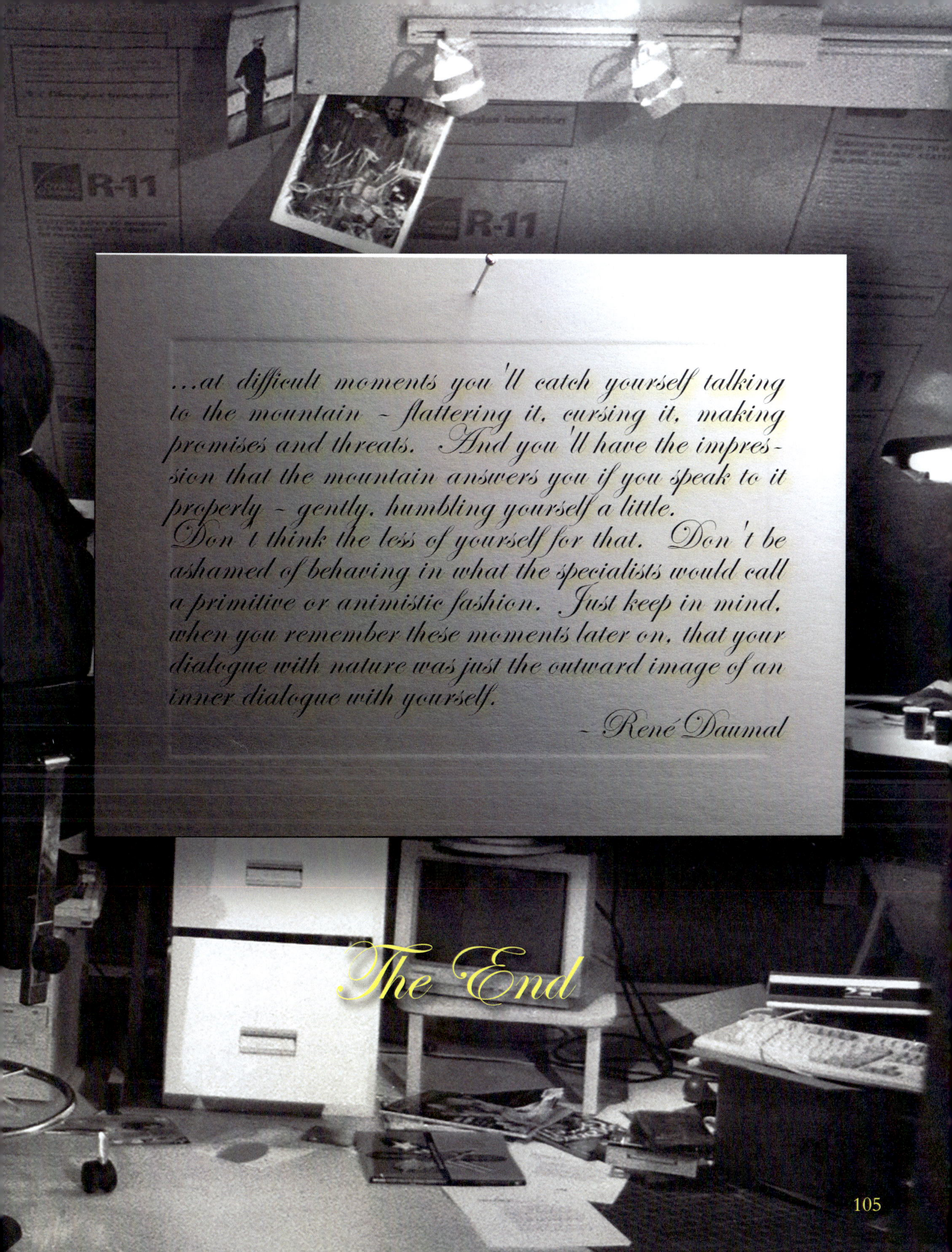

...at difficult moments you'll catch yourself talking to the mountain - flattering it, cursing it, making promises and threats. And you'll have the impression that the mountain answers you if you speak to it properly - gently, humbling yourself a little.
Don't think the less of yourself for that. Don't be ashamed of behaving in what the specialists would call a primitive or animistic fashion. Just keep in mind, when you remember these moments later on, that your dialogue with nature was just the outward image of an inner dialogue with yourself.

- René Daumal

The End

About MOUNT SHASTA:

Peter Santino fell in love with *Mount Analogue*, René Daumal's classic French metaphysical mountaineering adventure back in the late 1960s. For the next 30 years he dreamed of finding someway of making it into a movie, even to the point of writing the publishing house in Paris in a fruitless attempt to find the rights holders. Then, in the 1990s, he decided that as an artist it was possible for him to make his own version of the tale and publish it as a kind of movie on the World Wide Web. Using Macromedia Flash® (now Adobe Flash®) Santino was able to stream *MOUNT SHASTA* as a sequence of still photographs with narration and a sound track. The story was broken into chapters and posted to his website, www.santino.tv, as they were completed – in the manner of a serial.

MOUNT SHASTA, a Photo-Novella for the Internet still exists on that website, www.santino.tv, in exactly the same Flash format as back in 2001.

It's worth taking a look at the streaming version if for no other reason than the beautiful soundtrack by bassist Bill Andrews. Santino chose the sequence of still photos because technology at that time did not allow video to be streamed efficiently at any resolution greater than that of a postage stamp. Working in this way allowed for the narration and music and also connected the work to the classic *foto-novelas* of Mexico and South America and served to acknowledge the great Chris Marker film, *La Jetée* (1962).

Garamond typeface is used for front & end matter and Chapter headings. The body of the book (captions) is Arial with some Edwardian Script ITC.

About the Cover:

The cover image and design is an original photograph and design by Peter Santino, realized as an homage to the first City Lights edition (May 1968) of Mount Analogue by René Daumal. That original cover imagery is credited as © 1967 by Casey Sonnabend & Michael Bowen.

Santino wanted the cover image to make MOUNT SHASTA jump out from the display shelf in the same way that Mount Analogue did for him back in 1968 when he wandered into City Lights Books in San Francisco's North Beach. That paperback jumped into the hands of a young mountaineer who still has that copy and still to this day, kicks himself that he did not request the man behind the counter inscribe within:

"Sold this day to Peter Santino – Lawrence Ferlinghetti"

Gismonda typeface (Andreas Höfeld, www.fontgrube.de) is used on the cover in an attempt to come close to an odd, almost Art Nouveau font used in 1967.

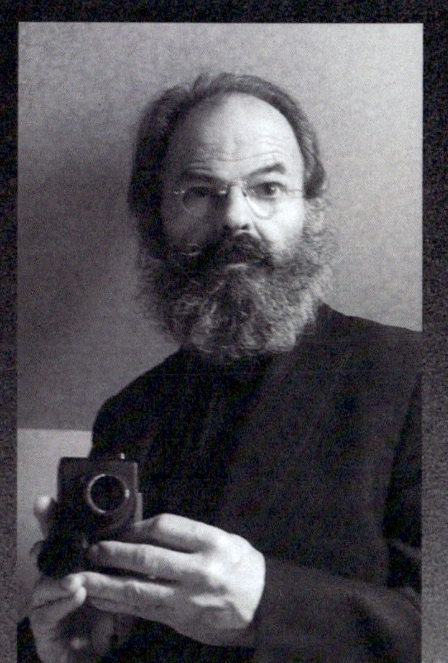

Peter Santino lives in his hometown of Eureka, county seat of Humboldt, west of the mountain, on the far North Coast of California.

Returned home after international and national exhibitions of his art; returned home after years of living in Seattle, New York City and Tuscany.

Peter Santino is also the author of:
LADY-FAME; or, The Fluke (2014)

Santino's drawings, paintings, photographs and three-dimensional works are archived at:
www.santino.tv

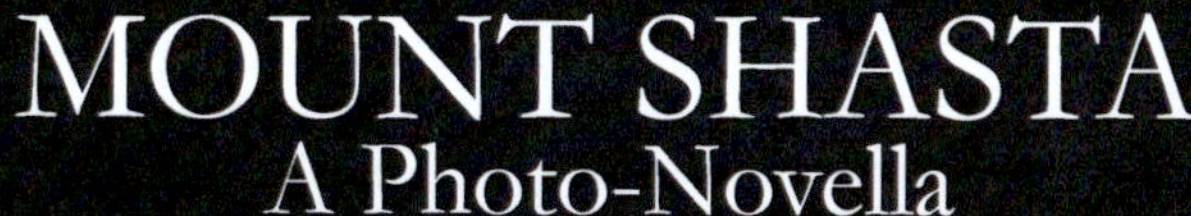

MOUNT SHASTA
A Photo-Novella

Printed in the USA
CPSIA information can be obtained
at www.ICGtesting.com
LVRC081637260224
772870LV00032B/213